NIGHT MOVER

Other Books by David Wise

NIGHT MOVER

HOW ALDRICH AMES
SOLD THE CIA TO THE KGB
FOR $4.6 MILLION

■

DAVID WISE

HarperCollins*Publishers*

HarperCollins books may be purchased for educational, business, or sales promotional use. For information please write: Special Markets Department, HarperCollins Publishers, Inc., 10 East 53rd Street, New York, NY 10022.

FIRST EDITION

Designed by Chris Welch

ISBN 0-06-017198-7

95 96 97 98 99 ❖/RRD 10 9 8 7 6 5 4 3 2 1

CONTENTS

CONTENTS

A photograph insert follows page 182.

To Sterling

"I simply delivered myself to them with the information that I had. It was . . . a switching of loyalties."
—Aldrich H. Ames
August 8, 1994

1

CAUGHT!

On the morning of February 21, 1994, Aldrich H. Ames left his house in Arlington, Virginia, and stepped into his $40,000 red XJ6 Jaguar. Ames loved his Jag; it was the third one he had owned. He revved up the engine, then headed for the headquarters of the Central Intelligence Agency in nearby Langley.

It was Presidents' Day, a federal holiday. The fifty-two-year-old CIA man was relaxed, dressed in a casual jacket, shirt, pants, and loafers. Although he had been called into the office unexpectedly, he did not plan to be there for very long. He had to get back and finish packing; he was, after all, scheduled to leave for Moscow the next day on official CIA business. It was to be an important meeting on drug trafficking with the Russian federal security service, one of the successors to the KGB.

At that precise moment, nine miles away in Alexandria, Special Agent Leslie G. Wiser, Jr., of the Federal Bureau of Investigation, and Mark J. Hulkower, a young assistant U.S. attorney for the eastern district of Virginia, pulled away from the federal courthouse in an FBI radio car. They had just come from the chambers of United States Magistrate Barry R. Poretz.

Wiser spoke into the microphone. A counterintelligence agent, he had headed the FBI's ten-month investigation of Aldrich Ames.

"We got the warrant," he said.

Ames turned right when he pulled out of his driveway, headed up the hill, and took another right on Quebec, a one-way street. About a block and a half from his house, Ames came to a stop sign. The car ahead of him had stopped at the sign, but, oddly, it had not started up again. Alongside it was another car that was waiting to turn left. The street was completely blocked. Ames waited impatiently for the car ahead to move. Suddenly, two more cars with flashing red lights appeared behind him. The Jaguar was boxed in.

The moment that Rick Ames had feared for nine years, the moment he often dreaded in the small hours of the night, had finally come—and he knew it. In that split second his life changed forever.

Special Agents Mike Donner, Dell Spry, and Aaron McGee of the FBI approached the car.

The window on the driver's side was down because Ames was smoking a cigarette.

Spry held out his credentials. "FBI. You're under arrest," he told Ames. "Get out of the car."

Ames, in a state of total shock, sat frozen behind the steering wheel. Agent Donner repeated the order. "Get out of the car."

Life imitates art. "There must be some mistake," Ames said, lapsing into B-movie dialogue. He repeated "There must be some mistake" a few times. Then the door of the Jaguar opened slowly. Ames got out, moving like a man in a slow-motion video. Agent Donner helped him out of the car.

Ames was holding his cigarette, and Aaron McGee reached over and took it out of his hand.

"You're under arrest for violating U.S. espionage statutes," Dell Spry said. It was 10:30 A.M.

Half a dozen other armed FBI agents surrounded the CIA man.

Ames spread his hands wide, a look of incredulity on his face.

"Espionage, me?" he asked. "I hear what you're saying, but you've got to be kidding."

They were not.

As Ames stood against the Jaguar, Dell Spry put the handcuffs on behind his back. Under arrest and in custody now, Ames was placed in one of the FBI cars. He was driven to the FBI's northern Virginia office in nearby Tysons Corner.

Les Wiser's car had only gone fifty feet from the courthouse in Alexandria when his radio crackled. "The suspect is secure," a voice informed him. It had all happened in seconds.

At the same moment, an army of FBI agents had silently surrounded the Ameses' $540,000 house on North Randolph Street, in an upscale neighborhood of the northern Virginia bedroom community just across the Potomac from Washington.

Upstairs in the bathroom, Ames's dark-haired Colombian-born wife, Rosario, was putting on her makeup. Their five-year-old son, Paul, was also in the house. Rosario's mother, Cecilia Dupuy de Casas, visiting from Bogotá, was asleep in the guest room.

The doorbell rang, and the housekeeper answered it. Rosario was surprised; she wasn't expecting anyone. She peered down and saw a man and a pregnant woman in the front hall. Rosario went downstairs. The visitors asked her to step outside.

They identified themselves as Special Agents Yolanda M. Larson and John Hosinski of the FBI. They told her that her husband had just been arrested for espionage. They said she was also under arrest for espionage. They had asked her to step out of the house so that her son would not see her being arrested.

They told her she could go back inside to tell her mother and get her coat. She was told to remove her jewelry and leave her purse behind. Accompanied by Yolanda Larson, Rosario ran upstairs, woke her mother, and told her that Rick had been arrested and the FBI had arrested her as well. Paul was waiting in the hall when Rosario came back downstairs. She grabbed a camel's-hair coat, then hugged and kissed her son.

"I have to go with these people," she said, "but don't worry, I'll be back soon."

Outside, she realized the house was surrounded. There were

FBI cars everywhere, and men with walkie-talkies in the front yard and on the street. She, too, was put in an FBI car.

Ten minutes away, in McLean, the telephone rang in the home of Nancy Everly, Rick Ames's married sister. A calm, attractive woman with strawberry blond hair, Everly was very fond of her older brother. Because of the holiday, she, too, had the day off from her job as an executive of a computer company.

"It was around ten-thirty in the morning. The phone rang. It was Paul," she said. "He didn't say anything except 'hello.' I kept asking, 'What's going on?' but he left the phone. Then a man picked up."

"Who's this?" the man asked.

"This is Aunt Nancy, who are you?"

"FBI. Your brother and his wife have been arrested. Can you come and pick up the child?"

Stunned, Everly managed to ask: "Why were they arrested?"

"Conspiracy to commit espionage."

Everly bolted for the door.

Two FBI agents were waiting on her doorstep.

"They questioned me briefly. They were surprised I knew of the arrest and was on my way over. They asked me how I knew. I told them Paul had called me. They hadn't expected that." The FBI dragnet had not figured on Paul Ames, age five, picking up the phone and calling his aunt.

Everly drove to her brother's house in her black Buick, followed by the two FBI men.

"When I got to the house it was full of people. Agents were coming down the stairs with Paul's knapsack full of videotapes. They had helped him pack.

"I tried to get Cecilia to come with me. She is very excitable and volatile. She wouldn't leave. No, she had to call the ambassador and the president of Colombia. Paul was sitting in my car outside with the FBI agents. I finally left and drove him back to my house. The FBI said they would bring Cecilia to my house, which they did."

As Wiser and Hulkower were approaching the Ameses' house in Arlington, a second message came over the radio: "Suspect two is in custody."

The FBI, according to plan, had arrested Ames away from his home so that he could not destroy evidence. In the FBI car that was taking Ames to the bureau's resident agency in Tysons Corner, Ames repeated to himself, almost like a mantra, "Think . . . think . . . think."

In the car, Ames, too, could listen to the FBI's communications. He heard a report come over the radio: "We've secured the house."

Ames knew that all kinds of incriminating documents, computer disks, and letters were in the house—and in his computer—containing details of much of his nine years of spying for the KGB. Now they had him, and Rosario, and the evidence. It was over.

Slouched low in the FBI car, Aldrich H. Ames, veteran of thirty-one years in the CIA, secret millionaire, and Moscow's most valuable mole in the entire history of the cold war, uttered only two words:

"Oh, fuck."

2

I G O R

As much as anywhere, it had begun with Shurygin.

In the dark, subterranean world of counterintelligence, a world of black mirrors and distorted images where nothing is quite what it seems, the truth is at best fleeting, relative, and always elusive. If it exists at all.

And yet, in some way, the seeds of Ames's treachery must have been planted in those long drinking sessions with Shurygin, some as long as a whole day. Drinking bouts and meetings that went on for almost two years, during Ames's whole time in Mexico. Later, the FBI would suspect that Shurygin was the key to everything that followed, although it could never prove it, of course. There were too many black mirrors.

But this much was clear: In Shurygin, Rick had found more than a target. He had found a friend, a drinking partner, a soul mate. And Shurygin was reporting it all back, in great detail, to the Center, in Moscow. To the KGB.

*   *   *

When Rick Ames reported in to the Mexico City CIA station in October 1981, his career, to all outward appearances, was on track. He was forty years old, a GS-13 earning $36,320 a year.[1] In his previous post in New York, he had impressed his superiors in Manhattan—and at Langley headquarters—by helping to handle Arkady Shevchenko, the undersecretary general of the United Nations for political affairs and the highest-ranking Soviet official ever to defect to the CIA. And he had won his second overseas tour, a must for agency officers seeking to rise in the Directorate of Operations (DO), the agency's clandestine arm.

But if his career seemed to be going well, his personal life was not. His twelve-year marriage to his wife, Nan, whom he had met when she, too, worked for the CIA's Directorate of Operations, was breaking up. Nan had quit the agency several years before and had a good job in New York. Ensconced in their apartment on Manhattan's East Side and absorbed in her own career, she had refused to follow her husband to Mexico City.

So Rick was a bachelor in Mexico, although not by choice. While Ames was assigned to Manhattan, the CIA had paid most of the rent on the expensive apartment. But once Ames left New York, the subsidy ended; the couple had to pay the full amount. More than one colleague remembers Ames complaining while in Mexico about the high rent he was paying in Manhattan.

In Mexico City, Ames moved into a penthouse apartment over a book factory, a warehouse in the rabbit warren of little streets, all named for rivers, that ran behind the American embassy on the broad Paseo de la Reforma. It was very small apartment, and the only one in the building, which was located in a semi-industrial

---

[1] GS stands for General Schedule and is the pay scale for civil servants throughout most of the federal government. Although the CIA is exempt from the civil service, it follows the GS pay scale. In May 1982, within months of Ames's arrival in Mexico, he was promoted to a GS-14 at a salary of $44,029. While a GS rank might not mean very much to persons in the private sector, within the federal government and the CIA, it is the shorthand that at once defines and limits the income, rank, prestige, and importance of a career employee.

area near Sullivan Park. But it had the advantage of being only a ten-minute walk from the embassy.

Alone in Mexico City, with his marriage on the rocks, Ames indulged in three extramarital affairs early in his tour. And he began drinking. In New York, his drinking, according to CIA colleagues, had not been a problem. It became a problem in Mexico.

When Ames reported in to the CIA station on the fifth floor of the American embassy in Mexico City, he was under diplomatic cover, supposedly a State Department officer in the political section with the rank of second secretary. His real job was chief of the Soviet counterintelligence branch in the Mexico City station. His reports went back to the CIA's Soviet East European (SE) division at headquarters. In the jargon of the agency, Ames was the station's SE/CI branch chief.

In the CIA, Latin America is regarded as something of a dumping ground for less-than-brilliant officers. An assignment to Central or South America is not considered career enhancing. But Ames was only nominally assigned to the Latin American division, although he was under its jurisdiction in Mexico; his home base was the Soviet division.[2]

Counting clerical personnel, the CIA station in Mexico City in 1981 had some two dozen employees, of whom about a dozen were case officers. They all knew each other. And within the CIA station, David T. Samson became Ames's closest friend.[3] A tall,

---

[2]Within the CIA, the common expression was that SE division "has no territory" of its own. Outside the Soviet Union and the bloc countries, its officers, attempting to recruit Soviets and gather intelligence around the world, were always seconded to other geographic divisions. Thus, an SE officer attempting to recruit a Soviet diplomat in, say, Burundi would be assigned to the Africa division. After the collapse of the Soviet Union in 1991, the CIA changed the name of the SE division to the Central Eurasia (CE) division.

[3]Samson retired from the government in 1990. He has since remarried, begun a new career far removed from anything to do with intelligence, and cut all ties to his past work, from which he has sought to distance himself. Interviewed in 1994, he insisted he had no intelligence connection when he served in Mexico. He was, he noted, listed as a foreign service officer, both in the American embassy and on the Mexican government's diplomatic list.

husky Californian, Samson had gone to the University of California at Berkeley, then earned a master's degree at UCLA, and joined the agency. He had served in Singapore and Turkey before Mexico. His own marriage had ended in divorce in 1980, and the two bachelors immediately gravitated toward each other.

"The Mexico embassy is the largest in the world," Samson said. "It was a well-run and competent embassy. John Gavin was the ambassador the whole time Rick was there. The press dismissed him as 'an actor friend of Reagan's.' But he is half Mexican, has flawless, beautiful Spanish, and he wrote his honors thesis at Stanford on Latin American economics. In *Psycho*, Gavin played the guy in love with the girl who gets stabbed in the shower at the Bates Motel.[4] He was smart, very knowledgeable about Mexico, and stunningly handsome, which makes a difference in Latin America. The women melted around that guy."

But if the embassy itself ran smoothly, the same was not true of the CIA station. Both in Langley and in the rest of the embassy, the Mexico station had an all-thumbs reputation, rather akin to a baseball club that could never climb out of the cellar. "The station," one CIA man recalled, "was a weak spot. Within the embassy, the station was known as 'The Gang That Couldn't Shoot Straight.'"

About a month before Ames arrived, Francis Cote MacDonald, a career CIA officer, was promoted to chief of station. The new COS[5], then fifty-five, was a corpulent, chain-smoking native of Brockton, Massachusetts, universally known as "Mac." Short,

[4]In the classic Alfred Hitchcock thriller, Gavin's lover, Janet Leigh, is killed by the motel owner, Norman Bates (Anthony Perkins), whose shadow is cast on the shower curtain just before the murder in one of Hollywood's more memorable scenes. Gavin follows the trail to the motel and discovers the killer. Some Mexicans were dismayed by Gavin's appointment in March 1981, however, in part because the actor had become widely known in Mexico in a TV commercial for Bacardi rum. "Perhaps we should name Cantiflas to Washington," one Mexican official said.

[5]In the CIA, the officer in charge at an overseas embassy is known as the chief of station, or COS, with each letter pronounced separately. The deputy chief of station is known as the DCOS, again with each initial pronounced separately.

white-haired, and jovial, MacDonald had spent most of his career in Latin America. "He was greatly distracted by his twenty-one- or twenty-two-year-old Mexican girlfriend whom he married while he was station chief," one colleague recalled.

Distracted or not, MacDonald noticed that his newest officer was embarrassingly drunk at a party they both attended. Since there were no foreign nationals—that is, Mexicans or other diplomats—present, MacDonald was less worried about Ames spilling CIA secrets than he was about him cracking up his car on the way home. The next day, MacDonald called Ames in for a chat. He did not, however, see fit to report Ames's alcohol problem to headquarters.

MacDonald thought that Rick Ames considered himself superior to everyone else. Maybe it was because MacDonald was a street-smart Scotsman from Brockton, reacting to an officer with the name of Aldrich Ames, which sounded preppy, rich, and Ivy League, although Ames was, in fact, none of these. Or perhaps it was because whenever MacDonald talked to Ames, he had the feeling that Ames was just tolerating him. For whatever reason, MacDonald took an almost instant dislike to Ames.

Lawrence M. Wright, the deputy chief of station, shared MacDonald's view of Ames. "He thought he was more intelligent than the rest of us," Wright said. "As an operations officer he was mediocre. I did not find him really imaginative. Intellectually, I suppose he was above average. But he was borderline lazy."

A tall, slender native of Ottawa, Kansas, Wright joined the CIA out of law school, volunteered for Vietnam, and had served in South America and Spain before Mexico. Some of his subordinates derided the fact that he displayed autographed photos of Generalissimo Francisco Franco on the walls of his home. To Wright, the photos of Spain's fascist dictator were simply mementos of his CIA tour in Madrid in the early 1970s. But one reason that MacDonald did not report Ames's alcoholism to Langley may have been the fact that Wright, at the time, had a serious drinking problem himself. "He was always looking for drinking partners," one station officer recalled. "He would disappear for whole afternoons or days." Under the circumstances, it would have been awkward for either MacDonald or his deputy to report Ames for drinking.[6]

When Ames arrived in Mexico, Ronald Reagan had been president for nine months. He had rewarded his campaign manager, William J. Casey, with the job of Director of Central Intelligence. A blustery, fast-talking, self-made millionaire, Casey had served in the Office of Strategic Services during World War II, infiltrating agents into Nazi Germany. For the rest of his life, he remained fascinated by covert action. A buccaneer, he saw the CIA as an instrument of secret power, there to be used to carry out American policy across the world, whether the enemy was communism in Central America and Afghanistan or Islamic fundamentalists and terrorists in the Middle East.

If Congress had placed restrictions on covert action against Nicaragua, the law could be brushed aside, like an annoying gnat on a summer day. The agency had the money and the power; Casey would use it.

Irwin Rubenstein, a veteran foreign service officer who served in Mexico at the same time Ames did and knew him well, said the embassy and the CIA station were under pressure from Casey and the Reagan administration.

"In this period of 1981–82 there was a feeling in some circles in Washington, led by Casey, that Mexico was going down the drain," Rubenstein said.

To Casey, "It was going to be another Iran and by God, it was not going to happen on my watch. CIA did a study saying communists and/or the military would take over and there would be riots in the streets. Embassy political officers, Arthur Shankle, and I really fought this and Gavin supported us."

Dissatisfied with the political and intelligence reporting coming from Mexico, the president's Foreign Intelligence Advisory Board

---

[6]Wright recovered from his alcohol problem. He retired from the CIA in 1992, returned to his hometown, and later that year was elected district attorney of Franklin County, Kansas.

sent representatives to Mexico City several times. The CIA called in a Latin American specialist, John R. Horton, to write a report on the situation in Mexico. "Horton did a report saying the end of the world is not coming. Casey was furious. The Horton episode got into the press."[7]

The Mexico station, in short, was operating in a fishbowl. Ames, as the Soviet division branch chief for counterintelligence, was regarded as an outsider by the other officers in the station, who worked for the Latin American division. On top of that, Ames grumbled that the Latin American division was headed by his old nemesis, Dewey Clarridge.

Sometimes mocked, sometimes feared, Clarridge was a legendary figure in the CIA, as much for his sartorial splendor and personal style as for his career. A dandy who once wore a monocle, Duane R. "Dewey" Clarridge made up for his short stature with an aggressive, tough-guy manner that masked his Ivy League credentials (Brown University and a graduate degree from Columbia). His speech was peppered with expletives, of which "bullshit!" and "fucking asshole!" were among the milder exemplars.

As station chief in Rome in the early 1980s, Clarridge cut an unforgettable figure on the Via Veneto. "In Rome," one CIA man recalled, "he bought every white suit he could find. He wore the white suits in Rome, and later at CIA headquarters, with colorful handkerchiefs in his breast pocket. It was in style in Rome, but in Washington he looked like an ice cream vendor."

Casey had personally selected Clarridge for what he considered a crucial cold war arena south of the border. On a trip to Paris in 1981 for a meeting of station chiefs, Casey had been impressed by Clarridge's crisp, confident manner. He brought him back to

---

[7]Horton, a widely respected DO officer for most of his career and former station chief in Mexico, resigned in 1984 after refusing to submit to Casey's pressure to alter the report. Casey insisted that the document warn that Mexico's economic and political problems were a threat to its internal stability and, indirectly, to the security of Central America. Horton said the data did not support that doomsday conclusion. *New York Times*, September 28, 1984, p. A4.

Langley as division chief for Latin America. Clarridge would have ultimate responsibility within the CIA for the agency's ill-fated covert operation in support of the contras, who were attempting to dislodge the leftist Sandinista government in Nicaragua.[8] The CIA operation, financed by nearly $4 million diverted from secret arms sales to Iran, violated several laws passed by Congress in an effort to block aid to the contra rebels.

Ames's fear and loathing of Clarridge dated back to Turkey in the early seventies, when Clarridge was deputy chief of station in Ankara and Ames was a junior officer on his first overseas tour. Clarridge gave Ames a bad fitness report, endorsing what Ames's supervisor had written. Ames was not cut out to recruit agents, the report said. It recommended that he not be sent overseas again and that he be assigned instead to work at headquarters for the rest of his career. Clarridge considered Ames a misfit, in the wrong business. Now Clarridge had turned up as his division chief in Langley.

In his office in room 521 of the U.S. embassy in Mexico City, Ames had a number of responsibilities, both offensive and defensive. First, he was supposed to try to recruit Soviet or Eastern European intelligence officers or diplomats to work for the CIA. Second, he was required to spot Americans coming into Mexico who might be working for the Soviets. The KGB maintained a huge espionage establishment in Mexico, and the CIA, the FBI, and the Defense Intelligence Agency (DIA) knew that Mexico City

---

[8]Clarridge was caught up in the Iran-contra scandal. In 1987, he was demoted by CIA director William H. Webster for his role in the affair. Clarridge was indicted in 1991 on seven felony counts of perjury for lying to Congress about a November 1985 shipment of eighteen Hawk missiles to Iran, part of the arms-for-hostages deal. The federal indictment charged that Marine Colonel Oliver L. North disclosed the planned shipment to Clarridge, who arranged for a CIA airline to deliver the missiles, which Clarridge then told House investigators were "oil-drilling equipment." Before Clarridge could be brought to trial, however, he was pardoned the day before Christmas of 1993 by President George Bush, a former CIA director, during Bush's last weeks in the White House.

was where the KGB preferred to meet Americans it had recruited. For the KGB, Mexico was a much safer place to meet agents than the United States, where the FBI kept a close watch on Soviet diplomats known or suspected to be intelligence officers.

In addition, Ames supervised a supersensitive technical operation. As the SE/CI branch chief, he was responsible for the take from the CIA's wiretaps in the Soviet embassy in Mexico City. "The technical stuff was in place in the Soviet embassy for years," one intelligence veteran said. "Rick Ames did not have to put it in. But he had to get the transcripts to Langley."

To help him, Ames had a staff of four—a secretary, two intelligence assistants (IAs), and a Russian-language translator to transcribe the tapes of the electronic intercepts. Ames read Russian, and spoke it, although not fluently. For street work, Ames could also call on a "close support team," a surveillance group of Mexican nationals working for the CIA.

But for his primary offensive mission—targeting and recruiting a Soviet—Ames was on his own. Soon after arriving in Mexico, Ames selected his target. As Langley headquarters was soon to learn, the Mexico branch chief had aimed high.

As his target for recruitment, Ames had selected an astonishing choice: none other than Igor I. Shurygin, chief of counterintelligence in Mexico for the Komitet Gosudarstvennoi Bezopasnosti, the KGB.

On the Mexican government's diplomatic list, he appeared with his wife, Irina, as "first secretary" of the Soviet embassy on José Vasconcelos Street. In fact, Shurygin was a Line KR, or counterintelligence, officer reporting to Directorate K of the KGB's First Chief Directorate, the intelligence agency's foreign espionage arm.[9] In the Soviet embassy, he was Rick Ames's opposite number.

---

[9]In the CIA, the First Chief Directorate was usually referred to as the FCD. KGB officers referred to the directorate as the PGU, pronounced "peh-geh-ooh," the initials in Russian of the First Chief Directorate (Pervoye Glavnoye Upravlenie).

Since Ames must have understood that Shurygin's job was, if at all possible, to recruit a CIA officer—perhaps to recruit *him*—Ames's decision to target Shurygin was, at the very least, bold.

Physically, at least, the KGB's counterintelligence officer fit the older stereotype of a Soviet spy. He was short, about five feet nine, and looked like a potato farmer. Perhaps it was for that reason that his CIA code name was GTPOTATO.[10] He was a man of medium build, with brown hair, blue eyes, and a light complexion.

But if Shurygin appeared a bit rough-hewn, the resemblance to a cartoon Boris the Spy ended there. Shurygin mixed easily in the diplomatic community, and his dry sense of humor made him friends. He quickly became a power in the diplomatic club.

In Mexico City, as in many Latin American capitals, the social life of the embassies centered on the diplomatic club. The Mexico City club, the Asociación Mexicano de Consejeros, Secretarios y Agregados Diplomáticos, was universally known by its Spanish acronym, AMCOSAD. In addition to its well-attended monthly luncheons, the club sponsored social events, such as trips to Acapulco and other resorts. The KGB and the CIA found the club mutually useful, not only as an innocuous arena to meet and attempt to identify each other's officers but for other intelligence purposes as well. The club was an ideal place to make casual contacts with other diplomats, one or more of whom might be devel-

---

[10]Shurygin had a CIA code name because he was a target of interest, not because he was a recruited agent. Code names are changed frequently for security reasons. The GT prefix is a digraph, a two-letter combination, used to indicate a sensitive Soviet or Eastern European source. Digraphs may also be used simply to indicate the geographic origin of a source. Digraphs, as well as code names, also change over time. In the 1960s, for example, the CIA assigned the digraph AE to Soviet cases. By the 1980s, the digraph for Soviet cases was PD. More sensitive cases were assigned a CK digraph, which the CIA changed to GT after Edward Lee Howard, a dismissed CIA officer, defected to the Soviets in 1985. To avoid confusion, the more recent GT digraph will generally be used in this book to describe sensitive Soviet cases.

oped as an "access agent."[11] Typically, half a dozen officers from the CIA station would show up at the monthly luncheons of the club, which were held at different hotels in the capital.

Shurygin ran for election to the club's board, and won. Affable as he was, always friendly to his fellow diplomats, Shurygin was vague about his own career. He could hardly say that he was a Line KR officer in the KGB. He had served in Spain, and hinted at a naval background. He sometimes mentioned that he had been posted to Cuba as a Soviet adviser to Fidel Castro's government. And the CIA knew that Shurygin was closely involved with the Cuban mission in Mexico City.

Ames, of course, was well aware that Shurygin was the KGB counterintelligence chief in Mexico—the CIA's computers tracked that sort of thing, building up dossiers on Soviet intelligence officers as they turned up in various countries.

And so the game began. "Ames started having seventeen-hour drinking sessions with Shurygin," one CIA source said. "They would go out and literally drink for a day in Mexico City."

Shurygin was an "American targets" officer; that is, he specialized in assessing and recruiting Americans. So while Ames was supposedly developing Shurygin, the Russian was developing Ames.

It was an odd ritual dance, a coming together of two professional spies, each of whom knew exactly what the other was attempting to do. It was a dance as familiar to the professionals in the cold war as a sedate fox-trot was to the older members of a country club.

[11]As the term implies, an "access agent" is someone who for one reason or another has entrée to a target of greater intelligence interest. The CIA recruits two kinds of agents: access and FI agents, short for Foreign Intelligence Reporting Sources. Access agents, through their work or social contacts, have access to a target of interest. An access agent might be a diplomat or a friend of the target. For example, the CIA might learn that a Venezuelan diplomat lived next door to, and had become friendly with, a high-ranking Soviet embassy official. Perhaps the Venezuelan could be persuaded to act as an access agent and keep the agency informed of what the Soviet was saying and doing— whether he might be critical of Moscow, for example, and ripe for recruitment. An FI agent, on the other hand, would report directly to the CIA—for example, from inside an embassy, a government ministry, or a political party.

First, the target is "developed," through socializing, and drinking, and long talks into the night about life, love, sports, women, and politics. The vodka flows, the camaraderie grows. When the pretense that each is a diplomat is finally dropped, the talk may turn to espionage tradecraft, and even war stories. *Remember when Ivanov got drunk in Zaire? He was trying to bug the home of the CIA station chief, and he fell into the septic tank? Yes, and I heard in Langley that the COS was so busy screwing his secretary that he never heard the splash!* And so on, strange fraternity brothers trading anecdotes.

As the dance goes on over weeks and months and the friendship deepens, neither man may actually make the recruitment attempt, "the pitch."[12] Each may ultimately decide that the other is not vulnerable to, or ultimately interested in, becoming a traitor, a risky profession. In that case, better not to make the pitch, because the target—if he reports it to his superiors—may be quickly sent home in order to end the recruitment attempt and place him beyond temptation. Then neither man will be able to drink and dine with each other at fine restaurants on the expense account, nor send any more glowing reports to headquarters about the excellent developmental they are each bringing along. There is, in all this, more than a faint echo of *Our Man in Havana*.

For the better part of two years, Rick dutifully filed his contact reports to Langley about his meetings with Shurygin; the Russian in turn was surely reporting every scrap of information he learned about Rick Ames to the KGB.

"Ames thinks the first look the Soviets got at him was in Mexico," said one CIA colleague. It was the first chance that Ames had ever had to spend an extended period of time with a Soviet intelligence officer, and vice versa. In New York, several years earlier, Ames had met and become friendly with Tomas Kolesnichenko, the chief New York correspondent of *Pravda*, the

---

[12]Occasionally, the CIA will attempt a "cold pitch" to a Russian or other target who the agency thinks might be a likely prospect for recruitment. A CIA officer, often sent in from another country, will approach the target on the street or in some other public place and try to persuade him or her to become a spy for Langley. It is a dangerous ploy, and when it fails the CIA officer usually finds it advisable to get out of town, fast.

Communist party newspaper. They had lunched regularly in Manhattan, about once a month. Ames regarded Kolesnichenko as a developmental; he hoped to recruit him for the CIA.

To his friend David Samson, Ames raved about the *Pravda* man in New York. He had learned a lot from him about the Russian people, their history, politics, and culture. But the *Pravda* correspondent knew Rick under an alias. And he would probably not have been KGB; *Pravda* generally resisted the KGB's efforts to plant people on its staff. Of course, the journalist would be required to report his friendship to the New York resident of the KGB, who might monitor the relationship and co-opt the *Pravda* man, requiring him to file reports. But all of that was indirect; in Mexico, for Ames, in the meetings with Shurygin, it was *mano a mano* with the KGB.

Except that the long nights with Shurygin soon became more of a party than a contest. In the shrewd KGB counterintelligence officer who looked like a potato farmer, Rick Ames had found a drinking partner and a friend.

In the CIA station, Ames might act as though he was smarter and better than his supervisors, but in truth he felt that his talents had not been adequately recognized by the agency. He was slow to reach the level of a GS-13, slow to make his 14. He had never held an important job at headquarters. Rick Ames was not on a fast track. Attention was not being paid to him. But now Igor Shurygin was paying attention, a lot of attention, and listening.

What did Rick tell him? In Mexico, Ames had gradually begun to share his political views, and his disillusion with the CIA, with his close friend David Samson. "He was very cynical about the way the U.S. political establishment manipulated the Soviet threat," Samson said, "and cynical about the cold war in general. He said it the whole time we were in Mexico. The U.S. had superiority—militarily, politically, strategically, and in intelligence—yet we portrayed it otherwise. Rick argued that the Russians were not really a danger. The danger to peace and ourselves was that the Soviets would be provoked into irrational behavior." According to Samson, however, Ames "was not pro-communist, a socialist, or a radical. He was a liberal Democrat."

Samson said that Ames's disenchantment went deeper than criticism of American foreign policy, however; he had begun to lose faith in the work he was doing and in the agency itself. "He saw the agency's lack of accountability as a threat to U.S. democratic institutions, given the agency's terrific resources, capabilities, and the cloak of secrecy. "I think Rick had reached the point where he was disgusted by the culture of the DO and the agency. At some point Rick felt what he was doing as a CIA officer was wrong." These were subversive thoughts, had Ames voiced them openly in the embassy and the station. Samson, who considered himself a Republican and fairly conservative, sharply disagreed with Ames's view that the Soviets were not a threat. But he had come to share the same disillusionment with his work as a CIA officer and with the agency.

It is not stretching the imagination to think that in the marathon drinking bouts with Shurygin, Rick confided some of these views to the KGB man. In their hours and hours of meetings and drinking together—vodka was, appropriately, Rick's drink of choice—Ames would hardly have confined himself to bland generalities. GTPOTATO must have learned a great deal about Rick's political views, his frustration with the CIA, and his troubled marriage.

In retrospect, some veteran CIA officers speculated that Rick had been recruited by the KGB in Mexico. The FBI actively investigated that possibility and carefully examined Ames's relationship with Shurygin. It found no evidence that Ames had begun working for the KGB while he was in Mexico.

But surely during Ames's time in Mexico, Moscow learned through Shurygin that Aldrich Ames was vulnerable, a prime target for recruitment. There was no need to rush matters. Ames would be much more valuable to the Soviets when he returned to headquarters after his tour in Mexico was over. The KGB could wait.

On the beach in Mexico, perhaps at Acapulco, David Samson remembers a time when he was bantering with Ames and asked casually, "in the sense that one person asks another how he would rob a bank, 'If you ever went to work or walked in to the

Russians, how would you do that?' And he said, 'Well, I would recruit myself in such a way that they would never know my identity, and that way I would be safe. I would do it through dead drops and nonhuman cutouts, maybe electronic voices on a telephone.'"

It was just a conversation between two friends, kidding around on the beach. But Igor Shurygin *did* know Rick Ames's identity, and so did the KGB in Moscow. The Center had Igor's detailed assessments of Ames. Shurygin had patiently laid the groundwork. In time, the reports from Mexico by the man who looked like a potato farmer would help to change history.

3

ROSARIO

It was the voice that had first attracted David Samson.

It was near the end of 1981, close to the holiday season, and the monthly luncheon of the diplomatic club was just breaking up when he heard her voice, flawless American English wafting across the room.

Samson had separated from his wife four years earlier, and the divorce decree had come through in 1980. He was, in traditional bachelor fashion, always alert to a new young woman in town.

He ambled over and discovered the voice belonged to a darkly handsome, black-haired woman with olive skin and brown eyes. He chatted her up and discovered that Maria del Rosario Casas Dupuy had just arrived in Mexico City from her native Colombia. She was a cultural attaché at her embassy, vivacious and friendly, and new to the diplomatic service. Samson was taken with her. He told her he was from the American embassy, which was true as far as it went. A big man with a bushy mustache, sandy hair, and horn-rimmed glasses, Samson grew up in Sacramento, the son of an engineer. He was then thirty-eight; Rosario was twenty-nine.

He decided to check her out further, as a possible CIA source and as a possible date. Soon, they started seeing each other.

Rosario told Samson that one of her forebears had been an Arab; her relatives had come from Spain, where many have Moorish blood. People frequently asked her if she was Lebanese. Samson was not the only one attracted to the Colombian diplomat. "People loved to be around her," he recalled. "She didn't fit the stereotype at all. The typical Latin woman knows how to get her nails done and go to parties. Rosario was intellectual. She read more than any ten guys put together.

"I dated Rosario occasionally that winter and spring," Samson said. The two were not having an affair, however, and by the summer of 1982, "I had a Mexican girlfriend I was head over heels about."

But Samson was increasingly interested in Rosario, if not for romance, for her apartment and her potential as a station asset. He had done some significant favors for her. Once, Rosario Casas had a financial problem; somehow her salary from the Colombian embassy was delayed. Samson lent her a thousand dollars or so, which she paid back.

Rosario loved music. Samson offered to obtain high-quality stereo equipment for her at a big discount through catalogs available to embassy employees. He remembered getting her a Nakamichi tape deck and speakers that way.

One good turn deserves another. Rosario lived in a small apartment in an elevator building only four blocks from the American embassy, near "El Angel," the independence monument on the Reforma. It was a one-bedroom place with a balcony. It would make an ideal safe house for the agency. Samson told Rosario that he would like to use her apartment for meetings and he would pay her $200 a month. Since he would use the place only during the day, when she was at work at the Colombian embassy, he assured her she would not be inconvenienced. Rosario agreed and began receiving the payments.

Rosario Casas was not in the espionage business, and she may not have realized at first that Samson was an intelligence officer.[1] In the beginning, Rosario probably did not know that she was being manipulated, in classic fashion, by the CIA. She was naive when she first arrived in Mexico City, with no diplomatic training and no background in intelligence. But once she had agreed to accept money, she was gradually drawn deeper into the web.

When the CIA began paying her, she signed a secret written agreement pledging never to reveal her confidential relationship with the United States government. As in all such agreements with agency assets, the document did not spell out any operational details; it did not refer to the apartment or her monthly payments. But at some point, Samson assumed, she must have realized that he was more than an ordinary embassy officer; conventional American diplomats did not go around renting safe houses.

By October 1982, if not sooner, Rosario Ames had been recruited by the CIA. She was recruited by David Samson, who served as her case officer.[2]

Much later, in interviews, Rosario claimed that her work for the CIA had been limited to allowing a friend to use her apartment. At the time, facing a prison sentence and a long separation from her young son, Paul, Rosario was attempting to minimize her role for the CIA. In terms of her public relations, the less she knew about spies, the better. But in fact Rosario did more than let the agency use her apartment.

David Samson was developing Rosario as an access agent for the CIA.

[1]After Aldrich Ames's arrest as a Russian spy, American counterintelligence officials considered the possibility that Rosario Ames was a KGB officer or agent who had actually recruited her future husband in Mexico City. Some gruff old CIA hands, long retired, were convinced of it. There is no evidence, however, that Rosario Ames was ever recruited or employed by the KGB in Mexico or later. The FBI looked into that possibility and discounted it. Rather, the record suggests she was what she appeared to be, a Colombian cultural attaché. She was, however, recruited by the CIA.

[2]Rick Ames was never Rosario's case officer. Early on, in the weeks after his arrest in 1994, CIA officials privately claimed—erroneously as it turned out—that he was.

Samson questioned her, casually at first, about Cuban and other diplomats. After she signed the secrecy agreement, however, the questioning became more pointed and quite specific. That was part of the process; once someone agrees to take money, the CIA case officer feels freer to ask questions. Samson had no doubt that Rosario realized by then that he was an intelligence officer. And at some point that she understood he worked for the CIA.

He regarded himself as her case officer and Rosario as his asset, in the jargon of the intelligence world. An FBI affidavit filed the day of the Ameses' arrest said that Rosario "was a paid source for the CIA" in Mexico City.[3]

And Samson had a major target in mind for his new asset, an important KGB man who was an officer of the diplomatic club. He wanted Rosario to report on GTPOTATO, Igor Shurygin.

But how to get her next to Shurygin? The Soviet counterintelligence chief was a member of the board of the diplomatic club. Samson, the club treasurer, encouraged Rosario to run for election to the board. If you are on the board, he told her, you can get a lot of information about what's going on. Rosario had some interest in seeking election to the board in any event; she was a friend of Olga Peñaranda Reyes, the club's president, who was first secretary of the Bolivian embassy.

"The station was interested in Rosario getting elected to the board," a CIA source said. "We wanted people close to us to be near him. She was being developed as an access agent. She may not have been aware of it, but that was where the station was trying to take her. Our objective in our effort to get her on the board was Shurygin."

The CIA ran into one unexpected snag in its maneuver to put Rosario next to Shurygin. Her boss, the Colombian ambassador, was Ignacio Umaña de Brigard, an old-line aristocrat who thought

[3]While perhaps technically true, the term was somewhat misleading. Rosario was a CIA source in Mexico City, since she provided information to Samson, and she was paid. However, she was being paid for the use of her apartment as a safe house, not for the information she gave. The FBI affidavit also stated that Rosario had "been under development since June 1982" by the CIA.

the world of Rosario. "But," Samson said, "as Rosario explained it, the number two man in the embassy was Carlos Osorio, whom she thought was lazy, did nothing, and bitterly resented Rosario, who became the ambassador's girl Friday. Osorio's family had political clout in some province of Colombia and got him appointed to the Ministry of Foreign Affairs. He was always sandbagging her. When she ran for election to the diplomatic board, Osorio supported the person who ran against her. The ambassador was infuriated by that."

To Samson, Rosario had confided her frustration over the situation at the embassy. "If the ambassador needed a speech, she had to write it, even though she had other duties seeing artists, professors, and cultural types. She ended up doing all Osorio's work. He was sent home by the ambassador and eventually sacked." And Rosario won the election.

After that, Samson questioned Rosario about Shurygin. Since Samson was the club treasurer, he attended board meetings with Shurygin; he did not need to ask Rosario to report on those. But he hoped that as a new board member, she would have a chance to chat with the Russian at the monthly club luncheons. After the luncheons, Samson would ask her, what had Shurygin said? Did he say anything interesting? Would she be sure to let him know if he said anything more about that?

Samson himself, of course, could talk to Shurygin. But, he reasoned, a Soviet might tell an attractive woman from a third-world embassy a good deal more than he would tell a male from the U.S. embassy, someone whom he probably suspected was a CIA officer. A lot of guys will tell more to a woman, Samson thought, maybe talk more about their personal problems; a sensitive woman would pick up more than a CIA guy would normally get.

With Rosario on the club board, Samson knew, there was a chance that GTPOTATO would pursue her as a target for recruitment by the KGB, to run her against the CIA. Had that happened—and there is no evidence that it did—Samson would have intervened to discourage it. Nor did the CIA plan to run Rosario against the KGB as a double agent. The agency ran very few double-agent operations; they were time-consuming and trouble, in part because headquarters would have to get all sorts of interagency clearances for the information passed to the Soviets.

There was also a danger, of course, that Shurygin would try to recruit Rosario as a Colombian source. But there is no reason to think he did, or that the CIA ever asked her to spy on her own country, or that she would have. Samson did not ask Rosario for information about Colombia; nor did she volunteer any. If they gossiped occasionally about events in her embassy, it was, from Samson's viewpoint, just another way to build rapport with his asset.

But Samson did press Rosario about Cubans she had met in the diplomatic community. What did they want from you? he would ask. Did they say anything interesting?

Rosario's increasing involvement with the CIA, and her acceptance of money under a secret agreement to let the spy agency use her apartment, were not circumstances she could have imagined when she left Bogotá late in 1981 to accept the diplomatic appointment in Mexico City. A sheltered, intellectual woman, her background was in academe, not foreign affairs. She had, in truth, become a diplomat almost by accident.

Maria del Rosario Casas Dupuy was born in Colombia on December 19, 1952, to a prominent family originally from Ibagué, a city ninety miles west of Bogotá. She was the daughter of Pablo Casas Santofimio, a mathematician and university rector who became a well-known and respected political figure in Colombia, serving as a senator, the governor of Tolima state, and secretary general of the Liberal party. Short, dark-haired, and thickset, with an Arabic appearance, he looked the part of the successful politician and university official that he was. He died of a heart attack early in December 1983, a few hours after seeing his wife off on a flight to Mexico City, where she was planning to visit Rosario.

Cecilia Dupuy de Casas, Rosario's mother, seemed at first glance an unexceptional Latin matron, dark-haired, plump, and jolly. She did not fit the matronly image, however. Although she came from a conservative, aristocratic background, Cecilia ran a sort of bohemian salon in her home in Bogotá, a meeting place for students, professors, and musicians with colorful names like Chocolate Armenteros and Ismael Quintana. She befriended and helped several poor salsa musicians. Cecilia had a collection of five thousand LP records and with Rosario would listen for hours to salsa and Cuban music. Rosario was extraordinarily close to her widowed mother.

Rosario had two younger siblings, Claudia and Pablo, but her mother always seemed to pay the most attention to her oldest daughter.[4] "They were pathologically close," according to one relative, who preferred not to be named. "Rosario spent more time with her mother than with people her own age, and her mother dominated her."

In the fall of 1972, Rosario, almost twenty, enrolled in Princeton University, partly in an effort to break away from her parents. But she returned to Bogotá after one semester to resume her studies at the University of the Andes. Her mother enrolled with her.

By all accounts, Rosario was a superior student at the university, from which she graduated summa cum laude in 1976. Her graduation thesis was entitled "The Recreation of the City in Baudelaire, Eliot, and García Lorca." Jaime Jaramillo, the dean of the School of Philosophy at the time, recalled Rosario as an outstanding and exceptionally bright student.

Rosario and her mother both joined the university faculty. Rosario, who speaks five languages, taught classical Greek and worked toward her Ph.D. at Bogotá's National University, where she completed her graduate thesis, "Esthetic Problems in Hegel with Respect to Literature." All the while, she continued to live at home.

Despite her academic accomplishments and rarefied literary interests, Rosario was not all work and no play. Besides her penchant for Caribbean music, her Colombian friends say she liked to have her Tarot cards read and she carefully followed her astrological sign, Sagittarius (the Archer). She wore V-necked sweaters, Scotch-plaid pleated skirts, kneesocks, and flat shoes to class, which made her appear more like a high school student than a

---

[4]In 1994, Claudia Casas was a physician in Bogotá. Her younger brother Pablo was an official of Colombia's defense ministry.

candidate for a Ph.D. She had an active social life; there is some evidence, in fact, that she met Rick Ames on the rebound.

"Rosario was very nice, but a little shy," said her close friend Flavia Falquez. "She was a very sweet person, but she didn't open up to people very easily. She was famous for being very intelligent. She was very smart, very analytical. She ended up leaving Colombia broken-hearted because she had fallen in love with a professor at Los Andes University who was a real ladies' man."

A few years after graduating from the University of the Andes, Rosario had been named head of the Literature Department. "She was also sick and tired of the intrigues at the university," Falquez added. "There were many people after her position as department head.

"Since Rosario's father was a politician, she met the president at that time, Julio Cesar Turbay Ayala, who invited her to have lunch at the presidential palace. When she realized there was a chance of getting a diplomatic post, she jumped at it." In Mexico City, Falquez said, Rosario, because of her political clout, had importance beyond her rank. "The ambassador at the time, Ignacio Umaña de Brigard, trusted her and even left her in charge of the embassy on various occasions. She first started going out with a pilot. Later she said she met an American who was a political attaché at the U.S. embassy."

The "political attaché" was Rick Ames. "They met through the diplomatic club," said Irwin Rubenstein, of the embassy's political section. "Guys were attracted to her. A new woman in town, dresses nicely, fluent in English. At first, Ames was not in the picture at all. My guess is she dated three to five guys. I'm guessing."

It was David Samson who introduced Rick to Rosario. He thought it happened at a luncheon of the diplomatic club. "I don't remember exactly when it was," Samson said, "but by the summer of '82 I had introduced them. Rick really wasn't interested in her until maybe December or January. He didn't date her, in other words, until about six months after I introduced them."

Ames's interest in Rosario may have been piqued when they both attended the Marine Ball in November 1982. David Samson was there with his Mexican girlfriend and Rosario, and they were joined by Rick and his date, a woman from the American embassy. It was not long after that evening that Rick and Rosario began seeing each other.

Ames, as a member of the CIA station, knew exactly what Rosario's relationship to the station was. When he began dating Rosario, he told Samson immediately, since Rosario was Samson's asset. "Everyone was delighted they found each other," Samson recalled. "It never crossed my mind this was the end of his marriage. But it became apparent by April or May that it was very serious. I assume they were together at both his apartment and hers."

Now an interesting three-cornered game began between Rick, Samson, and Rosario. Ames and Samson both knew, of course, that Rosario had been recruited by the CIA. But she had also signed an agreement not to reveal her relationship with the U.S. government. The two CIA men were curious. In their discussions, they wondered aloud: Would Rosario protect the secret, or would she tell Rick?

Some months later, Rick revealed to Rosario that he was not really an embassy political officer but, like Samson, worked for the CIA. Rosario, in turn, disclosed her secret to Rick. The revelation by Ames that he worked for the CIA could not have come as an enormous surprise to Rosario; she knew that Samson was a CIA man and that Rick was his closest friend.[5] Twice, they had all flown to Acapulco together for fun in the sun; Samson took his Mexican girlfriend on one trip and his daughter on the other.

But as the secrets were revealed among the three friends, a

---

[5]In an interview in the Alexandria, Virginia, jail with Sally Quinn that ran in the *Washington Post* on October 19, 1994, Rosario said she learned that Rick was a CIA man only when he proposed marriage to her. She professed to be shocked that he was a spy. "I guess I had some sort of stereotype of what CIA people were like. . . ," she said. At the time Rick proposed, it should be noted, Rosario was already on the CIA's payroll. In earlier interviews, with the *Los Angeles Times* on April 20, 1994, and National Public Radio on April 21, Rosario Ames, without revealing David Samson's name, confirmed that she knew that the person to whom she made her apartment available in Mexico City was a CIA man.

change had become inevitable in the CIA's relationship with Rosario. Samson had been developing Rosario to become an access agent, but that was obviously no longer possible now that Rick and Rosario were being seen openly together at social affairs. Word was getting around on the diplomatic circuit that Rosario Casas was involved with the Americans.

Her usefulness as an access agent was obviously impaired. Moreover, it was against CIA rules for an agency officer to have a personal relationship with a station asset—not that the rule bothered Ames, who simply ignored it.

But the point was proven sometime during that summer of 1983 when a group of Cubans accosted Rosario at a luncheon of the diplomatic club. By that time there were rumors that Rick and Rosario were making plans for a future together. "Jesus Christ," one of the Cubans complained, "why are you getting married to this gringo?" A non-Cuban diplomat who was present defended Ames. Rick, he said, is a great guy.

But if Ames was happy with his new romance, there were still plenty of problems in his life. For one thing, talk of a wedding was premature; he was still married to Nan. He was still drinking heavily. And a new CIA station chief had taken over in Mexico City, with a new deputy. Neither of them regarded Aldrich Ames as a great guy.

4

RICK

Al Wedemeyer, at fifty-six, wanted to end his CIA career with a tour as chief of station in Mexico City. The living was easy, the climate warm, and there would be a lot less paper to shuffle than at headquarters where, in 1982, he was serving as deputy chief of the Latin American division.

Dewey Clarridge, his boss, was delighted to send Wedemeyer off to Mexico in place of Francis MacDonald. Clarridge regarded Wedemeyer, a West Pointer, as a fine person and a fine officer. He was the son of a famous father, Gen. Albert C. Wedemeyer, who had replaced Joseph Stilwell as commander of U.S. forces in China during World War II. True, the senior Wedemeyer after his retirement had become somewhat less revered as an archconservative and professional anticommunist.

But his son Al not only came from a distinguished military family, he had served in Venezuela, Chile, and Panama, where he had been chief of station. He had the background and experience to take over the Mexico City station, especially when Mexico was so much on Bill Casey's mind. Moreover, Wedemeyer had one other quality that would make him a splendid choice: He was terrified of Dewey Clarridge. He could be depended upon to follow orders from his division chief. There would be no static from the Mexico City station with Al Wedemeyer as COS.

A tall, thin man with wavy gray hair, Wedemeyer, according to his embassy colleagues, was from the start insecure in the job of station chief. "He was a very pleasant gentleman, scholarly and serious," said one. "But he was nervous, and jittery, and seemed unsure of himself."

"He was very timid, worried about everything," said another. "Always talking about, what will 'they,' i.e., headquarters, think about this. He had all these nervous mannerisms. He would walk around literally wringing his hands and making hissing noises like the Japanese. A sort of inhaling noise through the nose.

"He had a couple of lucky breaks as an ops officer. He was doing a liaison job, working with the intelligence agency of a host country. It's a real numbnuts job, nobody wants it. He got lucky because the service he was dealing with had recruited a local Communist party member who turned into a gold mine. Al got the credit. It was his agent, even though it was handed to him. It was common knowledge in LA division."

Wedemeyer had some reason to be nervous; at headquarters, Casey kept the pressure on the Mexico station. On one trip back to Washington, Wedemeyer was called in by the volatile CIA director. An embassy colleague recalled the episode, which Wedemeyer had related to him.

"Casey's first words were not hello, but, 'Last month you sent in forty-eight reports. This month you only did forty-two. What the fuck's wrong with you guys?'"

Wedemeyer's deputy, who replaced Larry Wright, was John W. Sears, a CIA veteran who had grown up in Latin America and had served in Mexico before, as well as in Brazil, Argentina, and other posts in the region. Ames hated him.

One reason was that Sears, along with Wedemeyer, finally reported Ames's drinking to Langley. At a reception at the U.S.

embassy for the diplomatic club, Ames got drunk. Sears took David Samson aside.

"Look at Rick, that's inexcusable," Sears said. At the party, Ames engaged in a loud and boisterous argument with a Cuban intelligence official.

It was too much. The CIA station sent a message to headquarters recommending that Ames be assessed and counseled for alcohol abuse when he returned to the United States.

But Ames's alcoholic performance at the party paled beside another incident in Mexico City, when he got into a traffic accident. Ames was so drunk that he could not answer police questions or even recognize the embassy officer who had been sent to help him.

It was after the argument with the Cuban official that the CIA station cabled headquarters about Ames's drunken behavior and recommended that he be counseled for alcohol abuse. Ames suspected that his drinking had been reported to headquarters by the Mexico City station, and he worried about the effect the report might have on his career. (As it turned out, he need not have worried.) Although Ames blamed Sears for blowing the whistle on his drinking, he also disliked Wedemeyer, whom he regarded as a nervous nitpicker.

Ames did some of his drinking at lunchtime. Ames and Samson were the only officers in the CIA station assigned for cover purposes to the embassy's political section. At first, they sat in on the weekly staff meetings of the State Department officers, and Rick got to know several of them well. Gradually a friendly luncheon group formed with Ames, Samson, and several of the foreign services officers. A core group of four lunched frequently at restaurants in the Zona Rosa, an upscale section of the city across from the embassy. They were Irwin Rubenstein, J. Richard "Rich" Thurman, and the two CIA men. Sometimes they would be joined by other foreign service officers.

"Ames created the impression of being very, very bright," Rubenstein said. "I knew his father had been a professor. Ames read a great deal. We'd go to lunch, an hour, two hours, he'd go back to work. We didn't see Rick that often. Because of circumstances or personality he was much more of a loner. He wasn't leading the high life.[1]

"I knew his marriage was shaky. His wife had a well-paying job in New York, and they discussed it and she decided to stay up there. They planned to meet periodically in places like Miami, South Padre Island, New Orleans, Acapulco, and they did for a while. They did meet a couple of times in some middle spot. I would ask, 'How's your wife?' And he would say, 'I haven't seen her for a few months.' You could tell they were drifting apart and the marriage was shaky. If a couple splits up geographically for any length of time, the marriage isn't going to last. I've seen foreign service couples where that happens.

"He was alone and drinking a lot," Rubenstein remembered. "At lunch we drank bulls. They're called Texas iced tea or Long Island iced tea in the U.S. They're served in a beer mug. They would take gin, vodka, rum, and tequila, any two of those, a little sugar-water syrup, club soda, a few drops of dark beer, to give it color, a lot of lemon juice. When you got it, it looked like iced tea. Very smooth and had a kick to it. If I'd have two, he would have four."

After a four-bull lunch, "Rick might slur his words, but he was not staggering. He went back to work.

"Some months later, Rick said to me when we were walking over to lunch that he had been seeing Rosario. 'Oh?' I asked. 'Is this serious?' 'Yes.' I was surprised and delighted. I noticed that when I would see them at a party, he was drinking much less. I thought, how great. The stability of a nice young lady, a nice relationship."

Aside from the lunches, Ames socialized with his fellow workers in the embassy's drama group. Irwin Rubenstein remembered one opening night when Ames had starred. "Rick performed in a play popular in the early '80s called *Mass Appeal*, it was on

---

[1]Four days after Ames's arrest in February 1994, the *Wall Street Journal* reported that Ames and the political officers "frequently went for long lunches where they discussed books—mainly contemporary fiction and political science." Rubenstein called Rich Thurman. "We both laughed. I asked, how did that get in there? Rich said he told the *Wall Street Journal,* because 'I couldn't say we talked about sex and football. So I told them we talked about books.' But what do you think four or six guys talk about?"

Broadway, about an old priest who was a drunk, and a young one disappointed with the old priest.[2] Rick played the old priest. He was great. He really dazzled everybody."

Over two years in Mexico, Ames was involved in a wide range of CIA clandestine operations and counterintelligence schemes. Most of them fizzled, although that was not uncommon, since only a small percentage of CIA field operations actually succeed. Few of Ames's operations had any measure of success, however, although some were foiled by bureaucratic opposition or the usual workings of Murphy's Law.

Ames had suggested that the station photograph all visitors to the Soviet embassy. "For some reason, the station had decided years before to dispense with that program," a CIA officer said. "In the past, people going in and out of the Soviet embassy were photographed. There was a lot of controversy over the photo identified as Oswald, for example.[3] Ames wanted to start that program again. Wedemeyer vetoed it; he said the station would drown in photographs."

Ames initiated one plan designed to identify any American KGB agents who came into Mexico to meet their handlers. The station was able to gain access to airport landing cards that incoming passengers must hand in to Mexican immigration authorities. Ames's plan was to collect the cards of everybody who arrived in Mexico on a Friday and went back on a Monday. Most vacationers, Ames reasoned, would stay for a week or more, not a weekend. Nor would most business travelers stay only for a weekend. So if someone came just for a weekend, it might indicate that the visitor was a spy.

[2]*Mass Appeal*, by playwright Bill C. Davis, was produced off-Broadway in 1980 and then moved to Broadway in 1981, where it had a six-month run. Ames played the role of Father Tim Farley, the alcoholic old priest who is persuaded to look at himself anew by an idealistic young seminarian.

[3]Lee Harvey Oswald was in Mexico City September 26–October 3, 1963, and visited the Cuban and Soviet embassies. At the time the CIA photographed visitors to both embassies. But for reasons that remain unexplained, the picture that the CIA identified as Oswald was a photograph of another man. The CIA never produced a picture of Oswald taken at either embassy.

The station approved, and the plan went briefly into effect. Because the operation involved surveillance of travel by Americans, the CIA station had to clear it with the Department of Justice. Word came back from the attorney general's office in Washington: The CIA could not collect the landing cards; the dragnet scheme was overbroad and intrusive. After having run for a few weeks, the operation was discontinued.

In another abortive operation, Ames learned—perhaps through the wiretaps he handled on the Soviet embassy—that a Soviet diplomat had been assigned by Moscow to temporary duty in Mexico City. The CIA had "pitched" the Russian—attempted to recruit him—some years earlier. The Russian had told the CIA officer who made the pitch to get lost.

The Mexico station decided to have another try, and the CIA man whose overtures had been rejected flew in, contacted the Soviet, and arranged to meet him. Ames and another CIA officer would be nearby, monitoring the meeting.

Here the plot, as in all counterintelligence operations, becomes rather complicated. Once again, the key was Igor Shurygin, GTPOTATO; if anyone from the Soviet embassy showed up to conduct countersurveillance—to watch the meeting—it would be Shurygin, the CI chief. If Shurygin did not appear, it would be a sure sign that the target had not told the KGB of the meeting and perhaps this time was considering the CIA offer. If Shurygin did show, the plan was to pitch him as well. The elaborate scheme flopped; the meeting never took place, and the CIA man from Langley flew back to headquarters, mission unaccomplished.

Undaunted, Ames designed an even more elaborate operation. This time, the target was a Soviet journalist, an Armenian correspondent in Mexico City for a Moscow newspaper. A CIA access agent, an American who had been born in Armenia and knew the journalist and was now living in the United States, was imported and set up in a villa in Acapulco. The apparently wealthy access agent invited his old friend, the Soviet newsman, to visit him. The station's plan was for the American to introduce the journalist to another station asset, a Mexican man who would develop and try to recruit the Soviet correspondent when he returned to Mexico

City. The visit to the villa took place, and the American introduced the reporter to the third party, the station asset. But when the asset later tried to contact the Soviet newsman in Mexico City, he did not respond. Apparently a good time was had by all in Acapulco, at CIA expense, but the Armenian journalist was never added to the agency's rolls.

Ames supervised another failed operation to plant a bug in the home of a Soviet-bloc diplomat. First, the CIA would have to break in to the man's apartment to hide the device. After listening to the tapes of the bug and learning as much as possible about the target, the station hoped to recruit the diplomat. The operation had been planned under Francis MacDonald, "Mac," Ames's first station chief, but was carried out after Wedemeyer took over.

The night the bug was to go in, Ames had the help of the station's close support team, the Mexicans who conducted surveillance for the agency. The team would get into the apartment, plant the tiny transmitter, and get out. Other members of the team would provide backup; they were posted in the neighborhood, alert to any countersurveillance or the unexpected return of the diplomat.

"Rick was in the field supervising the operation," a CIA man recalled. "He was in radio communication with the station. Al was back in the station at the command post, sweating blood, walking back and forth and carrying on that we were going to get caught. Well, we weren't. The bug went in beautifully." After a day, the bug stopped working, however, and the recruitment never took place.[4]

Ames had better luck with a few of his other operations in Mexico. He reportedly was effective in identifying Soviet intelligence officers who came to Mexico City to meet American double agents. These were American citizens recruited by the FBI or the

---

[4]The CIA's miniature room bugs are often hidden in a small block of wood that is concealed in, or underneath, a piece of furniture, for example. For this reason, a bug is usually referred to in agency parlance as "a block." With a long-life battery a transmitter can work for a couple of years, picking up and broadcasting all conversations in a room.

Defense Intelligence Agency in the United States, sometimes after they had been approached by the Russians to spy. Others were Americans simply recruited by the two agencies and floated to the Soviets to see what would happen.

Then there was the Ames operation that worked too well. For a time, Ames was the case officer for a moribund station asset the CIA had planted inside the PRI, Mexico's ruling Institutional Revolutionary Party. The agent was supposed to report on Mexican politics. He seldom bothered. Although Ames was a Soviet division officer, he was ordered to handle the man. Ames devised an incentive system, paying the agent more money for better information.

A CIA colleague remembered what happened next: "The Mexican was galvanized; headquarters loved his reports and the agent was showered with money. He was earning $50,000 a year. Suddenly someone, either at headquarters or in the station, said, 'Hey, this guy is making more than we are.' They cut down his payments. Rick was humiliated. He had to go back and tell the guy the agency was reneging on the deal."

Ames had one major success in Mexico, although it was not something the agency necessarily wanted to know. Ames discovered that the head of the station's close support team had never been investigated. Hired by the CIA years before, the team leader, a Mexican, was involved in many of the station's operations. But nobody had ever subjected him to a security investigation and a polygraph test. According to a CIA source, "Rick said, 'This is nuts,' and insisted the guy be investigated. It turned out the guy had been working for the KGB for years and had reported everything to the Soviets. He was fired on the spot.

"It meant that all of our ops that the surveillance team was involved in were compromised. There was a huge flap. This happened under Al Wedemeyer. It implicated so many previous station chiefs that it was hushed up. OS [the Office of Security] never really followed up. The Latin American division swept it aside."

In retrospect, the discovery that the head of the CIA's surveillance team in Mexico was working as a double agent for the KGB explained why the station's effort to bug the home of the East

European diplomat had failed. The head of the surveillance team never admitted he had sabotaged the bug. But the CIA assumed that the device had stopped working after a day because the chief of the team told the KGB exactly where to look for it.

Since Ames had pushed for the investigation that pinpointed the team leader and exposed a serious KGB penetration of the agency in Mexico, it is further evidence to suggest that he probably was not yet working for the Soviets during his assignment in Mexico. But for the better part of two years, he quietly continued his contacts with Igor Shurygin, the KGB counterintelligence chief in Mexico City. And all the while, Shurygin was assessing Ames and reporting on him to the First Chief Directorate in Moscow.

David Samsom was astonished when, early in 1983, he realized for the first time how close his friend Rick was to Shurygin. "I left Mexico in July of 1983," Samson said, "and about four months before, Rick made a comment to me about Shurygin. I said I'd grown fond of Shurygin, whom I knew from the board of the diplomatic club, and he said, 'Yes he's a great guy.' I was surprised. I realized he knew Shurygin very well."

Samson, by now, realized something else about his friend. Ames's alienation from the agency was growing deeper, and his political views seemed ever more sympathetic to the Russians. Not that Samson ever suspected, even for a moment, that Rick would sell out to the Soviets.[5]

But Rick's disenchantment would surface on their trips to Acapulco. "I remember the first time we went to Acapulco," Samson said, "with Rick and Rosario and my Mexican girlfriend. Rick and I when we get a couple of drinks would go at each other politically. Rosario was alarmed. My Mexican friend laughed. She said, 'Don't worry, this is how they are when they get together.'

"Rick always argued that the Soviets weren't as aggressive as we made them out to be in the cold war. He said we still have strategic superiority, and we knew it and they knew it. He said

---

[5]"Certainly I realized Rick was deeply disillusioned with the agency," Samson said. "But I never thought or suspected that he would do what he did. I don't approve of treason."

Reagan was talking about fighting the evil empire, but it struck terror into the Soviets because they knew we already had superiority. It would make them cornered rats, and it was dangerous to put them in that threatening situation. The Soviets would not start a war unless we threatened them.

"I told him I thought that was bullshit. While the Russians were not Hitler, clearly they were a threat. In Carter's time they perceived weakness on our part and went into Afghanistan. I argued that the Reagan administration's apparent policy of attempting to spend the Soviets into the ground was correct. In retrospect, I still believe that."

Aside from politics, the two friends continued to talk about the CIA. Ames, according to Samson, complained that the agency was a danger to the country. "He felt the agency routinely lied to Congress. Agency officials bragged about co-opting the intelligence committees. Rick felt Congress has no incentive to control intelligence. Members of Congress are only interested in money and reelection. And he made the point that the agency does favors for Congress and for important constituents. Some of it involves procurement stuff—who gets the contracts to make the secret radios for the CIA, and the plastic bubbles they put in embassies to foil electronic eavesdropping.

"Rick saw the agency as a threat to U.S. national interests, because its actions embarrassed the U.S. abroad. He considered the agency a threat to democratic institutions in foreign countries. Because of its subversion of mass media, intervention in elections, and all the rest."

But if Ames was disillusioned with the CIA, he made no move to quit and find something more to his liking. Rather, Ames began to worry that his CIA career was going down the tubes in Mexico. Each year, CIA officers receive a Performance Appraisal Report (PAR) from their supervisors, and these evaluations (known as Fitness Reports in the agency's earlier years) are crucial to their careers. Ames knew he had received unfavorable evaluations.

Not only had Sears and Wedemeyer reported his drinking to headquarters, he had been reprimanded for taking Rosario to an embassy party attended by several CIA officers. It rankled Ames.

Mac, the previous station chief, had taken his Mexican girlfriend, whom he later married, to parties. And one officer, the son-in-law of a senior CIA official, had lost a briefcase full of classified documents in a taxi and was never reprimanded, as far as anyone in the station knew. It was unfair, Ames felt. The disparity in the treatment of station officers, said one colleague, "made Rick wild."

In July, Ames's good friend David Samson left Mexico City to return to headquarters. Before leaving, Samson turned Rosario over to another CIA man, her new case officer.[6]

Within a few months, it was time for Ames to go as well. His tour was over, and he would have to return to Langley to face whatever the future might hold. Irwin Rubenstein had a particular reason for remembering the farewell party for Ames. All the luncheon regulars were there, and other friends from the embassy. "At his party," Rubenstein said, "Rick had a bull-making contest and all the ingredients were lined up. The gin, the tequila, and so on. He had a jury to judge. I won! It was the only bull I had made in my life."

But the merriment at Rick's party only masked the truth. By October 1983, as Ames's two-year tour in Mexico ended, he was an angry and bitter man, trailed by unfavorable evaluations, outraged at what he thought was unfair treatment by his superiors, and fearful that he was approaching a dead end in his CIA career. He was still drinking too much, and not only in the marathon sessions with Shurygin.

But he had made some decisions. He had, by now, proposed to Rosario. He would go to New York and ask his wife for a divorce. Rosario had promised to join him in Washington. He was under financial pressure, but he was sure he would somehow find a way, once back at headquarters, to build a new life for the two of them.

[6]With her friend David Samson gone, it was not the same. Rosario saw little of the new CO and ended her relationship with the CIA in December. By that time, however, she was preparing to come to Washington to be with Ames.

5

"SUCH MEN ARE DANGEROUS"

Cummins Catherwood was born on Philadelphia's Main Line in 1910, went to the right prep school, and became a wealthy financier, philanthropist, banker, oilman, patron of the arts, avid yachtsman in the Newport-to-Bermuda races, and a pillar of the Philadelphia establishment. In 1947, with a gift of $15 million, he established a small family foundation in Bryn Mawr designed "to promote scientific research" in educational institutions.

That same year, Congress created the Central Intelligence Agency. To carry out its covert activities, the CIA needed various fronts, "proprietaries," and other organizations that might serve as conduits for the agency's money, so that its clandestine source could not be traced. The agency soon discovered that obscure foundations were ideal for this purpose.

It was the height of the cold war, and dozens of foundations were happy to serve as fronts for the CIA, thereby discharging their patriotic obligation in the battle against international communism. One of them was the Catherwood Foundation.

In 1952, Carleton Cecil Ames, a Ph.D. historian, was teaching at the River Falls State Teachers College in River Falls, Wisconsin, a rural community about twenty miles east of St. Paul, Minnesota. At age forty-six, he had settled into a comfortable life on the little campus. He was married, and he and his wife were raising three young children, a son and two daughters.

The future looked pleasant, if predictable. As it happened, however, Carleton Ames was one of a relative handful of academic experts in the United States on the new nation of Burma, which had won its independence four years earlier. Officially, Burma was neutral, but it had been one of the first nations to recognize Communist China and leaned to the left. Clearly, Burma would bear watching, and the CIA needed spies who understood the country's culture and history.

In 1949, Carleton Ames had written his Ph.D. dissertation at the University of Wisconsin: "Impacts of British Rule in Burma 1900–1948." He received his doctorate that same year. He was made to order for the agency.

And so it came to pass that Ames, a tall, distinguished-looking man with a great mane of white hair, found himself recruited into the CIA, a professor turned spy. With his family, he moved to Washington for a year of training in his new profession.

Then in 1953, Carleton and his family were sent to Rangoon. Carleton Ames was a CIA officer in the Directorate of Operations.[1] Most CIA spies overseas have diplomatic cover and operate under the protective umbrella of American embassies. Carleton Ames, however, went to Burma as a "NOC," (pronounced "knock") a CIA acronym for Non-Official Cover. To work as a NOC is potentially the most dangerous of CIA jobs, because if caught and

---

[1] In those years, the DO was known as the Directorate of Plans. The name was changed in 1973. The Directorate of Operations, the CIA's espionage arm, is also known as the Clandestine Services. To avoid confusion, the CIA's espionage directorate will be referred to throughout as the Directorate of Operations, or DO.

arrested, a NOC can be imprisoned or executed. The worst that a CIA officer under diplomatic cover usually faces is expulsion after being declared persona non grata.

In Rangoon Carleton Ames posed as a college professor visiting Burma to write a book. He was doing so, Ames told anyone who asked, on a grant from the Catherwood Foundation.

It was probably on the trip to Bhamo, a river port up near the Chinese border, that Rick at age twelve or thirteen learned the truth about his father. At least that is what his sister, Nancy Ames Everly, thinks.

Carleton told his wife, Rachel, that he would have to leave Rangoon and go up north. "He was gone for several weeks," Mrs. Everly said. "Rick went with him." She thinks that as the oldest of the three Ames children, and a bright kid, Rick must have realized his father was a spy. "Whether Carleton told him on the trip north, or Rick guessed, I don't know. Rick never said. Father was most private."

We were sitting in Clyde's restaurant in Tysons Corner, not far from the FBI office in northern Virginia where they took Rick Ames the day they arrested him as a Russian spy. Nancy Everly, who is thirteen months younger than her brother, is an intelligent, sophisticated, and attractive woman, a successful executive of a computer company. She has survived the trauma to her family with great effort by separating her deep affection for her brother from the appalling crime of which he has been convicted. "It's the only way I can deal with it," she said. Mrs. Everly has regularly visited her brother in prison. She is devastated by what has happened.

The Ames family originally came from England and settled in Vermont. Rick's great-grandfather, George Ames, joined the Union army during the Civil War. Nancy Everly has a faded picture of him in uniform, at age seventeen, serving in the Army of the Potomac. George Ames was barely old enough to join up, and since the war was nearing its end, he did not fight in any battles. An unpublished biography written by his son noted wryly that the only action George's unit saw was a raid on a watermelon patch in northern Virginia. After the war, George married, moved to Green Bay, Wisconsin, and became a foreman in a logging camp.

His son, Jesse Hazen Ames, the grandfather of Rick and Nancy, was an educator who became president of the River Falls State Teachers College, now a campus of the University of Wisconsin. A building on the campus, the Ames Teacher Education Center, is named for Rick's grandfather.

Carleton Ames, Jesse's son, was born in 1905 in Brandon, Wisconsin, a small town about sixty miles northeast of Madison, the state capital. He earned his bachelor's and master's degrees at the University of Minnesota and began teaching history at River Falls, his father's college.

One of his students, Rachel Aldrich, caught his eye. She had grown up on a farm in nearby New Richmond, Wisconsin. At twenty, she was attractive, dark haired, and thirteen years younger than Carleton. They were married in 1938.

Rachel was the daughter of John Leo Aldrich, a farmer, and Mabel Luckman, the daughter of a lumberman and inventor. Rachel had lived on the farm until she went to college in River Falls, where she worked for a local family in return for her housing.

Aldrich Hazen Ames, Carleton and Rachel's first child, was born on May 26, 1941, in River Falls. As a child, and through high school, he was Ricky; after that he was called Rick. His sister Nancy was born the following year, and their kid sister, Alison, came along in 1945, a few months after the end of World War II.

Rick Ames appears to have had an average, fairly normal boyhood, although family and friends remember him as introverted and bookish. "Rick was a Cub Scout in Wisconsin," his sister Nancy said. "He did not do any sports then. He was interested in chess, he was an intellectual kid. He wore glasses as a boy of ten. Rick always had terrible eyesight. He kept to himself. Rick was a very private person."

Was he a good student? She hesitated. "He pursued his interests; he was not studious at school. He liked science fiction. He pursued knowledge for his own pleasure; it wasn't for good grades."

Rachel's father, John Aldrich, was a Catholic, and she was raised as one. Her own children were not. In River Falls, Rick went to Methodist Sunday school, and occasionally the Ameses attended services at the Methodist church. But they were not a religious family.

It was hardly a joyful, Leave-It-to-Beaver existence in River Falls. The Ames family was formal in style. Emotions were to be repressed, not shared. "The family placed emphasis on good manners," Nancy said. "It was partly the era, of course, but we were expected to be polite in our dealings with each other, and with parents and other adults. In our family, you never probed or pried, never asked, 'What are you thinking, how do you feel?'"

One of the things the family never spoke about was Carleton's alcoholism. Carleton Ames was a striking figure, six feet tall, a slender, courtly man whose hair had turned white by the time he was in his early thirties. It helped to give him an air of erudition. Like Rick, he wore glasses and was nearsighted. He also drank a six-pack of beer a night. Rick's father was not a falling-down drunk, at least not at home. He would be up in his study, reading and drinking quietly. Periodically, there would be an episode of binge drinking, and Carleton would disappear on a weekend. His absence was never explained to the children. It didn't have to be.

Within the family and to his friends, Carleton was called "King," apparently because he had once played a king in a college production. Nor was his wife known as Rachel. In the family, said Nancy, "It was King and Rae."

When the Ames family arrived in Washington in 1952 after the CIA had recruited Carleton, they moved into an apartment on North Capitol Street. Rick was ten, Nancy nine, and Alison six. The children attended public schools. Rick went to Keene Elementary School, then still racially segregated.

A year later, the family was off to Rangoon. The CIA station at the time was headed by James B. Burns, a hard-drinking Princeton graduate who was only twenty-six. Carleton was not based in the embassy with Burns, of course, since he was ostensibly in Rangoon as a professor engaged in research on a grant from the Catherwood Foundation.[2] Nor could Carleton afford to be seen going in and out of the embassy very often. But he reported to Burns, his boss, and the two families grew close. Beverly Burns, then married to the CIA station chief, became a lifelong friend of Rachel Ames. Rick baby-sat for the Burns's young son.

The CIA station in Rangoon was a busy place; the agency was deeply involved in an operation that it had concealed even from the American ambassador, William Sebald. Burma, once part of British India, was invaded by the Japanese during World War II. After the war, the British and the Burmese leader, Aung San, reached agreement on full independence for the country. Aung San was assassinated in 1947, but the following year neutral Burma became independent under a socialist government.

By 1953, when Carleton Ames arrived on the scene, there was growing tension over the presence of some twelve thousand Chinese Nationalist troops in northern Burma. The troops had fled the advancing Chinese Communist army. The Nationalists, led by General Li Mi, settled down to a life of banditry and opium-running.

The Burmese government pleaded with Washington to apply pressure on Taiwan to withdraw the troops. Privately, Burmese officials accused the CIA of aiding the Nationalist troops to keep Rangoon from becoming too friendly with Communist China. Ambassador Sebald, who had not been told the truth, repeatedly assured the Burmese government that the United States was not involved. But Burma was right; the CIA was supporting the

[2]Even forty years later, and well after the end of the cold war, the Catherwood Foundation was not a fount of information. A telephone call to its offices in Bryn Mawr, Pennsylvania, was answered by a woman who refused to give even her first name. A request was made to speak with Cummins Catherwood, Jr., listed as the foundation's president. "No. That won't be possible," the woman said. She confirmed that the foundation had provided assistance to the CIA, but that was a long time ago. Only the senior Mr. Catherwood, who died in 1990, would know about it. She did not believe his son would know.

Nationalist troops through a front called Sea Supply with the cable address "Hatchet."[3]

Except for the trip to Bhamo, only forty miles from the Chinese border, on which he accompanied Carleton, Rick was not exposed to much of this intrigue. Yet he was attracted, even at that early age, to the world of espionage.

He devoured a series of books by the British author Leslie Charteris about the swashbuckling fictional hero Simon Templar, "the Saint." The Saint was the James Bond of his day, a dashing, debonair British adventurer who traveled the world rescuing damsels in distress, smoking cigarettes, drinking highballs, and solving mysteries. In Burma, Rick Ames signed himself "Simon Templar."

And for twelve-year-old Rick, Rangoon was paradise. For the first time, the intellectual, chess-playing boy blossomed as an athlete. "There was a tennis and swim club, and most homes had tennis courts," Nancy recalled. "Rick learned to sail. He became a good sailor and an excellent swimmer." At thirteen, Rick won second place in the men's long-distance race at the Kokine Swim Club.

He also got his first taste of the good life. Rangoon, and the upper-class enclave just off the Royal Lakes where the Ameses lived, still enjoyed the atmosphere of the British raj. There were servants, a large Oriental-style house with louvered slats instead of solid walls, and some touches right out of Kipling. Once, a four-foot snake, a highly poisonous krait—a member of the cobra family—was killed in the house.

The Ames family left Burma and returned to Washington in 1955 in time for Rick's freshman year in high school. The Ameses moved to a house directly across the street from McLean High School in suburban northern Virginia. Rick went there, along with

[3]After Burma took the issue to the United Nations in 1953, the Nationalists withdrew some of the troops, but many stayed behind. Ambassador Sebald resigned in disgust and spent the next three years trying to persuade the CIA and the State Department to talk to each other so that the left hand of the United States might know what the right hand was doing in its international dealings.

a lot of other CIA brats. He was active in the drama, debate, and chess clubs, and began dating in his junior year. Rachel taught English at the school.

At McLean, Rick formed close friendships with two other boys, Wes Sanders and John M. Souders. All three had one or more parents working for the CIA. "They were called the Triumvirate," said Margaret Anderson, Rick's high school classmate and good friend, now a history professor at the University of California at Berkeley. "We knew all three had fathers who worked for CIA, and all three had summer jobs working for the CIA. The three boys were interlocking with our girl gang. Well, it wasn't much of a gang. We did things like put toilet paper on the French teacher's dogwood trees."

It was the late 1950s, and the McLean High School scene was straight out of *American Graffiti.* "We rode around in cars on Saturday night. We'd go to Tops Drive-in in Arlington.

"Ricky wasn't an athlete. He was in the drama club and the debate club. He played Cassius in *Julius Caesar.* 'Yond Cassius has a lean and hungry look; he thinks too much: such men are dangerous.' Wes was Brutus. I forget who played Caesar. Ricky was good."

Kathryn Strok Hartzler, another of Ames's friends at McLean, remembers Rick's role in the British farce *See How They Run.* "It all took place in a vicarage in a village in England. Another guy played the part of the Russian spy who went around yelling 'Tovarich!' Rick was the vicar who runs through the theater in his underwear chasing the Russian spy.

"There was very little drinking in our crowd and of course no drugs. The craziest thing we did was to go out and steal signs. I remember my favorite sign we stole was 'Rabbit Manure—25 cents a bushel.' We listened to Elvis, Johnny Mathis, Chuck Berry, the Kingston Trio, Harry Belafonte, and also classical music. I also remember a bunch of us, I think Ricky was one, got season tickets to the National Theater. We would go to art museums on weekends.

"There were about two hundred and fifty kids in the class. Ricky was respected among our crowd. There was a big arts focus at the school. Of course there were also the Dixie-playing, Confederate flag-waving types at the football games. But for a high school in the South in the fifties it was very cultural. The students were diverse. Many had traveled all over the world."

Margaret Anderson remembered Rick as a New Deal liberal. "I was a reactionary Dixiecrat who went to Swarthmore and came back a radical. Ricky always argued with me in my segregationist stage in a very civil way. When I came back from Swarthmore a pink, I argued with him then. I'm spouting Red slogans but uninformed. But Rick was knowledgeable. Rick argued me into a corner. 'C'mon, Peggy,' he said, 'don't you have any integrity at all?' He was remonstrating with me because I seemed to take on the political coloration of wherever I was. In northern Virginia, surrounded by Robert E. Lee, I'm a Confederate, when I go to Swarthmore, I'm a Red. His view was you should have some ideas of your own. Ricky was someone who knew what he thought, he had a set of ideals." Anderson was bewildered by Ames's treachery. "He was the opposite of someone who betrays his country because somebody gives him money."

Margaret Anderson said she and Rick "were just good friends, we did not date each other. In high school I was very close to him. We were going to get married. We had a pact. If neither of us got married by the time we were thirty, we would marry."

Other friends suggested that during Ames's teenage years his relationship with his father was troubled. One member of the Triumvirate, Wes Sanders, a playwright and director in Boston, warmly remembers Rachel Ames, a popular teacher at McLean. But, he said, "Rick never spoke of his father. He [Carleton] was a shadowy figure. His mother taught English at school and was a remarkable woman. I had her in English. Sometimes we would see the father at Rick's house, but he did not socialize with us."

Secluded in his study, Carleton was not closely involved with his children, either, although he would take time off to watch Rick in a debate in school or Nancy playing basketball. A friend who knew the family in Rangoon recalled, "Carleton was somewhat remote, but he was extremely proud of his children. When Rick went to get his 'B' in sailing I remember Carleton was very proud of him. But I don't remember him being a buddy to his children."

It was Rachel who ruled the roost. A liberated woman for that era, she and Carleton divided many of the household chores. "My father did the grocery shopping," Nancy Everly said. "He would do laundry and cook some of the time. He was a good cook, mostly meat and potatoes. He always had a garden. We always had corn and strawberries."

In 1957, after Rick's sophomore year at McLean, he obtained his first summer job with the CIA, working as a lowly records analyst, marking classified documents for filing. He held the same job for the next two summers.

His father's career, meanwhile, had gone downhill. Carleton had returned from Burma with an extremely negative performance appraisal. Rick later bitterly blamed Jim Burns, the Rangoon station chief, for his father's lackluster career at the agency.[4] But CIA records, according to the Senate Intelligence Committee report on the Ames case, reflect that "the elder Ames had a serious alcohol dependency." Rick himself recognized that Carleton had not achieved notable success at the CIA. "My father had a very honorable career," he told Dennis DeConcini, the chairman of the Senate panel, "but not a distinguished one."[5]

When Carleton returned from Rangoon, no CIA division particularly wanted him. For six months, he was on probation, his future uncertain. Finally, James J. Angleton, who had just become chief of the agency's new Counterintelligence Staff in 1954, took him on. "Angleton's staff became a parking lot for the Clandestine Services," said one veteran CIA officer. "A lot of people were put there who did staff busywork. Angleton occasionally complained about it."

There is some irony in all this, since Angleton, the CIA's legendary and controversial hunter of moles, had employed the father of the man who became the most notorious mole in the

---

[4]Asked about Carleton Ames, Burns, retired and living in Virginia in 1994, said, "Yes, I remember him." When questioned about Carleton Ames's relationship to the CIA station in Rangoon, however, Burns said: "What is this about? I don't think I can give you any information. Thank you [Hangs up.]."

[5]August 5, 1994, interview with Aldrich Ames by Senator Dennis DeConcini, Transcript, p. 4, in U.S. Senate Select Committee on Intelligence, *An Assessment of the Aldrich H. Ames Espionage Case and Its Implications for U.S. Intelligence*, November 1, 1994, hereinafter "Senate Interview" and "Senate Report."

history of the CIA.[6] Carleton's colleagues on Angleton's staff, then housed in temporary buildings by the Reflecting Pool on Washington's Mall, remember him snoozing at his desk after lunch. "The offices in summer were very warm," said one, "and I'd see him with papers in front of him, sound asleep."

William R. Johnson, a retired member of Angleton's shop, remembered him as well. "Carleton Ames was a colleague of mine on the CI staff. I didn't really know him, he was almost a transparent guy. He was an analyst. A kind of a faceless guy."

When Rick Ames graduated from high school in 1959, the senior class voted him "wittiest." That summer, he interned again at the CIA. In August, he went off to the University of Chicago. As in high school, he was active in a theater group, acting and producing. The following summer, he returned to Langley and worked as a laborer and painter at a CIA facility in Virginia. That fall, as John F. Kennedy was campaigning for president against Richard Nixon, Rick returned to the University of Chicago. But he spent so much time with the drama group that he flunked out of the university and took a job as an assistant technical director in a Chicago theater.

Early in 1962, Ames returned to Washington. Once again, he applied for a job at the CIA. It was a decision obviously influenced by the fact that Carleton was already employed there. "You know my father had worked for the agency," Ames told Senator DeConcini. "And that in a sense stimulated, played a strong role in my coming to work there."[7]

The CIA relies heavily on the polygraph, or lie detector, to screen both applicants and current employees. Although lie detectors are notoriously unreliable, many CIA employees *think* they work and are frightened to death of them, which makes their use at least partly effective. During his entrance polygraph on March 23, 1962, Ames admitted that the year before he and a friend,

---

[6]Aldrich Ames, it should be clear, was not the presumed mole whom Angleton hunted during the 1960s and never found, destroying the careers of several loyal CIA officers in the process. Ames did not begin spying for the KGB until 1985, a quarter of a century after Angleton's futile mole hunt.

[7]Senate Interview, p. 4.

both drunk, had taken a bicycle from a liquor store. Caught by police, they were released with a reprimand.[8]

Ames passed his polygraph. On June 17, 1962, at age twenty-one, he was hired by the CIA as a clerk-typist, his first full-time job with the agency. He was a document analyst in the Records Integration Division (RID) of the DO, where he worked with the files of a clandestine operation against an East European target. It was Ames's first real exposure to espionage operations against the Soviet bloc, and he became increasingly fascinated with the subject.

While working at the CIA, Ames enrolled as a part-time student at the George Washington University. He graduated in 1967 with a bachelor's degree in history and a B average.[9]

That same year Ames applied for the agency's Career Trainee Program. He was sent to "the Farm," the CIA's school for spies at Camp Peary, near Williamsburg, Virginia. There he learned the intelligence "tradecraft," from secret writing to agent recruiting and handling, that prepares trainees to become full-fledged case officers.[10] In October 1968, Ames completed his year of training and reported to Langley headquarters. From the start, he worked for the agency's covert side, the Directorate of Operations. He held a top-secret clearance for all of his thirty-one years with the CIA. Within the agency, he used the pseudonym Winfield Leggate.

In the CIA, Ames was always "Rick." No one ever called him

[8]The prank was of little consequence, perhaps, except that Ames's admission meant that the CIA—even before it had hired him— knew of an incident involving Aldrich Ames and alcohol, a behavior pattern that was to repeat itself over many years.

[9]While working for the CIA and completing college, Ames was arrested three times—for intoxication in April 1962, for speeding in 1963, and reckless driving in 1965. At least one of the driving violations was alcohol related.

[10]A psychological assessment of Ames, written before he was accepted for the Farm, found him to be an intellectual and a loner, poor qualities for meeting and recruiting agents. However, at the end of his training, Ames was assessed as a "strong" trainee and depicted as intelligent, mature, enthusiastic, and industrious. These findings were contained in a 486-page classified report on the Ames disaster compiled by Frederick P. Hitz, the CIA's inspector general, in 1994. Ironically, although the fact was not publicized, Hitz had been Ames's classmate at the Farm.

Aldrich. One of the minor mysteries of the Ames case is why, in an agency long dominated by high-WASP graduates of the best eastern establishment schools, many with reversible names like his, Ames preferred to be known as Rick. "Aldrich Ames," with its tony cachet and faint whiff of Rockefeller, might have been a name that would not only have advanced his career inside Langley but would also, later on, have helped to explain all those millions that began to flow into his bank accounts in the mid-1980s. An Aldrich Ames might not have had to explain a thing. But, then, neither did Rick.

Ames had met and found himself attracted to another CIA career trainee, a young, slender blond woman from upstate New York. Nancy Jane Segebarth had grown up in Orchard Park, a pleasant suburb of Buffalo, the daughter of an official of the Buffalo Savings Bank.

After graduating from Denison University in Granville, Ohio, in 1963, she had joined the CIA the following year and was assigned to the Directorate of Operations. Rick and Nancy Segebarth began dating.[11] They were married in May 1969 at a Unitarian church on Hunter Mill Road in suburban Oakton, Virginia.

Well before then, however, the Ameses' nuclear family had begun to break up. Alison, Rick's youngest sister, was hospitalized with a serious emotional disorder, and Rachel, who somehow felt she was part of the problem, distanced herself by accepting a teaching post in Karachi, Pakistan, for two years.[12] Carleton remained in Washington. It was a time of turmoil and strain for the family.

But for Rick, the future looked bright. He was promoted, and in October 1969 he was given his first overseas assignment, in Turkey. At age twenty-eight, with his new bride, Rick Ames would be put to the test. In the service of his country, he would be a spy in Ankara.

[11]Within the Ames family, Nancy Segebarth Ames was known as Nan, at least in part to avoid confusion with Rick's sister, Nancy Everly.

[12]Alison recovered, married, and had a son, but tragically died at age forty-one of breast cancer.

6

TOPHAT

In November 1961, seven months before Ames had joined the CIA, an unusual blip came across the radar screen of John F. Mabey, a thirty-eight-year-old FBI agent in New York City. A wiry, square-jawed graduate of Notre Dame, Mabey at the time was head of the Soviet counterintelligence squad in Manhattan. The tidbit of information that reached him that month was unusual, and potentially exciting.

For some months, the FBI had been tracking a Soviet military intelligence officer assigned to the United Nations. His name was Dimitri Fedorovich Polyakov, and he was a colonel in the GRU, the Glavnoye Razvedyvatelnoye Upravlenie, the military equivalent of the KGB. Edward H. Moody, an FBI agent working with Mabey, had succeeded in placing two or three access agents around Polyakov at the UN. The Russian casually mentioned to one, an American, that he would like to meet the commanding general of the First Army, headquartered on Governors Island. Prompted by John Mabey, Lt. Gen. Edward J. O'Neill, the First

Army commander, invited Polyakov to a party, along with about thirty other guests from the United Nations. At the cocktail party, the GRU man took the general aside and asked if he could be put in touch with the CIA representative in New York. The general thought it could be arranged.

In due course, General O'Neill invited Polyakov to another cocktail party. "I was invited," recalled Mabey, now retired and living in northern California. "I was supposedly the CIA representative. I took a girl who was a steno in the office, who was supposed to be my wife. I was introduced to him under whatever name I was using. Polyakov had been told the name. After the introduction it was obvious that Polyakov was avoiding me. Towards the end of the evening I decided to take the bull by the horns and go up to him."

The FBI man was blunt. "We've gone to a lot of trouble," he said quietly.

"I've changed my mind," Polyakov replied.

"We've gone to a lot of trouble," Mabey persisted. "I want to meet you at Fifty-ninth Street and Columbus Circle at midnight."

Polyakov shook his head. "I'll report this."

"You better be there."

Mabey had no idea whether his ploy would work. "At midnight I went down to Columbus Circle. It was a drizzly night, no one around. But he showed up, out of the shadows. He said, 'I have no time, I have to get home, my wife is waiting for me. If you don't leave me alone, I will report this to the UN and there will be repercussions.' And he took off."

That seemed to be that. Mabey reported the disappointing midnight encounter to his chief, Joseph L. Schmit, the top FBI agent in charge of counterintelligence in New York. "Joe Schmit was a wise old duck. He said let's just sit on this. So we followed him in the normal way.

"In January 1962, we made a decision to approach him again. It was a Saturday morning. We knew he usually worked half a day and came home at noon. We decided to make the approach on West Eighty-sixth between Columbus and Central Park." Polyakov and his wife and two sons lived on that block in the Cameron, a residential hotel.[1]

On the other side of Central Park, FBI agents were stationed across from the Soviet mission to the UN at 680 Park Avenue. Other agents were staked out near the hotel on the West Side. "I was waiting in the lobby," Mabey said. An FBI agent on Park Avenue radioed that Polyakov was on the way in his car. "His wife and children came in first and went up in the elevator. About ten minutes later he walked in. He saw me sitting in the chair. He got on the elevator and I walked right behind him and got on. There were two other people on the elevator. The elevator stopped and the two people got off.

"'I want to see you,' I said. We were alone. I said, 'Be in room so-and-so on the seventh floor within a half hour.' We had rented a vacant apartment. 'I can't,' he said, 'my wife is expecting me, we have plans.' 'Be there,' I said. He got off at the eighth floor."

Mabey waited, but Polyakov never showed. "I went up to the eighth floor, knocked on his door, and he answered."

The FBI man wasted no words.

"I'm expecting you," he said.

"I'm sorry, I'm delayed."

"You be there."

"Sorry, I have to go move my car."

"I'll be waiting for you."

Mabey went back downstairs to the FBI's apartment. Fifteen minutes later, there was a knock on the door.

It was Polyakov. "I can't spend any time," he said nervously. "I have to go back to her or she'll wonder where I am."

"Fine," Mabey answered, "but I'll see you at 110th Street and Broadway, at the entrance to Columbia, at nine o'clock tonight.

"I got up there, and there was nobody around. Then I saw his car. He pulled over to the curb, opened the door, and said get in. He put a finger to his lips. He whispered to me. 'We can't talk. The car might be wired.' I said, 'It wouldn't be us.' He kept shaking his

[1]The Cameron Hotel, then at 41 West Eighty-sixth Street, no longer exists.

head and his hand. He drove up to Grant's Tomb. It was desolate. He pulled over to the curb."

The Russian seemed to overcome his fear of a car bug as Mabey began talking. "I said, 'I can't understand your change of attitude. You indicated you wanted to talk to someone from American intelligence. Do you want to cooperate or not?' And he hesitated a moment and said, 'Okay, I'll cooperate.'"

Mabey pulled out a United Nations directory. "I opened the book. I said, 'We need a show of faith. Give me the GRU resident's name, your code clerk's name, and the names of the other GRU members.' So he did that. He pointed to the names. He said, 'He's the resident. I'm the assistant resident in charge of illegal operations.' I asked, 'Who is the KGB resident?' He did that."

Mabey pressed Polyakov to explain his motives. The GRU man said he was dissatisfied. "He said, 'I'm being overlooked in my work.' 'What do you expect out of this?' 'Nothing.'" But as it turned out, there was something. "Polyakov said he needed six hundred dollars. He said a GRU underling who had left New York for Moscow a few months before had given him six hundred dollars and wanted him to buy some things and bring them back. Polyakov spent the money and didn't have it. I said, 'Okay, we'll give you the six hundred dollars. I'll see you on the seventh floor in one week.' We were in the car for an hour and a half."

It was approaching midnight when the FBI man and the Russian drove away from the deserted monument. "We started downtown, and in the Eighties on Riverside Drive he said, 'Get out.' I found the nearest telephone and they sent a car to pick me up. We were all pretty elated."

Once Polyakov was recruited by the FBI, he had to be given a code name to protect his identity. Mabey thought about it and came up with his choice. Henceforth, in the bureau's files, Dimitri Fedorovich Polyakov would be known as TOPHAT.

Soon after TOPHAT began providing information to the FBI, Aleksei Isidorovich Kulak, a KGB officer under cover at the United Nations, volunteered his services to the FBI. Kulak, a scientific attaché in the Soviet mission to the UN, provided information to the bureau in the 1960s and 1970s. Over a fifteen-year period, the FBI paid him approximately $100,000. The FBI gave Kulak the code name FEDORA. In the pantheon of cold war spies, the code names FEDORA and TOPHAT became as intertwined as ham and eggs; one was seldom mentioned without the other.[2]

One week after the encounter at Grant's Tomb, Mabey met again with the Russian in the safe apartment at the Cameron. "We talked about everything," Mabey said. "He was disgruntled. He was forty-three and he felt he should have been a general by this time. He was from the Ukraine. He was in the artillery during World War Two, decorated in the war. I had been in the army, too, and we talked about that experience."

To Polyakov, Mabey was "John"; the FBI man never revealed his last name. "We had five or six meetings every week in the apartment. Then he asked that we change the meeting place, it was too close to home. We got an office at 607 Madison Avenue and subsequent meetings were held there every week.

"In the safe houses in New York, he gave us actual chemicals used by Soviet illegal agents in secret writing. He emptied his pockets once, and all the chemicals fell out. The FBI lab analyzed the chemicals. The lab was able, for the first time, to read letters we had intercepted from illegals[3] in a number of cases. He never gave us a document. He was afraid to get documents; he would not accept a camera."

TOPHAT talked for hours about Moscow's "illegals" in the United States, many of whom he had trained. Most Soviet spies in America had legal cover, as diplomats in Washington, at the United Nations and the Soviet UN mission in New York, or at the consulate in San Francisco. But both the KGB and the GRU had also successfully infiltrated illegals into the United States, spies

[2]"I personally chose the name TOPHAT from the first day he cooperated," John Mabey said. "It sort of started a series. Later, the name FEDORA was picked by someone else." As it turned out, the bureau's affinity for headgear did not end there. "We had HOMBURG and others," Mabey recalled.

[3]In KGB/GRU terminology, illegals are spies operating abroad without official cover.

with no diplomatic status. Often, the illegals adopted the identity of real Americans who were unaware that Soviet intelligence agents had stolen their names and backgrounds.

While spies under diplomatic cover could be followed and watched with relative ease, illegals were extraordinarily difficult to detect. For that reason, the FBI was interested in every scrap of information that Polyakov could provide.

The bureau was particularly interested in the additional details that TOPHAT was able to provide on two GRU illegals, a husband-and-wife team who had been dispatched to New York in the late 1950s. The FBI gave the episode the code name KOBCASE. It was not the bureau's finest hour. The two illegals, Margarita N. Tairova and Igor A. Tairov, clearly aware that they were being watched, had vanished from under the noses of the FBI. Worse yet, some American intelligence officials believed that the couple's detection of the FBI surveillance had led directly to the arrest of Lt. Col. Pyotr Popov of the GRU, the first Soviet intelligence officer ever recruited by the CIA. Popov was the last person to see Margarita Tairova before she arrived in New York in October 1957; he had put her on the plane in West Berlin and the FBI was waiting at the other end. As a result, KGB suspicion focused on Popov.[4]

TOPHAT told John Mabey that he had trained the Tairovs before they were dispatched to New York and had also trained another GRU illegal, Kaarlo Rudolph Tuomi, the key figure in another FBI case code-named KAROT. Tuomi, who had been "turned" by the FBI and persuaded to become a double agent, provided the leads

---

[4]Popov, code-named GRALLSPICE by the CIA, was arrested in 1958 and later executed. Counterintelligence mavens still debate the reason; the FBI surveillance in New York was only one possible explanation. TOPHAT, Mabey said, never voiced an opinion on whether the surveillance led to Popov's downfall. Betrayal by George Blake, the Soviet mole inside MI6, the British spy agency, was another hypothesis. However, George Kisevalter, the legendary CIA officer who handled Popov, was convinced that the GRU officer was caught by the inept action of George Payne Winters, Jr., a State Department officer working for the CIA who misunderstood his orders and mailed a letter in Moscow addressed to Popov at his home in Kalinin. The KGB fished the letter out of the mailbox, and Popov, the first important penetration of Soviet intelligence, was doomed.

that enabled the bureau to arrest another GRU husband-and-wife team of illegals, Robert K. Baltch and his wife, Joy Ann, who had taken the identities of a Roman Catholic priest from Amsterdam, New York, and a housewife in Norwalk, Connecticut.[5]

These were past cases, but TOPHAT also identified an illegal then in the United States whom the FBI gave the code name PEBBLE.[6] The FBI found and approached PEBBLE, who first promised to become a double agent but then disappeared. TOPHAT also told Mabey about another illegal he had trained who was sent to the United States, a woman whom the FBI had detected and given the code name GLEAM. She had committed suicide, but Polyakov did not know that. TOPHAT told the FBI about other illegals as well.

TOPHAT also revealed that the GRU was able to monitor the FBI's surveillance communications. When FBI cars followed the Soviets around New York and the bureau's agents talked to each other by radio, the Russians were listening in.[7]

Polyakov also provided Mabey with the names of four Americans who were spying for Moscow. They were Nelson C. "Bulldog" Drummond, a navy yeoman who sold secrets to the GRU for five years after he was recruited in 1957; Jack E. Dunlap, an army sergeant working at the National Security Agency who beginning in 1960 passed secrets to the GRU for three years; William H. Whalen, an army lieutenant colonel working in intelligence for the Joint Chiefs of Staff, who spied for Moscow for four years until 1963; and Herbert W. Boeckenhaupt, an air force

---

[5]The Baltches were arrested in July 1963. Baltch, whose true name was Andre Sokolov, and his wife were freed and flew back to the Soviet Union after the Justice Department conceded that the case against the two spies might have been tainted by evidence obtained through a bug placed in their apartment in Washington.

[6]The FBI uses the term "code names." In the CIA, code names are usually referred to as "crypts," short for cryptonyms.

[7]The Soviets learned in this manner that the FBI had bugged the car of Vladimir G. Krasovsky, the deputy KGB resident in Manhattan, TOPHAT disclosed. To disguise the source of the information, he said, the Russians waited for a moment when they knew that the FBI was watching. They then made a great show of kicking the tires of the KGB officer's car, pulling out wires, and pretending to have "discovered" the transmitter.

sergeant and code-machine repairman convicted in 1967 of betraying the secrets of the Strategic Air Command to Moscow. Dunlap committed suicide; the others were arrested, convicted, and given long prison sentences.

Early in May 1962, Polyakov informed Mabey that his wife was pregnant. She was returning with the two boys to Moscow. He would follow in June on the *Queen Elizabeth,* sailing to Cherbourg and going on by train to Paris and Moscow. He expected to remain there until his next overseas posting.

TOPHAT promised to stay in touch with U.S. intelligence. With the operation moving overseas, the CIA would have to be brought in. That was arranged through Sam Papich, the FBI's longtime liaison with the CIA. Polyakov made it clear there would be no face-to-face meetings in Moscow; it was too dangerous, given the KGB's pervasive surveillance of CIA officers working out of the American embassy there. However, he agreed to communicate through dead drops and newspaper ads.

Early in June, Polyakov boarded the Cunard liner for France. He traveled first-class. There was another first-class passenger aboard from the FBI: John Mabey. It was tricky; Mabey could not be seen on deck with TOPHAT because another GRU officer and his wife were aboard, also traveling in first class.

During the crossing, Mabey gave TOPHAT a short course in FBI codes and CIA dead drops. "I used the time to train him in our cipher system and to brief him on the dead drops in Moscow provided by the CIA. I gave him the one-time pad and a code phrase.[8]

"He did not accept all the Moscow drops. I described them, and showed him pictures of some. He said some were not secure. We agreed on three dead drops and signal sites, where chalk marks would be placed at prearranged times." As an experienced GRU

---

[8]For encoded communications, the FBI (and Soviet intelligence as well) used a one-time pad system, a complex but virtually foolproof code in which only Polyakov and the FBI would possess an identical tiny pad printed with random groups of numbers. With the aid of a code word or phrase, TOPHAT would create a grid from which he would choose numbers to add or subtract from those on the pad in order to encode or decode his messages.

officer, Polyakov needed no explanation of how all this worked. Ironically, the Russians and the Americans use the same system to communicate with their agents. A chalk mark on an agreed object, a telephone pole or a mailbox, for example, would signal that a dead drop, or hiding place, had been filled by either party and was ready to be emptied. This type of "impersonal" communication was by no means without danger, but it avoided the possibility of the spy and his case officer being grabbed while meeting face-to-face. Through dead drops, spies can pass money, documents, instructions, or other material in relative safety.

Aboard the *Queen Elizabeth*, Mabey and TOPHAT agreed to communicate through ads in the *New York Times*. As a senior GRU officer, Polyakov explained, he had access to the newspaper, even though Western publications were normally forbidden to Soviets.

"We gave code names to the signal sites and dead drops. Male names indicated the signal sites and female were the drops themselves." The ads would be in the form of messages from Ed Moody, the FBI agent who provided support to Mabey in the case, to "Donald F.," for Polyakov. Mabey told Polyakov what to look for. "The ads might say, 'Cousin Jane anxious she hasn't heard from you, and Uncle John would also like to hear from you.'

"After TOPHAT sailed back and returned to Moscow, we ran the ads and nothing happened. For two years, there were no signals." A typical ad ran in the *Times* public notices column on May 20, 1964, and ten successive days. It said:

"Moody—Donald F., please write as promised. Uncle Charles and sister Clara are well and would like to hear from you. Don't forget address Dave, Doug and spouses. Travelling? When? Where? We hope for family reunion soon. Regards and best wishes, brothers Edward H. and John F. Closter, N.J."[9] Translated, the message meant that the CIA had made a mark at signal site

---

[9] FBI agent Edward H. Moody lived in Closter, New Jersey. He was obliged to use his true name because the newspaper required that individuals placing personal ads identify themselves and provide their correct, verifiable name and address. Even the FBI, engaged in a high-risk clandestine operation, had to bow to the rules of the *New York Times*.

Charles to indicate that dead drop Clara should be emptied. TOPHAT was also reminded to check signal sites Dave and Doug.

For several months, the ad brought no response. "Late in '64 or early '65 we got word from the CIA that a signal had been made and they [the CIA in Moscow] had cleared a drop. There was a message encoded in the drop. He used the one-time pad and said he was secure, gave his current rank, and said there was a chance he would be sent to Athens."

TOPHAT never got the assignment in Greece. "Next thing we heard he showed up in Rangoon in November of 1965. As a military attaché. The CIA told us he was there. He came to our embassy because he had open contact with an American military guy in the embassy, an air force colonel. He came ostensibly to discuss the purchase of a car from an American who was being transferred home. Inside the embassy he said he wanted to be put in touch with American intelligence. He asked for me by name, John. He said, 'I don't want to talk to anyone else.'"

Mabey put another ad in the *Times:* "Moody–Donald F. I was extremely glad to learn of your good fortune. Everything is fine. I will call on you soon. John F."

Bureaucracy being what it is, "soon" did not mean right away. "It took us two months to get cover through State, and a visa, and to meet with CIA to get their support. I arrived in Rangoon in January 1966.

"I was John Morey in Rangoon. In New York, I was just John, but I needed a last name for the passport. I was under cover with the army military assistance program."

In Burma, Mabey contacted the air force colonel, who telephoned Polyakov. "He called him up and said, 'I have a car you might be interested in.' He came to the embassy and I was in the military attaché's office, sitting there. I got up to shake hands and he embraced me. There were almost tears in his eyes. He wanted to know where the hell I'd been.

"We met twice a week from January to April of 1966. The meetings were held in safe houses which were the homes of CIA people from the embassy. I would pick him up and drive to the safe house. The meetings lasted an hour and a half, two hours. I took notes on a yellow pad."

It was in Burma that TOPHAT began providing strategic intelligence. "He talked about missiles in Burma," Mabey said. "CIA gave us technical questions on missiles—the number, capabilities, and accuracy of Soviet missiles."

The Vietnam War was at its height, and many of the CIA's questions for TOPHAT dealt with the war. "I remember him telling me the only way to bring North Vietnam to its knees was to bomb Hanoi. 'That's the only way you're going to beat these people.' I passed that back. He gave us a description of the operations of the GRU in various Far Eastern countries. He answered a great many questions furnished by CIA and DIA."

Mabey met Polyakov's wife in Burma. "He claimed she never knew what was going on, but I could read her eyes that she did. Once, at his home, he introduced me to other Soviets. I asked him later, 'Isn't this dangerous?' 'No,' he said, 'I told my people I was recruiting you.'

"I can vouch for his sincerity and his dedication. Polyakov loved the Russian people, but not the communist system. He never would consider defecting. I had asked him that several times. He was family oriented, he loved his children. He wanted to help the U.S, but only to get back at the Soviet system. He was very hurt that he was passed over for promotions several times.

"We didn't pay TOPHAT. When he left the United States, he asked for a fur coat and some jewelry for his wife, and a good camera, maybe worth a couple of hundred dollars. A few trinkets is what it amounted to. The same thing in Burma, he really never asked for anything except an over-and-under shotgun. He gave us the make and everything else. We finally found one in Hong Kong or somewhere.

"I was there four months. All this time I was supposed to be CIA, not FBI. Around March, I convinced him I could not stay any longer and he agreed to be turned over to someone else. The turnover would be at the Inyalake Hotel on a certain day at a certain hour. A signal would be made on a bathhouse near the swimming pool. TOPHAT and the CIA man would meet casually at the swimming pool. I met the CIA guy when I returned to Washington. He was going to be sent especially."[10]

In the complex world of counterintelligence, spies being managed by two agencies often ended up with three code names. Thus, in interagency communications with the FBI, TOPHAT was code-named BOURBON by the CIA, and FEDORA, the other FBI source in New York, was called SCOTCH.

The CIA gave Polyakov a third code name, used only inside the agency: GTBEEP.[11]

There was more to the story, of course. TOPHAT was unaware—at the time, at least—of how his career and that of FEDORA had become caught up in the tangled history of conflict between the CIA and the FBI. The trouble had begun near Christmas of 1961, when Anatoly Mikhailovich Golitsin, a KGB major, appeared on the doorstep of the CIA station chief in Helsinki and asked for asylum. He was flown to Washington. Once there, he began spinning tales in Scheherazade fashion to James Angleton, the agency's counterintelligence chief, of a mole inside the CIA. Angleton believed him and launched his destructive mole hunt. When a second Soviet defector, Yuri I. Nosenko, fled Switzerland early in February 1964, Angleton became persuaded that Nosenko was dispatched by the KGB to deflect attention from Golitsin's charges.

Moreover, Nosenko said he had personally handled Lee Harvey Oswald's case when the former marine arrived in Moscow and asked to remain in the Soviet Union. After President Kennedy was assassinated, Nosenko said, he had read the KGB file on Oswald. He was certain that Oswald had not been recruited by the Soviet spy agency and was not acting for Moscow when he shot the president.

In an effort to break Nosenko and determine whether he was telling the truth about possible Soviet penetration of the agency

[10]James M. Flint was the case officer dispatched to meet Polyakov, along with Paul L. Dillon.

[11]At first Polyakov was AEBEEP. Once recruited, Polyakov became a sensitive source and rated a CK digraph, which the CIA changed to GT after Edward Lee Howard fled in 1985 and defected to the Soviets.

and about Oswald, the CIA held him under brutal conditions for almost five years, much of the time in a twelve-by-twelve-foot windowless concrete cell in a house deep in the woods at the Farm, the CIA's training base. Despite the horrendous treatment of Nosenko, he never changed his story. Eventually, he was released and rehabilitated by the agency.

But Angleton was convinced that Nosenko and the FBI's sources in New York were part of a KGB plot. FEDORA had seemed to support Nosenko's bona fides, which immediately made him, and by implication TOPHAT, suspect in Angleton's eyes. By contrast, J. Edgar Hoover, the FBI chief, had complete faith in both TOPHAT and FEDORA.

John Mabey had firsthand exposure to the CIA's skepticism. The huge volume of valuable information that Polyakov had provided to the FBI did not seem to matter. Even after five years, Mabey recalled, "Angleton still didn't think he was bona fide. I can remember Angleton sitting there with that sly look and saying, 'This is all bullshit.' He said it before I went to Burma, and then when I met him again after I came back. Before I went, their attitude was, sure, let's do it, but we don't believe it.

"When I came back, Angleton and his staff guys debriefed me. They interrogated me, they were almost hostile." Even within the FBI, Hoover's confidence in Polyakov was not shared by everyone. The most powerful doubter was William C. Sullivan, a confidant of Angleton's and head of the bureau's intelligence division. "Billy Sullivan believed Angleton," Mabey said. "That TOPHAT was bad."

At the CIA internal debates raged for years over the validity of TOPHAT and FEDORA. They were accepted as genuine by the CIA only after Angleton departed in 1974.[12]

In April 1966, it was time for Mabey to leave Rangoon, the city where Rick Ames, as a teenager, had learned to swim and sail a decade before. "Two or three days before I left, we had a regular meeting in a safe house," Mabey said. "We wanted to toast the

[12]The debates inside the CIA had their parallel in the FBI, which had great difficulty making up its mind about FEDORA, who returned to the Soviet Union in 1977 and died of natural causes about 1983.

occasion, but he almost never took a drink in my presence. He did have a couple of drinks once, a couple vodkas in Rangoon when he introduced me to his other friends, all GRU. He didn't smoke, at least in my presence. He was so straight, he could have been a priest.

"At the end, he thanked me for recontacting him. I couldn't give him a date for when he would meet the new man. I can't recall if he embraced me again. We shook hands and wished each other good luck. I left Burma, and that's the last time I saw him."

But at that final meeting, John Mabey had one parting word of encouragement for TOPHAT. As Mabey knew, although TOPHAT did not, the CIA would be taking over now, which meant that Dimitri Fedorovich Polyakov would henceforth be putting his life in the hands of the agency's Soviet division. To Polyakov, it simply meant dealing with a new case officer. But there was no need to worry, Mabey said.

"I reassured him his security would be okay."

ASSIGNMENT IN ANKARA

Rick Ames had a problem. The Soviet division was sending him to Ankara, but his wife's job was at headquarters. Nan Ames worked for the CIA's Directorate of Operations, the DO, at Langley.

It was October 1969. Married only five months, Ames did not want to go off to Turkey without his new bride. In Ankara, Ames would be reporting through the CIA's Near East division. He decided to talk to an NE division acting branch chief, Hugh J. McMillan.

A gregarious transplanted Canadian, McMillan had served in Bombay, New Delhi, and later in Alexandria, Egypt. He was working at headquarters until his next overseas tour.

He remembered the encounter. "I had known him, he seemed a nice young fellow, very deferential. One day he showed up in my office to ask a favor. He said he was in a predicament. 'I'm being assigned to Ankara and my wife won't accompany me unless she gets a job there.'"

McMillan said he would do what he could. "I managed to get

her a job in Ankara as an administrative assistant in the DO," he recalled. "I've found that wives who have busy hands are a lot less likely to go bananas in a foreign environment." But the job that McMillan arranged was at a lesser grade. "She was dropping from a twelve to a seven or maybe a nine, and she didn't like it."

Still, the branch chief's intervention had made it possible for the couple to serve overseas together. In Ankara, Rick and Nan moved into a flat upon the hill in Çankaya, above the American embassy on Ataturk Boulevard. At the time, the CIA station chief was John H. Leavitt, who had an unusual background. An American born in France, he volunteered in England for the Royal Air Force before Pearl Harbor and had flown in the RAF against the Nazis. Leavitt, who had diplomatic cover as a foreign service officer, was based in the embassy.

Rick and Nan both worked as civilians under army cover in a two-story brick building a few miles away, not far from Ataturk's tomb. The installation was ostensibly the headquarters for JUSMMAT, an acronym that stood for Joint U.S. Military Mission for Aid to Turkey. The CIA unit occupied the top floor, and there were Turkish officers on the ground floor. The building overlooked a farm field populated by about three hundred turkeys; on slow days, the CIA officers would amuse themselves by watching the birds chasing each other.

As part of the complicated bureaucratic arrangement under which the CIA allowed Nan to go to Ankara, she officially "resigned" from the agency but then went right back to work for the CIA's Directorate of Operations in the same office as her husband. In the brick building, Rick Ames worked initially for Robert J. Stevens, the head of the unit, who in turn reported to Leavitt at the embassy. When Stevens left in 1971, Ames acquired a new boss, Joseph F. Lynch.

Ames's job in Turkey, as throughout much of his career, was to try to recruit Russians or other Communist-bloc intelligence officers or diplomats. He did not recruit any Russians in Ankara. Veteran CIA hands say he could not be faulted for that; Soviets were difficult enough to recruit, and a young first-tour officer was not expected to do much more than try.

The Turkey that Ames worked in for three years beginning in 1969 was a nation in turmoil, racked by student and left-wing protests, terrorism, and recurring political crises. In 1971, Prime Minister Suleyman Demirel resigned, and martial law was imposed. As the violence increased in the streets, so did government repression, censorship, book banning, arrests, death sentences, and murder of terrorist suspects. But Washington's first priority was not to reform the government. Turkey was a staunch NATO ally, strategically situated on the border of the Soviet Union. It had the largest army of any NATO country other than the United States itself. Sitting astride the Dardanelles, it could bottle up the Soviets' Black Sea fleet in the event of war.

In addition to the U.S. Air Force base at Adana—from which Francis Gary Powers had begun the first leg of his ill-fated U-2 flight for the CIA in 1960—there was the NATO base at Izmir on the Aegean and U.S. nuclear weapons depositories around the country. Along the border, the National Security Agency had listening posts to eavesdrop on Soviet communications and electronic signals. American intelligence also had facilities in Turkey to monitor radioactivity in the atmosphere, to detect any Soviet nuclear tests. In Ankara, the Pentagon and the CIA maintained close and friendly liaison with the Turkish military and intelligence services.

Aside from bombings and curfews, life in Ankara had some minor inconveniences for the Ameses and other residents. An arid city built on a high plateau, the Turkish capital lacked an adequate water supply. Water would be cut off at various times of the day as it was pumped to other parts of the city, and some days there was no water at all.

In 1971, Hugh McMillan arrived in Ankara and joined Ames and Nan under army cover in the brick building. McMillan was a man of rather fixed opinions about gender roles, and he did not look with favor upon Nan, whom he thought harbored suspiciously feminist views. "In Ankara," he said, "Rick ran home and made his wife lunch and all the other meals and cleaned house. He had a ring in his nose."

According to McMillan, Rick was not a gourmet chef. He

recalled one occasion when the Ameses had invited him, his wife, Janice, and several other guests to a luncheon at their flat on the hill. "Rick had prepared what my wife calls possibly the worst meal she ever had in her life. It was weird. A buffet thing, different bowls and nothing went with anything else. He served Jell-O. I remember that because I hate Jell-O. And a bowl of peanuts. And salad."

By this time, Henry P. "Hank" Schardt, a former career army officer from the Midwest, had replaced Leavitt as the Ankara chief of station. And from the CIA base in Istanbul, the aggressive Dewey Clarridge arrived in July 1971 to take over as deputy chief of station. Clarridge regarded the move as overdue; in his view, Leavitt and Schardt were nice guys, but they did not know the spy business. The same month, another CIA officer, Alan D. Fiers, Jr., was assigned to Ankara. A decade later, both Clarridge and Fiers were to become embroiled in the Iran-contra scandal.[1]

The Ankara tour was not going well for Ames. Clarridge, it quickly became clear, disliked him. And only a few months after the new DCOS had arrived from Istanbul, Ames received sad personal news about his father, who had retired from the CIA in August 1967. Carleton Ames was living now in Hickory, North Carolina, with Rachel, who had retired from her teaching job in June 1969 after she had returned from Karachi. Late in 1971, Ames's parents visited him in Turkey and broke the news that his father was very ill with cancer.

Ames later told colleagues he considered his time in Ankara to have been "unhappy" and "unsuccessful," and because of this, he had even seriously considered leaving the CIA. To some extent, the problem was one of geography. Turkey was a tough environ-

---

[1]In July 1991, Fiers admitted in federal court that he told his superiors in the CIA about the diversion of millions of dollars in Iran arms-sale profits to the contras in Nicaragua. Fiers said that in 1987, Clair George, the agency's deputy director for operations, instructed him to lie to Congress about the CIA's role. In December 1992, George was convicted of two felony counts of lying to Congress. He was pardoned later that month by President Bush, who at the same time pardoned Clarridge, who was awaiting trial on perjury charges also stemming from the Iran-contra investigations.

ment for spies, and the Turks were serious about the United States not spying in their country. So partly it was Ankara, but Ames also blamed Clarridge, whom he detested and feared.

In looking back at his time in Turkey, Ames liked to tell his CIA friends about another young officer like himself, who was developing a Greek diplomat in Ankara. As one colleague recalled Ames recounting the story, "Dewey said, 'Go out and recruit that guy.' Dewey wanted to show recruitments. The officer said, 'I don't think he'll do it.' Dewey hammered the table and ordered him to recruit the guy. The officer went out and made a pitch, the diplomat turned it down, and his country complained to us. Dewey blamed it all on the officer's bad judgment. It got into his fitness report."

There was in fact a major flap in Ankara over the attempted Greek recruitment. Hank Schardt, the station chief, was back at Langley at the time, having left Clarridge in charge. Clarridge ordered the young CIA officer to make the pitch, the diplomat declined the dance, and the Greek ambassador angrily reported it to William J. Handley, the American ambassador to Turkey.

The Greek envoy had approached Handley at a cocktail party and asked, "What the hell is going on?" When Schardt returned from Washington, Handley, a career ambassador and former deputy assistant secretary of state, complained to him. Why was the CIA trying to recruit a diplomat from Greece, a NATO ally, in, of all places, Turkey? The embarrassed station chief fumed over Clarridge's gaffe, but nothing happened.

Dewey Clarridge was convinced that Rick Ames wasn't capable of recruiting anybody. The process was plain enough to the deputy station chief; when you are trying to recruit Soviets, you first recruit access agents. Ames, Clarridge thought, was incapable of even that. As Clarridge saw it, a Pakistani second secretary wasn't hard to recruit as an access agent; all he needed was a small stipend. And there was no danger to him; we were all allies. If he gets caught, he gets a slap on the wrist. But Ames couldn't even recruit a Pak.

Clarridge had tried talking to Ames, but to no avail. When you counseled him, Clarridge remembered, he would look at you through myopic glasses, and you knew what he was thinking: *You fucking asshole, I'm a hell of a lot smarter than you are.* So when Ames was arrested in 1994, Dewey Clarridge wasn't a bit surprised, not a bit. Ames's personality, Clarridge had concluded in Ankara, was not structured for agent handling; he should never have been recruited into the service.

Some CIA veterans, like Clarridge, had trouble accepting Ames into the club because he hadn't become a career trainee right out of college, like most CTs. Ames came up through the ranks as a maverick. Clarridge knew his background; Ames had started looking through indexes, doing file clerk stuff while he was still in school, and finally, aw shit, we'll give this guy a chance. Clarridge had been through these cases before. One case in Istanbul, he wrote a guy out of the service. He became an archaeologist. With Dewey Clarridge, it was a point of personal pride that everyone knew he was a big kick-ass guy.

During Ames's first year in Turkey, he was given a "strong" rating and promoted to GS-11. By the end of the second year, he was rated "proficient." But after Clarridge arrived, Ames's last fitness report, which Clarridge had signed, said that Ames was unsuited for field work and should spend the rest of his career at headquarters, where he would not have to recruit anybody. Ames, the report said, preferred "assignments that do not involve face-to-face situations with relatively unknown personalities who must be manipulated."[2] That comment, the CIA's inspector general noted later, "was devastating for an operations officer."[3] It was after receiving that evaluation that Ames considered leaving the CIA.

In the end, of course, he did not. In the summer of 1972, the Ameses packed up their apartment in Çankaya and left the arid hills of Ankara behind. If the future did not look particularly bright, he would doubtless be able to find a job of some sort at Langley. And he would be back in the familiar quarters of the mother ship, the Soviet division.

---

[2] *Unclassified Abstract of the CIA Inspector General's Report on the Aldrich H. Ames Case,* p. 9, hereinafter "IG Report."

[3] Ibid.

8

NEW YORK

Reston is an upscale, planned community in northern Virginia, halfway between CIA headquarters and Dulles airport. It was built on a vision of re-creating the atmosphere of small-town America in suburbia, in place of the usual developers' tracts.

Both the location and the concept were attractive to Rick and Nan Ames. After they returned from Ankara in 1972, they lived in an apartment for a while and then moved into a three-bedroom town house on Golf Course Island in Reston.

That summer, however, a sad family duty intervened. Carleton Ames was dying of cancer in North Carolina. Early in July, Rick and his wife, along with his two sisters, traveled to Hickory and, with Rachel, took turns at the hospital. On September 2, Carleton died at age sixty-seven.

Back at CIA headquarters, Rick was assigned to a desk job in the Soviet division, managing paperwork. In 1973, he was given Russian-language training, and after that he helped to support CIA operations against Soviet officials in the United States.

With no recruiting duties, Ames fared much better than he had in Turkey, receiving generally enthusiastic reviews from his supervisors. More evidence of his drinking surfaced in CIA records, however; at a Christmas party at headquarters in 1973, Ames got so drunk that he had to be helped home to Reston by escorts from the Office of Security. At the Christmas party a year later, Ames got drunk again and was discovered in what official records delicately termed "a compromising position" with a female CIA employee. The Office of Security duly made a note of both incidents, and the memos were routinely buried in the files.

Nan Ames, in the meantime, had left the CIA for good. Frustrated by the agency's notorious glass ceiling, she complained to friends that there was no future for women in the CIA—a problem that still plagues the agency in the traditionally male-dominated world of intelligence. But for Nan, the lesson of Turkey was an even more important factor. In order to accompany her husband, she had to agree to be downgraded. That experience persuaded her that it would be very difficult, perhaps impossible, to manage a two-career family with both partners working for the CIA. How could the marriage work, Nan wondered, with Rick traipsing around the world and his wife assigned to headquarters?

With her career as a spy over, Nan Ames found new interests. She became active in the Reston Community Association and plunged into local Democratic politics. In 1974, she was cochairperson in Reston of the successful congressional campaign of Joe Fisher, a liberal economist who upset northern Virginia's longtime Republican conservative, Joel Broyhill. Nan Ames worked hard in the campaign, ringing doorbells, talking to neighbors, distributing literature, and organizing coffees. After the election she went to work on Fisher's congressional staff.

The Ameses lived modestly in Reston and attended the Unitarian church. "They didn't seem at all concerned about material things," said their friend and neighbor Susan J. Williams, now a Washington public relations executive. "They were very into books and music. Rick was engaging, warm, and witty. His house, car, clothes, and lifestyle were very modest, everything was understated. They never went out to posh, fancy places. They were a friendly, outgoing, liberal-leaning couple."

In Reston, Rick supported a move by the county to build lower-cost housing in the community, right next to Golf Course Island, for blacks and less affluent applicants. "It was a big fight in Reston," another friend recalled. "Rick and Nan were very active on the side of the blacks. Their side won."

Susan Williams and her husband became good friends with the Ameses, who lived a few houses down. "My three-year-old son would wander over and watch Nancy planting her garden. We would go out to dinner or go to their house or have them to our place. Nancy and I were very close, but the four of us were also friends."

At Langley, Ames was doing nicely. He received four fitness reports rating him as a "strong performer." He also won commendations for motivation and effectiveness, although the evaluations noted a tendency toward procrastination and inattention to detail. Ames was not on the CIA's "fast track," but by 1976 the managers of the Soviet division were sufficiently impressed to award him another field assignment. This time, it was a plum.

Ames was selected for FR/New York. The FR stood for Foreign Resources, the name at the time of the CIA's domestic division in charge of operations against foreign targets in the United States.[1] Under the 1947 act that created the CIA, the agency was primarily seen by Congress and the public as an intelligence organization operating overseas; the FBI would continue to be in charge of the home turf. While that view was basically correct, it was by no means the whole picture. Despite popular misconceptions, the CIA does operate domestically. Although it has no law-enforcement powers, it has offices in large and medium-sized cities all across America. The most important of these domestic stations are in New York and Washington, where Soviet and now Russian diplo-

---

[1]FR/New York is now NR/New York, with the NR standing for National Resources. The change came about after the Foreign Resources division was merged with the National Collection division to become the new National Resources division.

mats and intelligence officers are traditional targets of interest.

While the Ameses were in New York, they rented their house in Reston for a time to Freddie Woodruff, a CIA colleague whose wife Meredith was the sister of Susan Williams's husband. Woodruff was born in Arkansas but grew up in Stillwater, Oklahoma, where he and his future wife were high school friends. Like Rick, he worked for the CIA's clandestine arm, the DO.

Ames was pleased with his new job. For a kid from River Falls, the assignment to Manhattan was a rare opportunity to enjoy New York, the culture, the theater, the restaurants, the good life, in a way that government workers could normally never afford. But the CIA would make it all possible.

In New York, Ames's mission was to suborn and recruit Russians working in that country's mission to the United Nations or in the UN secretariat. He worked in alias, not as Rick Ames. He could hardly introduce himself as a CIA spy, and almost certainly operated under commercial cover, posing as a successful business-man who could afford to live on Manhattan's expensive East Side.

Suddenly, Ames's life had taken a more glamorous turn. He and his wife moved into the Revere, a twenty-story luxury apartment house on East Fifty-fourth Street with a rather grand entrance and a uniformed doorman. Their apartment had a large living room and a beautiful view.

There were sound operational reasons for Ames's upscale address; an officer assigned to FR/New York had to live in a style that matched his or her cover; it would not do at all to be com-muting in by subway from Queens. Moreover, FR/New York required its officers to live within a reasonable radius of the UN and the CIA's New York base.[2]

Since Ames was a midlevel bureaucrat on a modest salary, the CIA subsidized the rent. In New York, because of the high cost of housing in the city, the CIA pays the entire rent of its clandestine

---

[2]At the time, New York, like other domestic offices, was designated a base; in the 1980s, it became a station, which was more prestigious. For one thing, the head of the office acquired the title of chief of station, which sounded bet-ter than chief of base. Within the CIA, a COS is a baron, outranking a base chief.

operators, then deducts a small portion, about 5 or 10 percent, of their salary.

If Ames, for example, earned $30,000 a year at the time, he might have paid only about $250 a month for an apartment that rented for $2,000 a month. In addition, he had a liberal monthly "revolving fund" for entertaining, dinners, theater tickets, and other expenses that he might incur in cultivating his Soviet targets. Ames, in short, was living well.

Nan Ames, with her successful political experience, landed a good job in New York. She began to carve out an impressive career of her own.

Rick Ames had no difficulty fitting in to life in Manhattan. Many of Ames's CIA colleagues assumed that he was a product of an elite East Coast college. Tall, broad shouldered, and articulate, Ames managed to give that impression. One of his supervisors in New York thought that Ames had come from an establishment background. "He seemed sort of Ivy League, upscale, he dressed nicely. He had the appropriately civil manners. He was an easy conversationalist. He had adopted the Ivy League mannerisms quite well. After his arrest, in talking to people who were more involved with him, I discovered he wasn't."

In 1976, when Rick Ames arrived in the Big Apple, George Bush was serving out his year as director of the CIA under President Gerald R. Ford. Later that year, Jimmy Carter would be elected to the White House.

Of more immediate concern to Ames were his new supervisors in Manhattan. When Ames reported in to FR/New York, Kenneth Y. Millian, a longtime CIA officer who had served in Japan and then in Latin America, was leaving after a two-year tour as base chief. He was succeeded by Peter Koromilas, another veteran CIA officer who had come to the city from the Washington base. Fluent in Greek, Koromilas spent most of his career in Greece and was regarded as a major player in the agency's operations in that country.

When the Greek colonels led by George Papadopoulos overthrew the elected government in April 1967, establishing a repressive military dictatorship, Koromilas was a branch chief in the

Athens station.[3] He was using the name "Peter Korom." Koromilas remained in Athens and then returned to Langley to work in the Foreign Resources division at headquarters in 1973 before moving to the Washington base and then New York.

He was an unlikely-looking spy, a short, round man with a graying fringe of dark hair surrounding his bald head. But Koromilas prided himself in his invisibility; he had a knack of sinking deep into the woodwork. His name had appeared in the press only once, and then fleetingly, in more than two decades.[4]

Koromilas and the CIA officers under his command in Manhattan operated out of a multitude of locations. The base itself, with appropriately James Bondish security, was in the Pan Am Building, under cover of an innocuous-sounding unit of the Department of Commerce. The CIA station ostensibly was an office dealing with international trade. The door was unmarked. "At one time we were listed on the lobby board," one of Ames's supervisors in New York recalled. "We had an arrangement with the Commerce Department downtown, if they received any inquiries about the office they would call us and alert us and we would call the person back. The inner door had a combination lock. The outer door was unmarked, and there was a secretary to handle people who wandered into the wrong office. UPS or someone trying to deliver a package to the wrong floor." Although Ames worked

[3]Presumably the White House and the CIA were not completely unaware that a coup plot might be brewing; Papadopoulos was said to have been on the agency's payroll for years. The degree of U.S. foreknowledge of the coup remains fuzzy; some senior CIA officials who were in Athens at the time insist the station was not involved. After the coup, however, there is little dispute that the Athens station was tight with the colonels, whose strongest support in the U.S. government came from the CIA.

[4]In November 1973, Papadopoulos in turn was ousted by the military and replaced by Gen. Dimitrios Ioannides, the strongman of the colonels. In August 1974, *Newsweek* and the *New York Times* reported that Koromilas was the American closest to Ioannides and that the CIA man had turned up in Athens around the time the Greek military staged the coup in Cyprus on July 15. After heading the New York base, Koromilas served as station chief in The Hague and in Cairo before he retired.

under Koromilas, he was not based in the Pan Am Building. FR/New York's Soviet branch, where Ames had his desk, moved around but ended up under commercial cover in an office building on Lexington Avenue just below Forty-second Street.[5]

FR/New York was not a small-time operation. The base had fifty-seven people assigned to it, counting secretaries and clerical personnel. And the CIA never lacked for funds. The agency's operation was the envy of the New York FBI office; in addition to the Pan Am Building and the Soviet branch on Lexington Avenue, the CIA operated out of a dozen well-appointed safe houses scattered around the East Side and elsewhere in the city. The bureau could not hope to match such affluence.

Posing as a businessman or consultant, Ames for the most part had to rely on the New York base to help him meet Russians. A CIA man who served in FR/New York with Ames explained how it worked. "We used access agents," he said. "These could be UN officials, people in different foreign missions, most of the time unpaid. An access agent would arrange a cocktail party and invite the target—perhaps a diplomat from the Soviet UN mission— along with one of our people. He would introduce the target to our man and, in effect, hand him off."

On the whole, Ames performed well for the CIA in New York, handling two major Soviet cases. But even before his tour had started, a Keystone Cop episode in New York nearly derailed his career. Sheer luck saved him.

Ames, still at Langley, was acting as case officer for a Soviet source in Manhattan whom the CIA was handling jointly with the FBI. Periodically, Ames would take the Metroliner to New York, meet with the FBI, and then travel by subway to a safe house in the Bronx to meet the Soviet.

On one of these trips, Ames was carrying a trick briefcase with a false panel to conceal classified documents, including a list of

[5]The office was on a high floor, which the occupants had good reason to remember. The building's elevator broke down, and for six months until it was repaired the CIA officers in the Soviet branch had to trudge up some seventeen floors.

"requirements," questions prepared by the CIA for the Soviet. On the subway, Ames realized he needed to buy batteries for his tape recorder. Suddenly, it was his stop. He leaped up, bolted from the train, and found a store where he bought the batteries. It was only then that he realized he had left his briefcase on the subway train.

The stop was near the end of the line. Ames ran back to the station, crossed over to the opposite platform, and waited, hoping to inspect each train as it came back downtown. No luck. Ames then rode to the last station and started desperately looking through trash bins. Perhaps someone thought there was money in the briefcase, and finding none, had tossed it aside.

After an hour, Ames went to the safe house and called his base chief.

"I have to come down and meet you immediately," he said. "We've got a real problem."

At the Pan Am Building, there was consternation. The safe house in the Bronx was near the Soviet housing complex in Riverdale, and there was even a chance that a Russian riding the train might have found the briefcase. If that happened, the tasking list alone, the questions Ames was carrying, might have enabled the KGB to identify the man. But it was worse than that.

Ames had been carrying some snapshots that the Soviet had given to him at an earlier meeting, showing the CIA source with some of his friends. If the KGB ever got its hands on the photographs, it was a death warrant for the man. If that was the good news, the bad news was that Ames had removed all of the materials from the false compartment, including the photographs. They were just lying in the briefcase.

Meanwhile, Ames and the base chief decided he should go ahead with the meeting. Ames did so but did not reveal to the Soviet the awful truth—that he had lost his briefcase. Instead, he told the CIA asset that the agency had instituted some new emergency contact plans, just in case something ever went wrong, not that it would. Ames gave the unwitting agent a new set of phone numbers. Then he returned to the base chief's apartment in Manhattan, where his boss and two FBI agents were waiting for him. The group was drafting an ad for the lost briefcase to run in small print on the bottom of page one of the *New York Times.*

While this was going on, the phone rang. It was the FBI. A schoolteacher in Queens, a Polish emigré, had found the briefcase and turned it in. "So it was a tremendous relief," Ames remembered. "I was going through agonies. . . . I was thinking, I am just going to have to quit, you know retire, or something, if anything happened."[6]

Nothing much did, of course. As was to be demonstrated throughout Ames's thirty-one-year career with the CIA, the agency has a degree of avuncular tolerance for its employees that would be the envy of workers in the private sector. Ames got a written reprimand, and he was asked to suggest procedures that might in the future prevent case officers from leaving their briefcases on the subway while en route to meetings in safe houses with Russian spies.

One of the first agents Ames was assigned to handle in New York was Sergei Fedorenko, a smooth, good-looking Soviet scholar working for the UN secretariat. His CIA code name was GTPYRRHIC. Ames was handling Fedorenko jointly with the FBI, which gave Fedorenko the code name MYRRH. Fedorenko, thirty-three, was to flit somewhat mysteriously in and out of Ames's life for two decades. Fedorenko was the son-in-law of Nikolai Fedorenko, former Soviet ambassador to the UN and to Japan; the senior Fedorenko spoke Chinese and had served as an interpreter when Stalin met with Mao Tse-tung in Moscow in 1949. Sergei Fedorenko had adopted the last name of his famous father-in-law, not an unknown practice in the Soviet Union.[7] Sergei's wife, Helen, was a celebrated beauty, so much so that a stunning, full-page photo of her, along with a short article, ran in *Vogue* in 1964, which

---

[6]Senate Interview, pp. 93–98.

[7]Under normal circumstances, the name change might have been expected to enhance Sergei Fedorenko's standing among Moscow's elite. In fact, he said, it proved a handicap because his father-in-law was not a popular figure in the Soviet foreign ministry. Sergei said he took the name at the insistence of Nikolai, who had never had a son.

did not please the dour Soviet foreign minister, Andrei Gromyko.[8]

Arkady N. Shevchenko, who was undersecretary general of the United Nations and Sergei Fedorenko's boss in the secretariat, remembered the fallout from the *Vogue* episode. According to Shevchenko, Gromyko already had it in for Nikolai Fedorenko. "He wore a bow tie, which Gromyko considered absolutely unacceptable for an ambassador. When Gromyko came to New York for the General Assembly, he [Fedorenko] would change his tie. The magazine photograph was on top of everything else." The appearance of the daughter of a senior Soviet diplomat in a two-page spread in an American high-fashion magazine was unheard of. "Gromyko was furious," Shevchenko recalled with a chuckle. "At least it was better than *Playboy*."

Although Sergei Fedorenko was a CIA asset in the mid-1970s, he hedged his bets in the spy war by feeding information to the KGB, including some unclassified data that had been given to him by Aldrich Ames. Fedorenko did so through Vladik Enger, a KGB officer working under cover at the UN.

Spying is a complicated business, and unknown to Fedorenko, the FBI and the Naval Investigative Service (NIS) were running a naval officer as a double agent against Enger. In May 1978 Enger and another KGB man were arrested in the woods in New Jersey as they looked for a package left by the navy man.[9] Enger and his

---

[8]The haunting portrait, by world-famous photographer Irving Penn, showed a dark-eyed beauty with a gaminlike resemblance to actress Audrey Hepburn. The accompanying text said, "Vivid, with a deeply romantic Russian look, Helen Fedorenko is a refreshing blend of brains, grave poise, and young exuberance. A world traveller at nineteen, she has lived, with her diplomat parents, in China, Japan, the United States—and naturally, Russia." *Vogue*, August 1, 1964, p. 98.

[9]The arrests set off a fierce argument within the Carter administration. Attorney General Griffin Bell wanted to prosecute the spies; CIA director Stansfield Turner and Secretary of State Cyrus Vance were opposed, arguing that negotiations then in progress on the SALT II arms-control treaty might be affected and that Moscow would only retaliate. Bell won, but in June the Russians disclosed the arrest a year earlier of Martha Peterson, a CIA officer in Moscow whom the KGB had caught in the act of filling a dead drop on a bridge that spans the Moscow River at the Lenin Hills.

accomplice were convicted of espionage and sentenced to fifty years, but were exchanged soon afterwards for five Russian dissidents.

Fedorenko departed New York for Moscow in 1977. Ames attended his farewell party at a safe house just north of the city and brought his asset a present, a black leather men's purse.

It was also during his New York tour that Ames tried to develop Tomas Kolesnichenko, the chief New York correspondent of *Pravda*, the Communist party newspaper. Ames, as he later told David Samson in Mexico, had been greatly impressed with the correspondent.

But Fedorenko and Kolesnichenko were only sideshows compared to the main event of Ames's tour in New York. The year before Ames had arrived in the city, Arkady Shevchenko himself had made contact with the CIA. The news was electrifying. The undersecretary general of the UN wanted to come over to the West. If it happened, he would be the highest-ranking Soviet ever to defect.

Rick Ames was assigned to help handle Shevchenko, the biggest fish ever to swim into the CIA's net. Arkady Shevchenko, a short, stocky, ebullient man with a quick sense of humor, was born in 1930 in Gorlovka, a coal-mining town in the eastern Ukraine where his father was a doctor. Even under communism, Shevchenko had a middle-class upbringing thanks to his father's status. He read Pushkin, learned to play chess and the piano, and hero-worshiped his older brother, Gennady. World War II shattered the family's pleasant life; young Arkady and his mother were sent for their safety to the remote Altai Mountains of Siberia, and his brother, a fighter pilot, was shot down over Warsaw and killed. After the war, Arkady was accepted at the prestigious Moscow State Institute of International Relations. He rose quickly in the Foreign Ministry and was sent abroad in 1963 on his first tour to New York as a member of the Soviet mission to the UN.

One of his colleagues in the mission was Aleksei I. Kulak, whom the FBI had recruited as FEDORA. "We were friends," Shevchenko said. "He said things about the leadership that I didn't want to hear. Things that were outspoken even for a KGB man. I knew he was KGB, of course." His friendship with Kulak aside, Shevchenko, in general, found it safer to give the KGB a wide berth.

In the spring of 1973, Shevchenko was back in New York with his wife, Lina, and their daughter, Anna, this time as UN under-secretary general for political and security council affairs. As such, he was the highest-ranking Soviet in the UN.

But Shevchenko, despite the perks of high office, including a dacha near Moscow, ambassadorial rank, and a good salary, was increasingly disillusioned with the Soviet system. He felt like a robot that no longer believed in the orders he had to obey.

Early in 1975, Shevchenko made his decision. He approached an American diplomat he knew and trusted. He said he wanted to defect. Soon after, the diplomat slipped him a note in the UN library. It told Shevchenko to go to a bookstore near the United Nations the next day. A CIA case officer was waiting for him.

They arranged to meet at a CIA safe house, a brownstone in the East Sixties. There, the CIA officer, following standard agency pro-cedure, urged Shevchenko to remain on the job for a while and spy for the United States. The agency always prefers an agent in place, who can continue to provide information, to a defector whose value, over time, diminishes rapidly.

After some hesitation, Shevchenko met again with the CIA man. He agreed to remain in place and to provide information. Shevchenko, who now lives near Washington, spied for the CIA for three years. He remembered four safe houses. The brownstone, "then the Waldorf-Astoria, in a rented room, an apartment in my dentist's building on the East Side between Third and Lexington, and an apartment in my building, two floors below mine."

Early in 1977, Shevchenko's CIA case officer told him he would be leaving New York. In June, he introduced him to a new case officer, a tall, square-shouldered man with a curled, waxed mus-tache. Shevchenko has long since forgotten the name the man used, but he knows now that his new contact was Aldrich H. Ames.[10] "I don't remember where I was introduced to Ames, but

[10]Ames later told his sister, Nancy Everly, that as a private joke, he and another CIA case officer who handled Shevchenko had used the names "Don and Phil," in honor of the Everly Brothers, a vocal duo and songwriters pop-ular in the 1960s, who are her husband's second cousins.

most likely it was in the safe house in my apartment building," Shevchenko said.

Shevchenko had considered his first case officer "more sophisticated, and I liked him more than Ames." But, Shevchenko added, "I think Ames acted quite professionally. I didn't like the change in case officers, but I understood it was unavoidable. The same person cannot be all the time with me."

And so, in June, Rick Ames took over the biggest case of his career. "I remember he was drinking a lot," Shevchenko said. "I was drinking a lot too. He made good company. It was the only way to get the stress off. I was drinking vodka, I think he was also drinking vodka, maybe Scotch, too. They always had a lot of drinks in all the safe houses where we met.[11]

"All in all I had a positive impression of Ames. He was friendly, he behaved normally. Obviously, he was not working for the Soviets then. If he had been, that would have been the end of me. I was in the Soviet mission every day. It would have been very easy for them to give me drugs. I would become sick, they would take me to Moscow."

In the summer of 1977, Shevchenko and his wife returned to Moscow briefly on home leave. It was a scary time. On a train trip to the Crimea to visit his mother, he realized a KGB man was in the same sleeping car, watching him. Soon after, at the beautiful wooded resort of Kislovodsk on the northern edge of the Caucasus Mountains, the surveillance became even more obvious.

Ames had been handling Shevchenko by himself as an interim case officer, but after the UN official returned to New York, James Dudley Haase arrived as deputy chief of base. He took over the Shevchenko case with continued help from Ames. Haase, then forty-six, was a short, heavyset ex-marine with a mustache and salt-and-pepper hair who was built like a right tackle. He had

[11]Whatever Ames's problems with alcohol before and certainly after his tour in Manhattan, none of his colleagues remember him drinking excessively during the five years he was assigned to FR/New York. His drinking with Shevchenko was considered part of the job. Russians are celebrated for their vodka consumption, and a CIA case officer who did *not* drink with a Soviet source might well arouse distrust.

just come from Ghana after tours in Laos and Uganda.

Shevchenko was getting increasingly edgy and pushing the CIA to let him defect. Then in March 1978 he got an ominous cable from Moscow summoning him home. Now he insisted to the CIA that the time had come. He had not dared to tell his wife, with whom he did not get along well, that he was spying for the CIA and planning to defect. A few nights later, carrying a heavy suitcase, he walked down a dimly lit fire stairs in his apartment building, ran out into the rain on East Sixty-fourth Street, and spotted a white car. Its signal lights were not flashing, which meant everything was okay. Shevchenko was spirited to a safe house in the Poconos. On April 11, the bombshell hit the press: The number two official of the United Nations had defected to the West.[12]

The CIA was elated over its coup, and there were plaudits for everyone who had worked on the case. Ken Millian, the base chief when the case had begun, retired on the strength of it. And the Shevchenko affair was a feather in the cap of Peter Koromilas, Jim Haase, Rick Ames, and the FBI agents who had also worked on the case. It was, in fact, the high point of Ames's career with the CIA.

Haase considered Ames bright and thought he performed well on the Shevchenko case. But he was less impressed with Ames's work on later cases; he felt Ames lacked initiative. To Haase, Ames would not follow up on things unless somebody told him to. The deputy base chief had tried talking to Ames about that, but with little result.

Ames fared much better with a new Soviet branch chief, Rodney W. Carlson, who arrived in the summer of 1979. The changing of the guard on Lexington Avenue, barely noticed at the

---

[12]Shevchenko's wife and daughter were whisked back to Moscow. A month later, he was told that his wife had committed suicide there and was found dead in a closet of her apartment. "It's possible they killed her," he said. "It is a mystery that may never be solved." Shevchenko remarried; his American wife, Elaine, died in 1990. He later married again, to Natasha, a Russian emigré. With the end of the cold war, his daughter was permitted to come to live in America, and his son, Gennady, was allowed to visit him in 1994.

time, was an event that was later to have a profound effect on Ames's career and the CIA itself.

Carlson grew up in South Dakota, went to Syracuse University, and earned a master's degree in Russian studies at the university's Maxwell School. He joined the CIA in 1958, and in June 1962, at age thirty, he was sent to Moscow to handle the agency's celebrated spy, Colonel Oleg Penkovsky of the GRU, code-named HERO. Carlson's cover was that of an agricultural attaché in the American embassy. At the ambassador's July 4 reception at Spasso House, Penkovsky was told to look for a man wearing a tie clip with red stones that he had been shown in London months before. Carlson wore the tie clip and made his first contact with Penkovsky. Later at a party at Carlson's apartment, the two men exchanged documents. But early in September, Penkovsky disappeared. The KGB had detected his spying months before, and he was arrested, tried, and executed. Five Americans, including Carlson, were declared persona non grata and expelled from Moscow.

But within the Directorate of Operations Carlson had made his reputation in the Penkovsky case, and he was posted to London, Tokyo, and Rome. Ames's new branch chief was a tall, thin man with dark hair and a Lincolnesque face. He was quiet and laconic, a respected veteran of the agency's Soviet division.

Carlson presided over some fifteen case officers and support personnel in the Soviet branch on Lexington Avenue. He knew of Ames's work in the Shevchenko case, and he was impressed with his performance in the branch. Carlson regarded Ames as a good street man.

While working for Carlson, Ames recruited some access agents at the UN. He did not recruit any Soviets, but then, neither did anyone else. FR was a tough environment; Carlson knew that. Unlike an overseas post, his people had no diplomatic cover, no support, really. Ames and the other CIA officers in the unit had to fall back on very vague cover. They ran around in different aliases, posing as businessmen, hoping that nobody would ask too many questions.

Carlson liked Ames, who developed into a sort of protégé of the branch chief, and over time they became good friends as well. In New York, Carlson met Nan Ames and thought her very attractive and career oriented. The Carlsons and the Ameses occasionally socialized together. Larry A. Fable was the FBI's liaison man in New York with the CIA base and dealt a good deal with Ames. When Fable retired, Rick and Nan and Carlson and his wife attended a party at Fable's house.

Late in 1979, a few months after Carlson became Ames's immediate boss, Jim Haase, the deputy chief of base who had worked with Ames on the Shevchenko case, moved up to become base chief. In 1981, Dean Almy, a CIA case officer who had served in Vietnam and elsewhere in the Far East, became chief of base.

By that time, Ames was preparing to leave Manhattan for his next assignment, in Mexico City. Nan balked at going with him. A liberated woman, established in her career, she was not ready to accept the idea of following her husband again to a foreign post.

Ames talked the problem over with a senior CIA colleague in New York. "He talked to me about the assignment in Mexico City," the CIA officer recalled. "Nancy didn't want to go with him. She was thinking in terms of divorce. She had another agenda in New York. She had her career, and she was involved in some political action group that was monitoring legislators; she would make trips to Albany and Washington with the group. Taking off for Mexico City would have disrupted that."

Over the past few years Ames had turned down several overseas assignments because his wife did not want to leave New York. He knew that his career would suffer if he did not soon accept a job abroad.

His CIA colleague remembered the pressures on Ames. "This was a dilemma for him; he wanted the Mexico assignment. He realized he had to get overseas and get more experience. I told him I thought he should take it. It was then that he said Nancy didn't want to go. He was thinking of a separated tour. I didn't think that was a very good idea for a marriage.

"I think their interests were pretty diverse. She was not sympathetic to the fact we had to work late hours, and work on weekends, sometimes spend weekends away. There was one weekend he had to go away and she was unhappy. A number of those types of things."

At the time, and later on, Ames told friends that his marriage was shaky. "Rick said they had grown apart," Michael Horwatt, a high school friend, recalled.

After debating what to do, Ames made his decision. He would accept the assignment in Mexico. Nan would keep her job in New York and remain in the apartment on East Fifty-fourth Street. Whether or not Ames or his wife knew it at the time, it was the end of their twelve-year marriage.

9

LANGLEY

Rick Ames had left his Volvo with his sister Nancy while he was in Mexico. When he came back to headquarters in October 1983, he moved into her basement bedroom in Vienna, Virginia, for about a month while he looked for an apartment.

"About two weeks into his stay," his sister recalled, "he told me he had met Rosario and was going to ask Nan for a divorce. He was in love, she was well educated, from a good family—this was not something he was doing easily. He was very upset that he would be the first in the family that he knew of ever to divorce. He went up to talk to Nan." He told his wife, who was still living in their apartment in Manhattan, that he wanted a divorce.

Soon after, Rosario followed Ames to Washington. She moved in with him into apartment 1009 of the Idylwood Towers, a high-rise building on Pimmit Drive in Falls Church, Virginia.[1] The next year, Mrs. Ames filed for divorce in New York; Ames did not contest it.

[1] As it happened, another Soviet spy, Edward Lee Howard, had lived in the same apartment building in 1981. Although both Howard and Ames worked

Because the Mexico City station had recommended that Ames be assessed and counseled for alcohol abuse, when he returned to Langley, he was called in by the CIA's Office of Medical Services. It would have been difficult for headquarters to ignore the problem once Ames came back from Mexico—his loud argument at an embassy party with a Cuban diplomat and the traffic accident where he was too drunk to answer the questions of the Mexican police had been reported to Langley.

Ames was called in by the medical office for assessment of his alcohol problem in November 1983. He denied that he had a serious drinking problem. Ames had no difficulty in persuading the counselor of this, as is evident from the fact that there was only one counseling session; he was never required to return to discuss the subject again.

"I was very cooperative with the counseling," Ames said later, "but it was just one session, and we talked about it. . . . I was not a serious case."[2] At the CIA, Ames added, "There were some real problem drinkers."[3] He was not regarded as someone in that cate-

in the CIA's Soviet division, it is unlikely that they knew each other; Howard was fired by the CIA in May 1983, five months before Ames returned from Mexico. But Ames was in Washington briefly in June 1982, so their paths conceivably could have crossed. When I telephoned Howard for *Newsweek* in February 1994, he noted that at Langley he had worked directly across the hall from the office that Ames later occupied. "The face is familiar," Howard said, "but I can't say I ever met him." It is, however, a small world. Ames answered an ad and rented his apartment in the Idylwood Towers from attorney William Bruce Gair, who knew Edward Lee Howard in Peru in the late 1970s when both worked for the Agency for International Development.

[2]Senate Interview, p. 70.

[3]Ibid. The unwillingness of the CIA to take Ames's drinking seriously had a precise parallel in the case of Edward Lee Howard, who went to see an agency alcohol counselor about his drinking in 1982 and was brushed off. The counselor, a retired case officer, did not regard Howard's drinking as very serious on the scale of alcohol problems at the agency. "I've got people who sit in the parking lot at headquarters, drinking," the counselor complained to him. "I've got one lady who filled her windshield wiper dispenser with vodka and rigged the line so the hose comes inside the car. When she's caught in traffic, she can turn on the wipers and squirt herself." The counselor told Howard not to worry.

gory. The medical office did not have the information about Ames's drinking in Mexico and did not request it—a pattern seen throughout the Ames case, in which the various divisions of the CIA did not bother to talk to each other.

Although Ames was never again counseled for his drinking problem, which only grew worse, he was given a blood test for alcohol by the CIA in February 1984. The test was designed to look at liver function to see whether Ames was showing any physical signs of alcohol abuse.[4] The blood test was normal.

But if Ames had slipped through the agency's alcohol screening, such as it was, there still remained the problem of what job he would receive in the Soviet division.[5] It was not unusual for case officers returning from posts overseas to face difficulty in nailing down a new job; the less desirable officers might literally go for months without being given a desk and assigned to an office. For these pariahs, the period of limbo was known as "walking the halls."

In the wake of the poor performance reports Ames had received in Mexico, he had convinced himself that his career was going rapidly downhill. It was Rod Carlson who saved him.

In July 1983, Carlson took over the key CI Group in the Soviet division. As such, he was responsible for counterintelligence operations against the KGB and the GRU worldwide.[6] Carlson invited Ames to head the Soviet branch of the CI Group. Counterintelligence, or CI, means protecting an intelligence agency against for-

---

[4]In February 1984, the following liver enzyme tests were performed on a blood sample taken from Ames: ALT, ALK, PHOS, AST, LDH, and GGT, as well as a total bilirubin test for jaundice. The tests can indicate a damaged liver, but not necessarily from alcohol. The GGT test is potentially the most accurate for detecting alcohol abuse; a high level of the enzyme may indicate that the liver has been processing abnormal amounts of alcohol, although it is not conclusive. Also, if a person stops drinking for a few months, the enzyme will not show up on the test at an elevated level.

[5]The Soviet division's formal name at the time was the Soviet/East European division, referred to in-house as SE or SE division.

[6]The CI Group's formal name was the Operational Review and Production Group, or ORP (pronounced as a word). But within the Soviet division, it was almost always referred to informally as the CI (for counterintelligence) Group.

eign espionage operations and attempting, in turn, to penetrate and undermine the opposition services.

Ames had now been given a very important and highly sensitive job at the very heart of the CIA's operations against Soviet intelligence. As Soviet branch chief, Ames was responsible for all CIA operations against the KGB and the GRU outside the Soviet Union. He supervised all the CIA assets inside the Soviet intelligence services who were working abroad.[7] By virtue of his position, he had access as well to the identities of CIA sources inside the Soviet Union itself. In short, he knew it all.

An understanding of the SE division's structure makes it clear why Ames had such complete access to anything he wanted. The division had three groups. Carlson's CI Group consisted of the Soviet branch headed by Ames; an East European branch headed by Jack P. Gatewood, who had worked with Ames in FR/New York and became his close friend; and a Production branch to handle reports.

SE division's two other groups were an Internal Operations Group, and under it, a USSR branch to manage CIA activities and cases inside the Soviet Union and an External Operations Group, in charge of liaison with CIA stations abroad outside the Soviet Union. Ames dealt on a daily basis with the division's Internal Group and the USSR branch, which handled the cases in Moscow. "There was a lot of paper going back and forth, a lot of interaction between the groups," a CIA man said. Moreover, assets recruited outside the Soviet Union, for which Ames had direct responsibility, would eventually go back to Moscow. And Ames knew who they were.

How did Ames, who in time became the CIA's most destructive mole, burrow his way into such a job? The answer sheds light on how compartmentation, an essential element in any secret agency to guard against penetration, can be just as dangerous as the perils it is designed to protect against. The purpose of compartmentation is to restrict secret information to those with a "need to know," thereby limiting the circle of people with access and reducing the

[7]Typically, the CIA sought to recruit KGB and GRU officers when they were stationed away from home, particularly in the third world, but in other countries as well.

chance that the information will escape into the wrong hands. But that structure, rather like watertight compartments on a ship, may also have been responsible in part for the prevailing bureaucratic mind-set inside the CIA, in which various components of the agency did not communicate with one another, even when there *was* a need to know.[8]

Rod Carlson picked Ames because, based on his knowledge of Ames in New York, he considered him to be very bright, well informed about the Soviet Union, a superior analyst and writer, and a good case officer. Ames, after all, had brought Arkady Shevchenko in from the cold. And while Ames certainly drank in New York, he had not evidenced an alcohol problem. On a personal level, Carlson liked Ames and considered him a friend. He thought Ames had the depth and background that made him a natural choice for the job.

As far as is known, nobody disagreed with Carlson's selection of Ames to head the Soviet branch. Carlson was an experienced case officer, and he had handled the biggest CIA spy of all, Oleg Penkovsky. Nobody told Carlson that Ames had an alcohol problem in Mexico City, nor did Carlson see the negative performance evaluations Ames had received there. None of the records reached Carlson. He could have asked for the files, but he knew Ames. Besides, Carlson and most agency managers considered the performance reports next to worthless, since they are subjective and tend to reflect personal bias.

In 1983, David W. Forden headed the CIA's Soviet division. A handsome man of fifty, with prematurely silver hair, Forden was a popular division chief, a New Yorker who graduated from Wesleyan University and had served in the CIA for almost three decades. He approved Carlson's selection of Rick Ames as Soviet branch chief. Like Carlson, Forden was unaware that Ames had a drinking problem in Mexico City; no reports about that had crossed his desk.

[8]Ironically, compartmentation and "need to know" proved no obstacle to Ames after he began to spy for the KGB. Repeatedly, even when he was moved into less sensitive posts, he was able to obtain classified documents and information outside his immediate area of responsibility.

And so it came to pass that Ames reported in to Langley head-quarters in room 4D18 to begin his new job as Soviet branch chief of the CI Group. In that capacity, Ames reviewed the cases of Soviet intelligence officers who had been recruited as CIA agents to try to determine if they were genuine. Was the Soviet a true asset, or was he being played back against the CIA as a double agent? Ames also examined each Soviet case to see if there were security problems evident, or whether a particular agent might have been compromised. Ames, for example, would evaluate the ways that the CIA's Soviet agents were contacted to make sure that the methods were operationally secure.

"Our main job was to oversee operations worldwide against the Soviet target," one of Ames's colleagues at the time explained. "Scanning traffic from all around the world to look for problems." The co-worker remembered Ames well. "Slicked-back greasy hair, glasses, a mustache, smoking cigarettes all the time, tobacco-stained teeth and fingers. He had a sort of offhand approach to things. Anything but a hard worker—pretty lazy. My image of him is sitting with his feet up on the desk, big stack of files, smoking and reading old files. Presumably at the request of the KGB, we now know. He liked to do that."

In his fourth-floor office at headquarters, Ames did more than read cables, however. It is a delicious irony that part of Ames's new counterintelligence responsibilities was to uncover moles inside the CIA. Specifically, he had the job of tasking the agency's Soviet assets to try to learn of any penetrations of the CIA.

Because Ames supervised cases involving moles working for U.S. intelligence inside the KGB, he learned of two major sources right in the Soviet embassy in Washington, agents feeding information to the FBI and the CIA under the very noses of KGB counterintelligence. The recruitment of the first of these sources marked the success of a new, joint approach by the agency and the bureau.

By presidential executive order, the CIA must advise the FBI when it conducts foreign counterintelligence operations in this country. In 1980, the CIA and the FBI went even further; although traditional rivals, they jointly established an operation, code-named COURTSHIP, to try to recruit Soviets stationed in Washington. The unit operated from an office building in suburban Springfield, Virginia.

The year after Rick went off to Mexico, Rod Carlson himself had been summoned down from New York by David Forden, the Soviet division chief, to take over a big case. Carlson was assigned as the CIA case officer for a Soviet agent who was being handled jointly with the FBI through COURTSHIP.

In November 1980, Lt. Col. Valery F. Martynov of the KGB arrived in Washington with his wife, Natalya, to take up his duties, ostensibly as third secretary of the Soviet embassy on Sixteenth Street, not far from the White House in Northwest Washington. In reality, Martynov was a Line X KGB officer, who had been sent to the United States to collect scientific and technical information.[9]

In 1982, Martynov was spotted by a CIA man working out of the agency's Washington station, FR/Washington, then located in an office building in Bethesda. The CIA man had an engineering background and would go to various technical meetings in the Washington area. A CIA source recalled how the case began: "Martynov showed up at a meeting, one in a series, and our guy chatted with him. Martynov missed the next meeting, but at one of the subsequent meetings he was there. The agency officer came back and said, 'This guy is different. This is a very unusual Russian.' COURTSHIP took him away and recruited him. COURTSHIP had power to do that."

The CIA gave Martynov the code name GTGENTILE.[10] The FBI called him PIMENTA. Carlson began handling Martynov in the early spring of 1982. Jim Holt, a handsome, white-haired Virginian, handled Martynov for the FBI. Carlson and Holt met with

[9]Line X was the designation given to KGB officers in the field who worked for Directorate T, the KGB division in Moscow in charge of collecting scientific and technical intelligence. The CIA and the FBI referred to these officers as Line X or S&T, shorthand for scientific and technical.

[10]Initially, in 1982, he was called CKGENTILE. It was changed to GTGENTILE after Edward Lee Howard, who of course knew the CK digraph, fled to Moscow in 1985.

Martynov more than fifty times in FBI safe houses and other locations. The meetings, on the average of one almost every two weeks, went on for more than three years.

Valery Martynov was a big man, about six feet tall and 190 pounds. He was the opposite of the stereotype of the dour Russian; he was jovial, with a friendly, cheerful manner. He was thirty-six and spoke fluent English. He and Natalya lived in the Hamlet North subdivision of Alexandria, Virginia, with their two children, a twelve-year-old son in junior high school and a daughter of five.

Martynov's motives were not clear. He may not have felt he was taking such a big risk; after all, only a handful of CIA officers had sold out to the Soviets over the years, so PIMENTA may well have thought that the risk of betrayal from within the CIA or the FBI was minimal. Money may have been a factor, of course; Martynov was paid, although not a lot, perhaps a few hundred dollars a month. But he was told that there was a much bigger escrow account in his name being held for him in the United States, money that he could have if and when he decided to defect.

An experienced intelligence officer who has read the file on the Martynov case discounted money as his primary motive. "Like all spies, including Aldrich Ames, I think it was the excitement, and the idea of doing something really secret. You can't believe what you are told about motivation, anyway, because people don't understand their own motivation. Martynov was intrigued by the game. He did not think spying for the Americans was wrong. Because he did not regard us as an enemy."

The FBI and the CIA had different priorities in the meetings with Martynov. The bureau was interested in detailed information about the KGB residency in Washington, headed during those years by Stanislav Andreevich Androsov. The FBI, for example, wanted PIMENTA's assessment of which KGB officers might be vulnerable to recruitment.

The CIA, in turn, was interested in any counterintelligence information that could be gleaned—KGB targets in America, KGB modus operandi, the identities of Soviet intelligence officers traveling to the United States on temporary assignment, what the visitors might have to say about the latest news from Moscow Center, and, of course, Martynov's S&T requirements and targets.

Martynov also turned over documents to the FBI and the CIA. He provided Xerox copies; he did not use a camera. From the CIA's point of view, Martynov's real importance was not so much what he could provide, although that was valuable, but his potential as a sleeper agent. "Here was a bright young guy who would move ahead," one SE division officer said, "and someday might become a very important agent."

In the meantime, he was important enough. The FBI was ecstatic over PIMENTA, its first major penetration of the KGB residency in Washington. The excitement in Division 5, the bureau's intelligence division, became even greater when the FBI recruited a second KGB source in the embassy. KGB Major Sergei M. Motorin was posted to Washington during the summer of 1980, like Martynov, as a third secretary. He, too, became a spy for the United States.

The FBI gave Motorin the code name DIONYSUS. Later, it became MEGAS. Inside the bureau, the cryptonyms PIMENTA and MEGAS became twinned, and as well known in the early 1980s as FEDORA and TOPHAT were a decade earlier. The CIA gave Major Motorin the code name GTGAUZE.

As Soviet branch chief in the CI Group, Rick Ames knew about both cases. He knew the code names and identities of both Martynov and Motorin. Around the end of 1984, Motorin's tour was over and he returned home. But he agreed to continue to provide information to the CIA through the agency's Moscow station.

Other important cases crossed Ames's desk now, located as he was at the very center of the CIA's most sensitive and secret operations. There was, for example, the case of Vladimir V. Potashov, a young disarmament specialist working in Moscow for the prestigious Institute of the USA and Canada Studies headed by Georgi A. Arbatov.

Potashov, who now lives in the United States, felt stifled by the Soviet system. "For ten years I had been thinking to come to the U.S. and remain here," he said. "But my father got a gold star for his work as director of the Kamaz River truck plant, the biggest diesel truck plant in the Soviet Union. I was afraid of what would happen to my father."

In 1981, however, the institute sent Potashov to Washington for three months, attached to the Soviet embassy. He had met Harold Brown when the former defense secretary and president of the California Institute of Technology had visited the Arbatov Institute in Moscow several years earlier. "I went to Brown, who was living in Georgetown, and told him I love Russian people but hate the Soviet government." Through Brown, Potashov was put in touch with the CIA and the FBI, which gave him the code name SUNDAY PUNCH. The agency persuaded Potashov that he could not remain in the United States; his father would be harmed, his girlfriend would be a target of the KGB. But he could be a valuable source in Moscow.

"I agreed to go back and write reports on the chances for zero option or other disarmament agreements with the United States. Money was not a factor. But after several meetings they told me money would be placed in a U.S. bank for me."

Arms-control negotiations with the Soviets started in the fall of 1981, and Potashov agreed to provide the CIA with his analyses of the U.S. position and any information he could glean on the Soviet negotiating position. That year, the Reagan administration unveiled a plan to deploy cruise missiles and Pershing II missiles in Europe. At the same time, Washington offered to halt the deployment if the Soviet Union scrapped its SS-20 and other intermediate-range nuclear missiles. This was the so-called zero option. Potashov, convinced that the Kremlin's leaders would use their SS-20s against Europe if the Soviet Union was threatened with collapse, urged his government to accept the deal. He secretly transmitted to the CIA his assessments of the Soviet reaction to the Reagan proposal.

In Moscow, Potashov did not use dead drops or personal meetings to send his information to Langley. Instead, he sent letters to false addresses. The CIA used dead drops and shortwave radio to send instructions and questions to Potashov. In his communications with the agency, Potashov used the alias "Paul Lansky." For the next five years, he worked as an agent of the CIA.

Rick Ames learned as well about a valuable CIA and FBI source inside the KGB in Moscow who had been recruited years earlier in San Francisco. Boris Yuzhin had first come to the United States in 1975 as a student at the University of California at Berkeley. He was already working for the KGB.

A CIA officer in the agency's San Francisco base spotted Yuzhin at a party, and the FBI took over. To find a pretext to contact Yuzhin, who was married, the bureau enlisted the help of a young woman he knew. A rental property she owned had been raided by police, who found in the house some pamphlets from the Soviet consulate. It was a slim reed, but just enough to give the bureau a reason to interview the young KGB officer, whose superiors might not have appreciated his friendship with a woman whose tenants were of interest to the police. As it turned out, the ploy was not really necessary—Yuzhin admired what he saw in American society and began volunteering information to the bureau.

The FBI assigned Bill Smits, who spoke Russian and was only a few years older than Yuzhin, as his case agent. In the San Francisco field office, Smits was known as the Count, possibly because he favored three-piece suits. Born in Bay Ridge, Brooklyn, he graduated from the University of Colorado and was earning his master's degree and doctorate in public administration at Golden Gate University while handling Boris Yuzhin. "He cooperated because he hated the KGB, the politics," Smits said. "He had no use for it. He saw it for what it was." The FBI gave Yuzhin the code name RAMPAIGE. The CIA called him CKTWINE.

In 1978, Yuzhin returned to San Francisco, this time as a KGB officer under cover as the San Francisco correspondent of Tass, the Soviet news agency. A CIA officer explained why the KGB man continued to spy for the United States: "He had been treated well, but he was considered a country boy from an inferior background. In the KGB you got promoted because of who you knew, not what you did. Yuzhin didn't have a protector. Even though he was a lieutenant colonel by the time he went back to San Francisco, he felt he was a quota bumpkin. They pushed a few along in a sort of equal opportunity program."

Yuzhin provided valuable information to American intelligence.

He revealed the existence of the KGB's Group North, an elite unit of senior Soviet intelligence officers who specialized in recruiting American and Canadian targets worldwide. The KGB group was a kind of SWAT team with authority to travel anywhere on its missions.

Yuzhin also gave the FBI and the CIA leads that helped Norway to identify and arrest Arne Treholt, a high-level Soviet spy in that country's diplomatic corps. In 1984, Norwegian police arrested Treholt at Oslo's airport as he was about to leave for Vienna to meet his KGB control. He carried a briefcase containing sixty-six classified documents. Treholt was convicted and sentenced to twenty years.

Bill Smits continued as Yuzhin's bureau handler, working under James Fox, who later headed the FBI's New York office.

The FBI had developed some serious doubts about Yuzhin, but now—unknown to the KGB man—he became the guinea pig in an unusual display of cooperation between the bureau and the CIA.

At the center of this counterintelligence ballet was another important CIA source in Indonesia, code-named GTJOGGER, whose identity was known to Rick Ames in his job as the CIA branch chief for Soviet counterintelligence. GTJOGGER was Vladimir M. Piguzov, a lieutenant colonel in the KGB and the number two man in the Soviet residency in Djakarta in the late 1970s.

It was GTJOGGER who disclosed to the CIA that a former agency officer, David H. Barnett, had sold secret CIA information to the KGB. Barnett, who grew up near Pittsburgh, joined the agency in the 1950s and was sent to Indonesia in the 1960s to run a clandestine collection operation code-named HABRINK. The operation enabled the agency to gather detailed information on a wide range of Soviet weapons, from SAM missiles to submarines. The agency was getting the information from an Indonesian navy officer on the CIA's payroll. Barnett quit the CIA in 1970, lost a lot of money in the shrimp business in Indonesia, and decided to sell his knowledge about HABRINK and other CIA secrets to the KGB, which paid him $92,600. The CIA turned over GTJOGGER's leads about Barnett to the FBI. The bureau investigated and Barnett was indicted. He pleaded guilty in October 1980, the first CIA officer ever to be charged with espionage. He was sentenced to eighteen years in federal prison and served a little over nine years.

The FBI was so pleased with the successful prosecution of Barnett that in exchange for the CIA's leads in the case, the bureau agreed to let the agency work with it on an FBI case. The CIA chose Yuzhin. And for the first time, the agency in turn allowed two FBI agents to come to Langley and read agency case files.

In 1981, a CIA officer flew to San Francisco and in a hotel room gave Yuzhin a tiny James Bond–like camera disguised as a cigarette lighter. Yuzhin smoked, so his having a lighter would not arouse suspicion. The CIA camera was tube shaped, with the lens at the opposite end from the flint. The specially designed lens, known as a tropel, was not much bigger than a dime. A CIA technician showed Yuzhin how to use the camera to photograph documents in the Soviet consulate. The gadget had special film that took ninety frames. Yuzhin photographed a number of documents and would then exchange the exposed film for a new roll.[11]

Some months later, Yuzhin committed a terrible blunder that nearly cost him his life. He lost the cigarette lighter. Yuzhin was frantic. Bill Smits remembered the scene. "I searched his car that night thinking he might have dropped it between the seats. We damn near tore the car apart." No lighter. Yuzhin thought maybe he had dropped it at a friend's apartment. The FBI entered the apartment and searched it, but found nothing.

In the meantime, a janitor in the Soviet consulate had found the lighter. Trying to light a flame, he took four pictures of himself. He turned the lighter in. The KGB immediately saw what it was. Yuzhin and a Soviet political officer at the consulate, Igor S. Samsonov, both smokers, headed the list of KGB suspects.

In 1982, Yuzhin went back to Moscow, still under suspicion. But lacking any real evidence that Yuzhin was the culprit who had dropped the lighter, the KGB did not move against him. The CIA hoped to stay in communication with Yuzhin, but he was wary now. "When he returned to Moscow," a CIA man said, "Yuzhin

[11]On one occasion, using another small camera provided by the FBI, Yuzhin managed to take pictures of his own reflection on the documents, not a good idea had the film fallen into the wrong hands.

would only agree to give a 'sign of life,' such as a chalk mark. No meetings, no dead drops." But for the moment, at least, as Rick Ames knew, Yuzhin seemed out of danger.

The most important CIA source to cross Ames's desk was Dimitri Fedorovich Polyakov, the FBI's legendary TOPHAT, code-named GTBEEP by the CIA. He had been turned over to the agency when the FBI's John Mabey had bowed out of the case in Burma in 1966. The Vietnam War was then in full swing. In Burma, Polyakov provided extensive data on the North Vietnamese and Chinese military.

After three years, Polyakov was posted back to Moscow, where he remained until 1973, when he turned up in India as a Soviet military attaché. The CIA's Paul L. Dillon, who had known Polyakov in Rangoon, was sent out to New Delhi as his case officer. Dillon, with a fishing rod and a tape recorder, would meet GTBEEP along a riverbank. As the CIA man played the part of a fisherman, Polyakov briefed him rapidly on the latest information he had collected from inside Soviet military intelligence.

After four years in India, TOPHAT/GTBEEP returned to Moscow in 1977. So valuable was Polyakov that the CIA provided him with special high-tech equipment that it reserved for its most important agents. In India, Dillon gave Polyakov a burst transmitter, which would allow the GRU officer, back in Moscow, to send messages in short 2.6-second bursts. The high-speed transmitter would make it much more difficult for Soviet direction-finding equipment to zero in on the location of the signals. In Moscow, Polyakov used the transmitter to send information to the CIA from a streetcar traveling past the American embassy. He was also given a clock for his Moscow apartment that lit up in response to a radio signal to inform him that a dead drop had been cleared by the CIA.

In 1979 he was posted back to New Delhi. By this time, Polyakov had been promoted to the rank of lieutenant general. Now his access to top-secret information was even greater; over the years, Polyakov provided extremely valuable political-military information, including data on Soviet strategic missiles, antitank missiles, nuclear strategy, chemical and biological warfare, crop diseases, and civil defense.

In 1980, General Polyakov returned to Moscow for the last time. He had successfully spied for the United States for two decades. Despite the initial skepticism of James Angleton, he had become accepted by the CIA as its most valuable spy in the cold war since Oleg Penkovsky. In the CIA's pantheon of spies, Polyakov was in a class by himself. Approaching retirement age, TOPHAT/GTBEEP could look back with quiet satisfaction on his perilous career as a spy for America.

For Polyakov, the worst danger seemed over now. He had spied for the CIA and gotten away with it. He could look forward to a peaceful retirement with his family and the comforts and perquisites accorded to a Soviet general. His secret was safe.

10

"AS MUCH MONEY AS I COULD EVER USE"

n March 1984, Rick Ames told his boss, Rod Carlson, that he wanted to see some action. The desk job as chief of the Soviet counterintelligence branch was too tame.

Ames asked for permission to supplement his work at head-quarters with some after-hours espionage. He offered to start meeting with Soviets in Washington; perhaps it would lead to a recruitment or two.

At the time, it did not seem an unusual request. CIA officers assigned to headquarters often volunteer for field work, even though it may mean putting in extra hours. But for a deskbound case officer, especially one who has been stationed overseas, the operational work adds a little excitement to the daily routine at headquarters.

Carlson approved, as did David Forden, the chief of the Soviet division.

Forden did not hesitate to sign off on Ames's request; the division had an active program of trying to penetrate the Russian embassy and the KGB residency in Washington. It welcomed initiative by junior officers. "We used everything we could," said one CIA Soviet specialist.

Ames had to clear his proposal as well with the station chief of FR/Washington, since the CI Group had no direct responsibility for assessing and recruiting Soviets in the capital. During these months, Ames had complained to CIA colleagues that he was broke; he was already in debt, and the divorce he had asked for was proving costly as well.

But no warning flags went up at Langley, and if any colleagues or supervisors knew or remembered that Ames had been reported for his boozing in Mexico City, they said nothing. Aldrich Ames, with financial, marital, and alcohol problems, an officer whose ultrasensitive job put him at the very heart of the agency's global operations against the KGB, was about to approach the Soviets in Washington with the approval and encouragement of the CIA. He was stepping into the mouth of the bear.

With the benefit of hindsight it seems incredible that someone with the access Ames had to the agency's innermost secrets, and as vulnerable as he was, would be allowed anywhere near a Russian. But other CIA case officers in sensitive positions have experienced financial or personal problems without going over the edge and betraying their country. Agency managers were unaware of the extent to which Ames had become cynical and disillusioned about his work for the CIA. Moreover, Ames *had* done well with Arkady Shevchenko in New York, even if his prolonged attempt to recruit Igor Shurygin in Mexico had seemed to go nowhere, ending up in a vodka mist.

In any event, Rick went operational that spring of 1984, with the full and even enthusiastic blessing of his superiors. But proposing to recruit a Soviet was more easily said than done, and the first hurdle was how to meet one. It had to be worked delicately and just right because all that followed might depend on the initial approach.

Ames went to Carlson with the problem. The chief of the CI Group suggested that Ames contact Sergei I. Divilkovsky, a Soviet diplomat whom Carlson had known in New York when the CIA man ran the Soviet branch in Manhattan. At the time Divilkovsky was in the Soviet mission to the UN.

In Washington in 1984, Divilkovsky was listed as counselor for press affairs in the Soviet embassy. He was a thin, professorial-looking man of medium height with thinning hair and glasses. He looked to be in his fifties.

Titles did not mean anything; Divilkovsky's embassy colleagues, Valery Martynov and Sergei Motorin—the two CIA and FBI sources inside the KGB residency—were listed as third secretaries. Whether Divilkovsky was KGB or not was a subject of some dispute within the CIA. But regardless of the answer, as a window on the embassy, a way in, he suited Ames's purposes.

As Carlson had advised, Ames telephoned Divilkovsky and said he was a friend of someone the Russian had met in New York—Ames referred to Carlson by the alias that the branch chief had used in Manhattan a few years earlier. Ames, of course, was also using a fictitious name, Rick Wells, and as cover said he was with the Intelligence Community Staff, a coordinating unit for the government's intelligence agencies. He would, quite possibly, have offered Divilkovsky a backstopped phone number that rang at the CIA and would be answered appropriately.[1]

Ames began having lunch from time to time with Divilkovsky. Under the rules, FR/Washington had to clear such contacts in this country with the FBI, which kept a close eye on Soviet diplomats. Ames was required to report all of his contacts to the CIA, which in turn would inform the bureau.

During the day, Ames continued to work at his job at headquarters. In April, Ames told the CIA that he intended to marry Rosario, whose name was not, of course, unknown to the agency, since she had been a paid source in Mexico. In August, Rosario was given a polygraph test—standard procedure for a foreign national marrying a CIA officer—and she passed. The agency's Office of Security did a background check on Rosario, some of

[1]Ames might have liked to tell Divilkovsky that he was with the "State Department," but the department, while providing cover for CIA officers overseas all the time, was fussy about doing so for operations at home. To use State Department cover would have caused an interagency flap if it became known.

whose friends reported she came from a "prominent, wealthy family in Colombia." OS did not, however, check in Colombia to verify Rosario's purported wealth.

Because Ames intended to marry a foreign national, the CIA's counterintelligence staff recommended that he be transferred from his job as Soviet branch chief for counterintelligence to a less sensitive job. The agency's deputy director for operations accepted this recommendation. Nothing happened.

In July 1984, there was a major change in the Soviet division. David Forden went off to Greece to be station chief in Athens.

The new chief of the Soviet division, replacing Forden, was Burton Lee Gerber, then the deputy chief of the European division (EUR). He was a tall, thin, soft-spoken man of fifty-one with wavy gray hair, glasses, and an almost academic, rather humorless manner. Born in Illinois, Gerber had graduated from Michigan State in 1955 with a bachelor's degree and disappeared into the CIA. He learned Bulgarian and was posted to Sofia under State Department cover in the 1960s. In the early 1980s, he served as chief of station in Moscow. He climbed the ladder at headquarters, and now, in 1984, he got his division. Photographs of wolves lined the walls of the new chief's office; Gerber liked wolves.

That summer, or perhaps in 1985—the CIA is not sure of the date—Ames had several drinks with his Soviet contact and then continued to drink at a CIA-FBI softball game. Ames got blind drunk and had to be driven home, leaving behind at the softball field his badge, some cryptic notes, a wallet containing his alias identification, and his jacket. Senior Soviet division officials either personally witnessed or learned of this episode. Nothing happened.

In the fall of 1984, Ames was sent back to New York temporarily to assist the CIA station there in targeting foreign diplomats arriving for the opening of the United Nations General Assembly. Traditionally, the event was a happy hunting ground for the agency's recruiters. "He had a very short trip because he brought Rosario with him," a CIA man recalled. At the time, the New York chief of station was N. John MacGaffin, who had arrived in Manhattan by way of the CIA stations in Lebanon and Jordan.

"The station had provided a safe house on Manhattan's East Side, somewhere near the UN," a CIA officer who served in FR/New York at the time recalled. "The safe house was a two-bedroom apartment with a pullout couch in the living room, so that three officers could have slept there. Ames and two other officers were assigned to the safe house." No one expected Rick to show up with Rosario. Besides, bringing an outsider to a safe house, someone who knew Ames worked for the CIA, had exposed the faces and identities of the other officers present. It was against every rule in the book.

When Ames moved into the safe house with Rosario, Janine M. Brookner was the CIA's UN branch chief in New York. As such, she was responsible for supervising both the safe house and Ames and the other CIA officers detailed to New York for the General Assembly.[2] One of the men assigned to the CIA apartment complained to her about Rosario's presence. Brookner confronted Ames, who claimed he had permission from headquarters. There was no way he could have gotten permission, Brookner replied. She then alerted MacGaffin, who threw Ames and Rosario out of the safe house. Headquarters was informed of the incident, but took virtually no action against Ames.[3]

[2]Brookner, as "Jane Doe Thompson," sued the CIA in 1994 for sex discrimination, charging that her career had been ruined after she reported that the deputy chief of station in Jamaica, while Brookner was station chief, had repeatedly beaten his wife unconscious, "to the point of strangulation." Amazingly, the agency then turned on Brookner. A ludicrous report compiled under the supervision of Bertram F. Dunn, the deputy inspector general, who was a former high-level CIA spook, said Brookner in tropical Jamaica "sometimes wore brief shorts and thin tee-shirts with no perceptible underwear," leading "some men" to "believe she might make a pass" at them. The inspector general's report, when it became public in court papers, was an embarrassment to the agency. In December the CIA agreed to pay Brookner $410,000 to settle the suit. The agency did not apologize.

[3]In a statement to Congress on September 28, 1994, CIA director R. James Woolsey told of the safe house incident and declared: "This violation was reported, yet again, nothing was done." A week later, Woolsey amended his congressional testimony to say that when Ames returned to headquarters, he received a "verbal reprimand" from his division chief, Burton Gerber. In a letter to the *Washington Post*, Ames said Gerber told him he had exercised "poor judgment."

In September 1984, around the time of the safe house incident, Nan Ames filed for divorce in New York on grounds of mental cruelty. The divorce proceedings, sealed under New York State law, began the following month. The couple had formally separated when Ames had returned from Mexico.

As part of the separation agreement, Ames had agreed to pay all outstanding credit card and miscellaneous debts, which totaled $33,350. Under a "property stipulation," Ames also agreed to pay Nan $300 a month for forty-two months starting in June 1985, which created a new debt for Ames of $12,600 over the three and a half years.

Rich Thurman, who had been part of Ames's regular luncheon group in Mexico, returned to Washington in 1983 as a division chief in the State Department's Bureau of Intelligence and Research. Thurman's work on National Intelligence Estimates, for example, sometimes brought him to CIA headquarters, and he renewed his friendship with Ames over lunch at the agency. Ames told Thurman and other friends that he had been taken to the cleaners by his wife.

Ames, according to the CIA's internal investigation of the spy case, believed "his divorce settlement threatened to bankrupt him."[4] Ames conceded, however, that his indebtedness had grown since Rosario moved in with him in December 1983. He had taken out a new-car loan, a signature loan, and there were mounting credit card payments.

A couple of months after Ames's awkward safe house encounter in New York, he began thinking of a possible solution to his financial problems. Between December 1984 and February 1985, according to Ames, the thought occurred that he had a valuable commodity to sell to the KGB.[5]

"I felt a great deal of financial pressure. . . ," Ames said. "The pre-

---

[4]Senate Report, p. 18, quoting classified report of the CIA inspector general on the Ames case.

[5]Senate Report, p. 20. Whether Ames had toyed with the idea of selling CIA secrets to the KGB at an earlier date, during his drinking bouts with Shurygin in Mexico, for example, is something that may never be known. But the December 1984 to February 1985 period are the dates that Ames has offered.

vious two years that I had spent in Washington, I had incurred a certain amount of personal debt in terms of buying furniture. . . for an apartment and my divorce settlement had left me with no property essentially. . . . It was not a truly desperate situation but it was one that somehow really placed a great deal of pressure on me. . . . Rosario was living with me at the time. . . . I was contemplating the future. I had no house, and we had strong plans to have a family, and so I was thinking also in the longer term. . . ."[6]

According to the CIA's own investigation, "Ames states that the primary motivating factor for his decision to commit espionage was his desperation regarding financial indebtedness he incurred at the time of his separation from his first wife, their divorce settlement and his cohabitation with Rosario."[7]

Or as Ames put it in plainer language: "I felt embarrassed and potentially humiliated to be in a situation in which I had sort of lost control of the household budget, and getting from one paycheck to the next was getting increasingly difficult."[8]

The CIA investigation cited several other factors that went into the mix: "the opportunity to meet Soviet officials under Agency sanction," his belief that "the rules that governed others did not apply to him," and "his fading respect for the value of his Agency work as a result of lengthy discussions with Soviet officials."[9]

This last reason was significant. The disillusionment with his work for the CIA that Ames had privately discussed in Mexico with his friend David Samson surfaced when Ames was questioned by the agency after pleading guilty to espionage. Moreover, Ames was now stating that his disenchantment was a direct result of his talks with Russian officials *before* he had begun to spy for the KGB. While Ames had met Soviets in New York, the only intensive, extended talks that he had with a Soviet official over a long period of time

[6]Senate Interview, pp. 13–14.

[7]IG Report, p. 14.

[8]August 8, 1994, interview with Aldrich Ames by Chairman Dan Glickman and Congressman Larry Combest, Transcript, p. 2, in House Permanent Select Committee on Intelligence, *Report of Investigation: the Aldrich Ames Espionage Case*, November 30, 1994, hereinafter "House Interview" and "House Report."

[9]IG Report, p. 14.

were those that had begun in Mexico four years earlier with Igor Shurygin, the KGB counterintelligence chief in Mexico City.

In December 1984, Sergei Divilkovsky, the Soviet diplomat who had been Ames's contact for almost a year, returned to Moscow. Before leaving, he handed Ames off to another Russian, Sergei Dimitriyevich Chuvakhin, who was listed as a first secretary of the Soviet embassy. Divilkovsky described him as a diplomat specializing in arms-control issues.

In April 1985, Rick Ames, just short of his forty-fourth birthday, an employee of the CIA for almost twenty-three years, reached his fateful decision. He would cross over and sell the agency's secrets to Moscow.

Ames arranged to meet Chuvakhin on April 16 at the Mayflower Hotel, two blocks from the Soviet embassy. That evening, Ames had several drinks in the bar as he waited. Chuvakhin, the CIA, and Ames had rather different agendas. Chuvakhin thought that Ames wanted to discuss broad U.S.-Soviet security concerns. The CIA thought Chuvakhin was being assessed for possible recruitment as an agency source. Rick Ames planned to use the meeting as a pretext to get a message to the KGB, offering to sell classified information.

When Chuvakhin failed to show, Ames left, walked two blocks east to Sixteenth Street, and boldly went inside the Soviet embassy, an ornate and imposing nineteenth-century structure once the home of George Mortimer Pullman, who designed the railroad sleeping cars named for him. In the rear of the lobby, there was a reception desk with closed-circuit television consoles, manned by grim-faced uniformed KGB guards. Ames handed an envelope to the duty officer and asked to see Sergei Chuvakhin. The envelope was addressed, not to Chuvakhin, but to the KGB resident, Stanislav Andreevich Androsov.

Ames, of course, knew who Androsov was. He did not speak his name—everyone assumes the FBI has the embassy bugged, except for a soundproof "bubble"—but the clear implication was that Ames wanted the letter delivered to the KGB chief. The guard nodded his understanding.

Chuvakhin appeared, the two men had a brief conversation, and Ames departed. Inside the envelope that Ames had left for

Androsov was a note describing two or three Soviets who had approached the CIA in Russia to volunteer information. Ames said he later revealed to the KGB that the CIA's Soviet division considered each of the Russians to be double agents under KGB control.[10] So Ames rationalized that he was not giving the Russians anything they did not already know. Of course, if he was wrong, the Soviet walk-ins were dead, or headed for Siberia.

In the statement Ames read in federal court in Alexandria, Virginia, on April 28, 1994, the day he was sentenced to life in prison, Ames sought to explain this initial act of treachery as nothing more than a scam designed to extract money from the KGB. "In April 1985," he said, "seeking money to pay debts, I conceived a kind of confidence game to play on the KGB. In exchange for $50,000 I provided the KGB with the identities of several Soviet citizens who appeared to be cooperating with the CIA inside the Soviet Union. I suspected that their cooperation was not genuine, that their true loyalty was to the KGB, and therefore, I could cause them no harm."

The statement was pure Rick Ames: an arrogant rationalization of high treason as a mere shell game. He, Rick, *suspected* the cases were bad; he would take the lives of the Soviets in his hands and sell them to the KGB. There would be no harm done—well, probably no harm—and the money would come in handy to pay for all that furniture he and Rosario were buying.

Along with the names, Ames included much more valuable items in his letter to the resident. He enclosed a page from an SE division internal directory with his true name highlighted. Most important of all, he revealed the key position that he then occupied as chief of the Soviet counterintelligence branch of the CIA. That information alone was worth its weight in gold. To the KGB it was incredible news, as though an American Kim Philby had freely stepped into its web.

---

[10]Ames told investigators after he was sentenced that the CIA had learned from one of its sources that such an approach would be made to the agency by false volunteers. He said the Soviet walk-ins seemed to match the advance description given to the agency.

The very CIA official in charge of detecting Soviet intelligence operations against the agency worldwide, the man who knew the identities of every mole working for the CIA inside Soviet intelligence—this officer was volunteering his services to the KGB! If the senior officials of the KGB in Yasnevo could have penetrated the organizational structure of the CIA, peered inside, and reached down deep into the woodwork to select any officer they wanted, they would have chosen Aldrich Ames. It was beyond good fortune. Ames was the kind of walk-in of which spies can only dream. He was Supermole.

If Stanislav Androsov, the KGB resident in Washington, had been so slow-witted that he had not identified the American having all those lunches with Divilkovsky as Aldrich Ames—whose true name and physical description Shurygin had reported in great detail to Moscow—he certainly knew now. Ames also turned over to Androsov the alias he had used when meeting with Soviet officials earlier in his career. Finally, Ames asked in his note for $50,000.

It was all very cool, and low key. Ames, for example, did not ask Androsov for a meeting or suggest a means of future communication. He would have assumed that the KGB knew a bit about how to do that and did not need, and might not appreciate, his advice.

Early in May 1985 Chuvakhin contacted Ames and scheduled another meeting. On May 15, Ames again went inside the Soviet embassy and asked for Chuvakhin. Instead, he was taken to a private room. A KGB officer entered and handed him a note saying that the Soviet intelligence service had agreed to pay him the $50,000. The note added that the KGB would like to continue to use Chuvakhin as its intermediary.

The KGB officer, the FBI believes, was Viktor I. Cherkashin, the Soviet counterintelligence chief in Washington at the time.[11] He was listed as a "first secretary" of the Soviet embassy.

---

[11]When Ames was debriefed by the FBI, he claimed he could not remember enough about the physical appearance of the KGB officer to allow the FBI to identify him. However, early in 1995, Cherkashin was interviewed on television by the BBC and described as the man who had "recruited" Ames. He praised Ames and invited his son Paul to visit Russia "for a couple of years." Paul was welcome to stay with Cherkashin and his wife, he said.

Two days later, Ames again met Chuvakhin, to whom the KGB had now given the code name SAM 1. The Russian handed him $50,000 in cash. Rick Ames, CIA officer, was now Rick Ames, KGB spy.

On May 20, John A. Walker, Jr., a retired navy warrant officer who headed a family spy ring, was arrested by the FBI. Walker, who had spied for the KGB for nearly eighteen years, was eventually convicted and sentenced to life in prison. The high-profile Walker case was only one in a series of dramatic spy cases that broke in 1985, which became known as "the year of the spy." None of these arrests and accompanying publicity appeared to deter Ames, who considered himself a professional, too smart to be caught.

Originally, Ames later claimed, he had conceived of his spying as a "one-time deal," which may well be true. "My initial intention had been. . . having done the scam, having gotten the $50,000, then I would stop."[12] But there was all that easy money, and more where it came from. The alcoholic—and Ames was not unfamiliar with the syndrome—may also plan to have just one drink.

In the event, Ames in mid-June gave away the store. He sold the CIA to the KGB and never even named his price.

As Ames described it, "I did something which is still not entirely explicable even to me: without preconditions, or any demand for payment, I volunteered to the KGB information identifying virtually all Soviet agents of the CIA and other American and foreign services known to me. To my enduring surprise, the KGB replied that it had set aside for me two million dollars in gratitude for the information."[13]

Ames later told the Senate Intelligence Committee, "I'm still puzzled as to what took me to the next steps. The main factor . . . I think, was a realization after I had received the $50,000, was a sense of the enormity of what I had done . . . the fear that . . . I crossed a line I could never step back." What had seemed a "clever plan" in April, Ames said, left him by June "as if I were sleepwalk-

[12]CNN interview, December 27, 1994.

[13]Statement of Aldrich Hazen Ames in United States district court, Alexandria, Virginia, April 28, 1994.

ing. I can't really reconstruct my thinking. It was as if I were in almost a state of shock. The realization of what I had done. But certainly underlying it was the conviction that there was [as] much money as I could ever use."[14]

By saying he had "crossed a line" from which there was no turning back, Ames was only recognizing that once he had passed information to the Soviets and accepted the initial $50,000 he was vulnerable to exposure by someone working for the CIA or the FBI inside Soviet intelligence who might learn his identity. As Ames himself put it, "What I had done could never be undone and. . . I would be forever at hazard because of it."[15]

Ames also realized he was vulnerable to pressure from the KGB to keep the information coming. But Ames knew from his agency experience that neither the KGB nor the CIA liked to use blackmail to extract information. It was sometimes done, of course; both sides were expert in taking compromising photos. But a source who was blackmailed was operating against his will and possibly unreliable over the long haul. Far better to have a volunteer or a recruit selling secrets for money. Ames had seen actual examples "of KGB guidance to their stations, to their residencies on how to handle things like this. In other words, they would not pressure me. They would not try and twist my arm. They wouldn't try and blackmail me."[16]

But Ames's realization that he had crossed a line from which he could never step back was not the main reason he felt impelled to go on spying. He was honest enough in retrospect to admit that the prospect of vast wealth was the primary engine that drove him.

On June 13, 1985, in his fourth-floor office, Ames wrapped up between five and seven pounds of cable traffic and other secret documents in plastic bags, took the elevator down, and pushed his laminated ID card into the turnstiles that block the exits from headquarters. The black-and-yellow-striped metal barriers rose, and Ames walked through to the parking lot. No guard asked to look inside the plastic bags. As Ames knew, the CIA no longer examined packages being carried out of the building. That had

[14]Senate Interview, pp. 19–20.
[15]House Interview, p. 7.
[16]Ibid., p. 5.

been tried several years before, but the time-consuming searches created bottlenecks at the exits and proved very unpopular with the thousands of employees hurrying home after work, and the policy was abandoned.[17]

Chadwick's is a Washington saloon and restaurant under the K Street Freeway along the Georgetown waterfront. Its location is convenient to the CIA; Ames could drive there in about fifteen minutes without getting stuck in downtown traffic. On that day in mid-June, Ames walked into Chadwick's, met Chuvakhin for lunch, and handed him the plastic bags. Inside was the most secret information that Langley possessed—the names of more than ten of the most important Soviet sources working for the CIA and FBI. By giving the documents to Sergei Chuvakhin, Ames had sealed the doom of many of them.

It was the largest amount of highly sensitive information ever passed to the KGB in a single meeting. The package, Ames said, included "virtually all of our intelligence officer cases. GRU officers, KGB officers around the world."[18] His decision to do this, Ames said, "was like the leap into the dark."[19]

Among the names that Ames handed over were those of the two KGB sources in the Washington embassy, Lt. Col. Valery F. Martynov, GTGENTILE to the CIA and PIMENTA in the FBI, and KGB Maj. Sergei M. Motorin, the CIA's GTGAUZE, whom the FBI called MEGAS. In time, both were shot.

---

[17]In August 1994, in the wake of the Ames debacle, the CIA ordered random spot checks of articles being carried out of the building. For what it is worth, it should be noted that briefcases and packages of visitors *entering* CIA headquarters are carefully inspected.

[18]Senate Interview, p. 23. The KGB was astonished, and at first suspicious, of the huge amount of material that Ames produced at the lunch. They could not believe he could get his hands on so many secret documents and just walk out of the CIA with them. After Ames repeated the feat, both in Washington and in Rome, the Russians came to realize that it was as easy as Ames said. "The KGB had tremendous difficulty at first to understand," Ames recounted, ". . . and they said how can you get this stuff. . . . But eventually. . . they came to believe me when I said, well, this stuff is just floating around." Ibid., pp. 89–90.

[19]CNN interview, December 27, 1994.

In his gentle, somewhat wide-eyed prison interview with Ames, Sen. Dennis DeConcini, the chairman of the Senate Intelligence Committee, wondered if Ames realized what he was doing. Their exchange is chilling:

CHAIRMAN DeCONCINI: When you gave these names, Mr. Ames, did you have any realization of the significance of what you were doing? As to the danger these people would be in?

MR. AMES: Yes I did.

CHAIRMAN DeCONCINI: Did you just rationalize that this was not—

MR. AMES: It did not. I did not agonize over it.

CHAIRMAN DeCONCINI: Did it occur to you that they might be killed?

MR. AMES: Yes it did. . . . The death penalty would be a certainty for at least some of them.

CHAIRMAN DeCONCINI: What do you think made you, I mean, you sound like a man of convictions, and someone that just wouldn't do something dramatic like that. Did your alcohol involvement have something to do with it?

MR. AMES: No.

CHAIRMAN DeCONCINI: Or your personal life?

MR. AMES: No.[20]

Ames told DeConcini that others in positions of trust had been under financial pressure. In retrospect, he said, he could have worked himself out of debt, he could have managed. "It was my own sense of failure, inadequacy, and fear that made me conceive of it as even greater than it was in reality. But other people may have been in even deeper financial straits." What he had done that day in June, Ames said, was "irrational."[21]

Perhaps, but in the world of black mirrors, Ames was crazy like a fox. The first question he must have asked himself before volunteering his services in April was to what extent, in becoming an agent of the KGB, he would be placing himself in danger

[20]Senate Interview, p. 25.
[21]Ibid., pp. 26, 27.

of exposure by a CIA or FBI mole inside Soviet intelligence.

Because of his considerable knowledge of Soviet spy agencies, Ames knew the danger was minimal; the KGB was highly compartmented. Aside from Androsov, the resident, Viktor Cherkashin, the counterintelligence chief, and of course Chuvakhin, who was acting merely as a postman, there was little likelihood that anyone else in the Washington residency, aside from perhaps a code clerk, would know the actual identity of the major source that the KGB had acquired inside CIA counterintelligence.

Back in Moscow, of course, Vladimir A. Kryuchkov, the chief of the KGB's First Chief Directorate, would immediately know. And Viktor M. Chebrikov, the chairman of the KGB, would have to be told. Chebrikov would probably inform Mikhail Gorbachev, the new leader of the Soviet Union, but without revealing the precise identity of the source. Beyond that, others in Yasnevo, the headquarters of the FCD on the Moscow ring road, would be aware that there was an incredible source in the deepest recesses of Langley, but they would not be told who it was.

So Ames was not too worried that he might in turn be betrayed by one of his own agents inside the KGB, and yet—and yet, there was always the possibility that there might be a leak, that in some unforeseen way one of the Soviets reporting to the CIA might hear a whisper of a mole. Two of the most valuable KGB sources of the agency and the FBI, Martynov and Motorin, had been operating right out of the Soviet embassy.[22] That was much too close for comfort, which is why Ames made sure that both their names were on the list he handed to Chuvakhin over lunch at Chadwick's in June.

Ames, in other words, having committed his first crime in April, systematically set out to kill the witnesses. As chief of Soviet counterintelligence, of course, he knew exactly who they were. Those who were not executed, he was sure, would be imprisoned in the gulag, where they could do him no harm.

He was frank enough about this with DeConcini. "I began to fear the possibility of detection," he said. "We had a number of

---

[22]Motorin had returned to Moscow, but Martynov was still in the Soviet embassy in Washington.

KGB sources. . . . I began as a secondary motivation to see it as useful or protective of me to compromise those cases, so they wouldn't be in a position to . . . hear something. I didn't assume they would ever be involved or become knowledgeable, but accidents happen. And two of them were in the [Washington KGB] residency, and could be a potential threat. And I think in another sense at that point I sort of just threw myself at the KGB—lock, stock, and barrel. Together with any and all information. . . . In a sense, I was delivering myself along with them."[23] It was, Ames said, "an act of, in a sense, a switching of loyalties."[24]

The KGB gave Ames a cryptonym, KOLOKOL, the Russian word for bell. Ames chose it himself.

A month before Ames handed his plastic bags to Chuvakhin, on May 16, to be precise—the same day Ames received his first $50,000 in cash from his luncheon partner—Oleg Gordievsky, the KGB resident in London, received a telegram summoning him home to Moscow. Gordievsky, who had worked secretly for MI6 since 1974, sensed a trap, but had little choice but to obey. In Moscow, he was drugged and accused—accurately—of being a British spy, but admitted nothing. The KGB placed him on leave while it pondered his fate.

Gordievsky's identity was in the plastic bags that Rick Ames handed to Sergei Chuvakhin on June 13 in Washington. Although he was being run by the British, Gordievsky also had a CIA code name, GTTICKLE. And Ames, there is now no doubt, provided information that identified GTTICKLE.

But Gordievsky had fallen under suspicion *before* the June 13 date when Ames says he turned over the big list of names to the KGB, so U.S. counterintelligence agents later had a problem in sorting this out. Could another mole inside the CIA, the FBI, or MI6 have betrayed Gordievsky independently of Ames? Or was Ames, deliberately or not, confused about when he revealed Gordievsky? Perhaps he had, after all, disclosed his identity in April or early May, leading to Gordievsky's recall to Moscow. Although the answers were not clear, Ames at the very least con-

[23]Senate Interview, pp. 20–22.
[24]House Interview, p. 7.

firmed to the KGB that Gordievsky was indeed a British spy.[25]

GTTICKLE was one of the lucky ones. On July 19, wearing old trousers and a sweatshirt, he left his apartment in Moscow on Leninsky Prospekt to go jogging. He was rescued by MI6 and spirited out of the Soviet Union in a daring "exfiltration," as such operations are known in the intelligence world.

A CIA man with knowledge of the case explained what happened when Gordievsky went jogging that day. "He had a plan for emergency escape, and he had signalled the Brits. The Brits went to Margaret Thatcher to get permission to exfiltrate him. In Moscow, a dozen cars drove out of the embassy at once and the KGB surveillance went after them, but there were too many to follow, and during this diversion they picked up Gordievsky."

Although details of Gordievsky's escape remain classified, the CIA man said he and other DO officers had been told by a senior agency official how it was done. "They got Gordievsky out in a specially built Land Rover, four cylinders instead of six, and they rebuilt the driveshaft so there was a space. He was in the British embassy in Moscow for a couple of days, and then they drove him north to Helsinki. Even if the Russians had examined the car, they would have only seen a bump where the driveshaft would normally be. Gordievsky was in that space. The real driveshaft was off to one side in the door."[26]

On June 13, the same day that Ames in Washington turned

---

[25]Some U.S. counterintelligence officials leaned to the view that Ames was the sole betrayer of Gordievsky. If Ames had provided confirmation of a report from another mole that Gordievsky was working for the West, it was theorized, the Soviets would not have allowed Gordievsky to remain free in Moscow. They would at that point have had evidence from two sources and would have arrested the KGB man, preventing his escape in July.

[26]Gordievsky has given a rather different version of his flight. In a memoir published in 1995, he said he signalled MI6 that he was ready to escape by standing on a Moscow street corner with a shopping bag until a British agent chewing a Mars bar walked by. He said he then took the train to Leningrad and made his way to a forest near the Finnish border. Two MI6 cars stopped and, he said, he climbed into the trunk of one for the trip across the border into Finland. Oleg Gordievsky, *Next Stop Execution* (London: Macmillan, 1995), pp. 9–24.

over the five to seven pounds of CIA documents to Chuvakhin, in Moscow the KGB detained Paul M. "Skip" Stombaugh, Jr., a thirty-three-year-old CIA officer who was on his way to meet one of the agency's key assets in the Soviet capital. That source was Adolf G. Tolkachev, a defense researcher who was a leading expert on stealth aircraft technology. To the CIA, he was a highly sensitive source known by the code name GTSPHERE. Tolkachev never made it to the meeting; he was arrested by the KGB.[27]

Tolkachev's identity, too, was among the documents that Ames turned over to the KGB in Washington that day. Given the measured pace of bureaucracy anywhere, it is improbable that the KGB in Moscow could have arrested Tolkachev the same day on the basis of the information that Ames carried out of the CIA and gave to Chuvakhin at lunch. The CIA concluded that Tolkachev had been betrayed by Edward Lee Howard, whom the agency had been preparing to send to Moscow when it dismissed him in May 1983. In September 1984, Howard traveled to Vienna and sold the secrets of the agency's Moscow operations to the KGB.[28]

But Ames's identification of Tolkachev as a CIA agent may have helped to seal his fate. It confirmed the information that the CIA presumes the KGB had already received from Edward Lee Howard.

In a period of a little more than a year, starting in May 1985, Ames lunched with Sergei Chuvakhin at least fourteen times. Ames got more than a free lunch—in addition to the first $50,000, Chuvakhin handed cash to Ames at some of their sub-

[27]The Soviet government announced on October 22, 1986, that Tolkachev had been executed.

[28]When I interviewed Howard in Budapest in 1987, he told me that Tolkachev "very well could be one of the assets I would have handled" in Moscow. When I asked Howard if he had caused Tolkachev's execution, he replied, "I don't believe I did that." See David Wise, *The Spy Who Got Away* (New York: Random House, 1988), pp. 261–62. In 1991, Howard invited me to lunch at his dacha near Moscow. As we drove from the city, we passed one of several identical Moscow skyscrapers, this one an apartment building called Golden House. "That's Tolkachev's house," Howard said, pointing. I may have remarked that Tolkachev did not live there anymore. There was silence for a moment. Then Howard said suddenly: "I didn't bust him, David. I know I didn't bust him."

sequent luncheons in amounts ranging from $20,000 to $50,000.

Ames continued to provide all sorts of secret information to the KGB at these meetings, including the identity of more Soviet sources, details of CIA double-agent operations, and information that Ames knew firsthand about the agency's operations in Turkey, New York, and Mexico.

Typical of the documents that Ames is assumed to have passed to Moscow at these lunches was a classified study prepared by the CIA in February 1984 entitled *Soviet Intelligence: KGB and GRU*. The report contained the CIA's analysis of both Soviet intelligence agencies and a detailed breakdown of their tables of organization. The document also included a description of Group North, the KGB elite unit that specialized in recruiting American and Canadian targets, the existence of which had been revealed to the CIA by Boris Yuzhin, the KGB officer in San Francisco.

Ames must have been amused at the reference to the difficulties faced by Line KR, the KGB's counterintelligence officers. The CIA report quoted "one recent Soviet defector" as saying that Line KR officers were supposed "to recruit a [CIA] counterintelligence officer, but as this is so difficult they concentrate on analysis instead."[29]

At first, as CIA procedures required, Ames filed the contact reports of his meetings with Chuvakhin, whom he was supposedly developing as an agency source. By July, Ames stopped filing, although he mentioned some of the meetings to his colleagues at FR/Washington. The lack of reporting began to annoy the FBI, which was aware of most, but probably not all, of the lunches. Two or three times, FBI agents went to the offices of FR/Washington to ask why it was not receiving reports of the Ames-Chuvakhin get-togethers, and the bureau finally sent a memorandum about the problem to the Washington station. The FBI never did get the reports from Ames, and neither agency followed up. Once again, nothing happened.

For Ames, the best lunch took place in October. As Ames

---

[29] *Soviet Intelligence: KGB and GRU*, unpublished CIA study, February 1984, p. 51.

recalled it, "I had lunch with him and he passed me a note, a package with money and a note from the KGB. Chuvakhin was not a KGB officer. And we never spoke of what was going on beneath the surface. We would exchange shopping bags, and we never so much as winked at each other. And in the note the KGB said that they had set aside $2 million for me."[30]

---

[30]Senate Interview, p. 24.

11

YURCHENKO

In Rome on the morning of Thursday, August 1, Vitaly Sergeyevich Yurchenko, a senior KGB official recently arrived on a mission from Moscow, told his colleagues at the Soviet embassy that he was going to take a walk and visit the Vatican museum.

Instead, he went to a pay phone across the street from the American embassy on the Via Veneto and telephoned a CIA officer. Yurchenko asked to defect. He was told to come into the embassy right away.

The CIA man could hardly believe his luck. Yurchenko was the walk-in of a lifetime, the highest-ranking KGB officer ever to come over in the entire history of the cold war. He was the newly appointed deputy chief of the First Department of the First Chief Directorate of the KGB, the official in charge of operations against the United States and Canada.

The well-dressed man who entered the American embassy that midsummer morning had clear blue eyes, thinning red hair, and a drooping handlebar mustache. He had the big frame and broad shoulders of an athlete.

His manner was breezy. He spoke reasonably good, although heavily accented English, and looked more American than Russian. He had in fact lived in Washington for five years, where he had been security officer of the Soviet embassy. In appearance, Vitaly Yurchenko would not have looked out of place in California, perhaps driving a van along the Pacific Coast Highway.

The first question always asked of a KGB defector was whether he knew of any penetrations inside the CIA or U.S. intelligence. Yurchenko knew of two. One had been a CIA officer. The other had worked in the National Security Agency, the nation's super-secret code and electronic eavesdropping arm in Fort Meade, Maryland.

Although Yurchenko did not know the CIA man's true name, he knew that his KGB code name was ROBERT. The CIA officer had been preparing to go to Moscow for the agency but was never sent. Yurchenko also knew that ROBERT had met with senior KGB officials in Austria in the fall of 1984 and had been paid for CIA secrets that he turned over to the Soviets.

Yurchenko did not know the name of the NSA employee, either, but he had actually met and talked to him. In 1980, when Yurchenko was stationed in Washington, the man had telephoned and then come to the Soviet embassy to sell secrets.

These key disclosures were summarized in a cable flashed from the Rome station to Langley on August 1. The cable landed on the desk of Burton Gerber, the chief of the Soviet division. At the highest levels of the CIA, from director William Casey on down, the news from Rome was electrifying, and to most officials a cause for elation.

But for Gerber and Gardner R. "Gus" Hathaway, the chief of the CIA's Counterintelligence Staff, the Rome cable was a mixed blessing, as though they had just won an auction prize of a double date with Michelle Pfeiffer and Typhoid Mary. On the one hand, the two officials were pleased to have a major-league KGB defector walk into their web. On the other hand, there was, well, a slight, small problem. Hathaway and Gerber both knew instantly who

ROBERT was. For more than two years, the CIA had been sitting on the Edward Lee Howard case; both men knew that he was a potential source of big trouble. And for almost a year, the CIA had known that Howard had confessed to having lingered outside the Soviet consulate in Washington, contemplating going in and selling the agency's secrets to the KGB. Howard had said so in a meeting with two CIA officials in September 1984.[1]

The problem was that neither Hathaway nor Gerber nor anyone else at the CIA had told the FBI about Howard. Only the FBI has the power to arrest spies. The CIA was confident that the matter could be handled internally. Instead of reporting a dangerous counterintelligence threat to the FBI, the CIA arranged to pay for a psychiatrist, who saw Howard in Santa Fe, New Mexico, where the former CIA man had moved after his dismissal in 1983.

It was all very awkward indeed, but the immediate practical need was to form a team to begin to debrief Vitaly Yurchenko, who was being flown during the night via Naples and Frankfurt to Andrews Air Force Base outside Washington. That responsibility fell to Burton Gerber.[2]

On August 1, when the cable arrived from Rome, Rick Ames was on top of the world. Not only had he risen to his highest job yet in the CIA—chief of the Soviet counterintelligence branch—but two days earlier, the divorce he had sought from Nan had come through in New York. In only nine days he would marry the woman he loved, Rosario. Moreover, the money—tens of thousands of dollars in cash—had already begun to flow into his pockets from the KGB at the delightful lunches with Sergei Chuvakhin.

Ames had very little time to enjoy his newfound sense of freedom. For on that same day, Burton Gerber called Ames in and showed him the telegram from the Rome station. Vitaly Yurchenko, the man in charge of Moscow's espionage in the

---

[1]At the time Howard "confessed" to hanging around the consulate and thinking about betraying his country, he had in fact already met with the KGB a few days earlier in Austria and sold them the secrets of the CIA's Moscow operations.

[2]Gerber made it clear to all that his name was "Burton." To annoy the SE division chief, Hathaway made a point of always calling him "Burt."

United States and Canada, had defected to the CIA and would arrive in Washington the next day.

Rick Ames, cool cat though he was, must have experienced at least a small chill, a *frisson* of fear, when Gerber called him in that day and showed him the telegram from the Rome station. Yurchenko had come over!

A defector is the mole's worst nightmare. There is always a chance that no matter how careful a mole may be to cover his tracks—not that Ames ever bothered—a defector will surface to expose him. Ames knew that, of course; it was one reason he had turned over more names of the CIA's Soviet sources to the KGB to try to eliminate those assets who might somehow learn his identity. From the cable, Ames could see at a glance that Yurchenko had not described *him*. The defector was clearly talking about someone else who had worked in the Soviet division, which could only divert attention from Ames and work to his advantage. Still, it was scary; Yurchenko was high up enough that he might know about Ames. Perhaps he was holding back that knowledge until he was safely out of Rome and in the United States. For Ames, Yurchenko was not good news.

It got worse. Gerber instructed Ames to meet Yurchenko at Andrews Air Force Base the next morning and personally take charge of debriefing the KGB man.

An agency colleague smiled as he recalled what happened on Friday, August 2. "Rick looked awful, nervous and hungover. He told me he almost missed the arrival, he'd overslept. I think when he first learned about the defection he was scared to death. He goes home that night and gets plastered, and sleeps through the alarm clock. At Andrews, there are all these senior FBI guys standing around on the tarmac. He must have thought that Yurchenko would get off the plane, point to him, and say, 'There he is!'"

It didn't happen. There was no confrontation on the tarmac. Yurchenko did not appear to recognize Ames. In a caravan of FBI and CIA cars, the defector was driven from Andrews to a CIA safe house on Shawn Leigh Drive in Vienna, Virginia. Ames rode in a CIA car with Yurchenko and Rodney L. Leffler, the acting chief of the Soviet section of the FBI's intelligence division. They took a roundabout route, designed to throw off any KGB countersurveillance.

At the safe house, Yurchenko asked for tea. The CIA didn't have any, so he sat at the dining room table sipping hot water as he spoke. Gerber, Ames, and other CIA officers were there, along with Leffler. Agents from the FBI's Washington field office were in the room as well.

Yurchenko's most important information, of course, was his knowledge of ROBERT, the former CIA officer who had revealed the agency's Moscow operations to the Soviets. Burton Gerber knew that ROBERT was Edward Lee Howard as soon as he had seen the cable from Rome the day before. The details that Yurchenko had provided—a CIA man who had been slated for Moscow and did not go—fit Howard alone.

Two years earlier, the CIA had fired the thirty-two-year-old CIA officer after he had failed a polygraph test that an agency spokesperson said later had picked up evidence of "drugs and petty theft." Since Howard had talked openly of selling secrets to the KGB, Yurchenko's news could not have come as a total surprise to the CIA. And the Soviet division was already aware of trouble in the Moscow station. In June, only six weeks before Yurchenko defected, at least one major operation had been blown when Adolf Tolkachev was arrested and his case officer, Skip Stombaugh, expelled for espionage.

Now, as Yurchenko spoke about ROBERT, the Howard case—the CIA's nasty little secret—could not be contained much longer. FBI agents were sitting there, right in the room. It was a great irony that the FBI had to learn of the existence of a renegade CIA officer not from Langley but from a senior official of the KGB. Even now, the CIA did not admit to the FBI that it knew exactly who ROBERT was. Computers would have to be checked, a search of all pertinent records instituted immediately, rest assured every effort would be made to pinpoint and identify the officer. And so on.[3]

---

[3]Not until Wednesday, August 7, did the CIA finally own up to the FBI that ROBERT was none other than Edward Lee Howard. By that time, Howard was on his way to Vienna to meet again with the KGB, which warned him that he was in danger—a senior officer who knew about him had defected to the West.

Yurchenko also spoke of MR. LONG, the KGB code name for the former employee of the National Security Agency who had come to the Soviet embassy in Washington in 1980. The walk-in said that the NSA, using submarines, had been able to tap into an underwater communications cable that the Soviet military used in the Sea of Okhotsk.[4]

The anonymous visitor had offered to reveal more but demanded payment in "gold bullion." In a scene right out of the Marx Brothers, Yurchenko at first thought the man was referring to chicken soup. The confusion was soon cleared up. The KGB then ordered the visitor to shave his beard and change into Soviet work clothes. They drove him away in a van and dropped him off when they were out of sight of the embassy. The FBI had seen the man enter the embassy, but at the time it was unable to identify the mysterious visitor.

Yurchenko remembered that the NSA man had red hair. He also recalled that he lived in a rundown house in the Washington suburbs somewhere near Beltsville, Maryland.

With Yurchenko's clues as a start, the FBI would begin a massive hunt for the NSA walk-in. It ended with the arrest of Ronald W. Pelton four months later.[5]

After this first session in the safe house, the interrogation of Yurchenko settled into a daily routine. Ames was in charge of the debriefings, which usually took place for four hours from 9:00 A.M. to 1:00 P.M. Gerber appointed Paul J. Redmond, Jr., an experienced CIA officer who had served in Malaysia, Yugoslavia, Lebanon, Greece, and Cyprus, to run the Yurchenko task force. Its job was to analyze and follow up on the mass of material the defector was providing. Redmond, a native of Massachusetts and a Harvard graduate, was a short, brusque man given to profanity in both English and Serbo-Croatian. He was also a smart counterintelligence officer, one of the few in the division who was not afraid to stand up to Gerber.

---

[4]The NSA's highly sensitive project was code-named IVY BELLS.

[5]Pelton was arrested on November 24, 1985, and tried in May 1986. A federal jury convicted him of espionage, and he was sentenced to life imprisonment.

To assist Ames in the daily debriefings, Gerber named another savvy CIA officer, Colin R. Thompson. A big man, over six feet, Thompson was a fifty-year-old Wisconsin native and Yale graduate, the son of Edward K. Thompson, the former editor of *Life* magazine. He had joined the CIA soon after college and served in Laos, Vietnam during the war, the Philippines, Thailand, and Cambodia. He then spent several years in the Soviet division at headquarters.

Ames and Colin Thompson were joined in some of the interrogations of Yurchenko by two FBI agents, Michael T. Rochford and Reid P. Broce. Ames and Thompson, the two CIA debriefers, received lists of questions every morning from the research section of Rod Carlson's CI Group. The debriefings were a slow and painstaking process. There would be page after page of written requirements from the researchers, and the two CIA officers had to go over every one with Yurchenko.

What no one knew, of course, was that Rick Ames was reporting back to the KGB everything that Yurchenko was saying to the CIA. The First Chief Directorate in Yasnevo had a window into the safe house in northern Virginia that was almost as good as a remote video camera.

For one month, Ames sat across from Yurchenko, debriefing the KGB man in the safe house in Vienna, Virginia, and a CIA office in Great Falls. According to the CIA's official biography of Yurchenko, he had, since April, been the deputy chief of the First Department of the KGB's foreign intelligence directorate. Since the First Department covered North America, that meant that Yurchenko was in charge of "the KGB residencies in the U.S. and Canada." Why, then, didn't Yurchenko blow the whistle on Aldrich Ames?

It is, of course, one of the central mysteries of the Ames case, part of a deeper riddle about Yurchenko himself. Many counterintelligence officers in both the FBI and the CIA lean toward the view that Yurchenko was a genuine defector who changed his mind, walked out of a Georgetown restaurant, and went home to Moscow three months after he arrived. (His young CIA guard did not follow Yurchenko out of the restaurant; he thought he should wait and pay the check.)

But in the wake of the Ames case, other counterintelligence experts think that the Yurchenko case is more complex. They believe that Yurchenko may have been sent by the KGB to betray Howard and Pelton in order to protect a bigger player, Rick Ames. Harry B. "Skip" Brandon, a veteran FBI counterintelligence official, was acting director of the intelligence division when it closed in on Ames in the fall of 1993. Brandon confesses he is puzzled about Yurchenko.

He offered still another scenario. "Is it possible they [the KGB] doubted Ames and sent Yurchenko here as a test to see if Ames would report Yurchenko's debriefing? Once it was determined that Ames was reporting on Yurchenko's disclosures, they told Yurchenko to come home." Brandon, a soft-spoken, round-faced man, an all-American straight-arrow FBI type, smiled at the convoluted thought. "That is just the James Jesus Angleton in all of us. The Yurchenko thing is still extraordinarily puzzling."

One former CIA officer who worked on the Yurchenko case theorized that the KGB man was sent to the United States to force Edward Lee Howard to flee to Moscow, which Howard did. With Howard safely in the hands of the KGB, the officer speculated, the loss of CIA assets in Moscow could be blamed on Howard.[6]

There may, however, be a simple explanation for why Yurchenko didn't yield up Ames. He may not have known. Edward J. O'Malley, former chief of FBI counterintelligence, confirmed that a recruitment of Ames's importance would have been very closely held inside the KGB. Ames's contact in the Soviet embassy "would go to the resident, and probably no one else would be told." The same secrecy would be maintained within the KGB in Moscow.

A former CIA official who has closely studied the question offered this explanation: "Yurchenko was put in charge of the Canadian section of the KGB's North American department. He was never in charge of the U.S. section. The agency's Yurchenko

---

[6]For a while, in fact, the CIA did attribute its agent losses to Howard. But after a time, the agency realized that other agents were disappearing that Howard never knew about. As it turned out, they had been betrayed by Ames.

biography was wrong. In the Canada job he would not know about U.S. operations."

Moreover, Yurchenko had only occupied his job in the department dealing with North America for a few months, since April 1985. When he walked into the American embassy in Rome, the CIA station naturally asked him to remain in the KGB as an agent in place. Yurchenko refused, and his reasoning was interesting. He claimed it was impossible to go back to Yasnevo because he would have to "read in" and learn his new job, and once he did that, they would never let him out of Moscow again; he would know too much. His answer, if true, suggests he had not had time to familiarize himself with the case files for North America. Even if he had, the Ames file might not have been available to him.

Many CIA officers, specialists in Soviet cases, say that the KGB has *never* sent one of its officers to the West as a false defector because of the high risk. A KGB officer would have too many secrets in his head and might reveal some unintentionally. And suppose a dispatched agent of this sort changed his mind and decided to remain in the West? If this analysis is correct, then Yurchenko, if he was indeed playing a role, would be the first false defector ever sent to the CIA.

That Vitaly Yurchenko was part of a KGB gambit to divert attention from Ames is a plausible explanation and would make a wonderful plot for a John le Carré thriller, but the more likely possibility is that in 1994, after Ames was arrested, Yurchenko was as startled as anyone else to learn that the CIA officer who had debriefed him was a Soviet mole.

Why Yurchenko chose to go back to Moscow may have more to do with an affair of the heart than with espionage. Yurchenko, who did not get along well with his wife, had hoped to rekindle a romance with Valentina Yereskovsky, a very attractive doctor married to a Soviet diplomat in Montreal. Yurchenko had known her when he was stationed in Washington in the late 1970s with her husband, Alexander S. Yereskovsky. To outward appearances, at least, the relationship was platonic; Yurchenko and Valentina, according to one counterintelligence officer, "would go out to McDonald's and sit in the park and eat hamburgers."

Yurchenko had seen Yereskovsky again in the spring of 1985 when she returned to Moscow for her daughter's wedding. Now a defector in the hands of the CIA, Yurchenko pleaded to be allowed to see her once more. Gerber assented, and the Canadian security service agreed to cooperate. Colin Thompson flew to Ottawa, then drove to Montreal. Another CIA officer and Yurchenko, along with two CIA security guards, flew to Plattsburgh, New York, and drove Yurchenko to the border. There, the Canadians took over. In Montreal, the Canadians watched Valentina Yereskovsky's apartment building until they had determined a pattern of her husband's movements. While her husband kept a luncheon engagement elsewhere in the city, Yurchenko called Valentina from a sidewalk pay phone within view of her building. She hung up. The Canadians took him up to the apartment. She was reluctant, but let him in for a few moments. Tearfully, she turned down his pleas to resume their relationship. Yurchenko came out of the apartment and seemed crushed.

Afterward, Yurchenko was increasingly unhappy. Yereskovsky's rejection was a bitter disappointment. He was discontented as well with his ham-handed CIA security guards and furious over leaks to the press about his presence in the United States and his revelations to the CIA. William Casey himself was responsible for many of the news leaks; he boasted noisily about the big-shot defector. So it was not entirely surprising that Yurchenko might have changed his mind about remaining in the United States.

What was surprising was that Yurchenko took the risk of going back, that he was not shot, and that he continued to work for the KGB and the SVR, albeit in a much lesser job, until he retired in the spring of 1993. Although it was not generally known or publicized, however, over the years several other Soviet defectors had returned home. Yurchenko was the most celebrated to go back, but by no means the first.

Before Yurchenko escaped and flew to Moscow, he provided a wealth of material to the CIA. Until he had been transferred to the North American department, Yurchenko had spent much of his career in Directorate K, the KGB's counterintelligence division. For almost five years, he had been chief of the directorate's Fifth Department, which had the job of uncovering moles in the KGB.

It was in his Directorate K job that Yurchenko had learned about ROBERT, who turned out to be Edward Lee Howard. After Howard met with the KGB in Vienna in September 1984, a cable reporting on his disclosures had crossed Yurchenko's desk.

The cable reported that ROBERT had revealed three Soviet moles who were working for American intelligence. First, Howard reported that an unidentified KGB colonel in Hungary was a CIA source. Howard had made a mistake, as the KGB was later to discover; the source was a colonel in the GRU, Soviet military intelligence, who had been recruited in Budapest.

The second source disclosed by Howard was an unidentified sailor, supposedly a KGB officer working for the CIA. The third CIA source was Boris Yuzhin. Howard described him to the KGB as a Tass correspondent in San Francisco, which was as good as naming him. In 1984, when Howard fingered him, Yuzhin was already under suspicion because of the camera disguised as a cigarette lighter that he had dropped in the Soviet consulate.

Since Ames was reporting these disclosures back to the KGB, the black mirrors were now reflecting upon each other.

Follow this: Howard had betrayed Boris Yuzhin, a CIA mole in the KGB. Yurchenko, in turn, had betrayed Howard and revealed Howard's betrayal of Yuzhin. Ames had betrayed Yurchenko, so that the KGB now knew with certainty, although it might have guessed it anyway, that the CIA was now aware that the KGB knew that Yuzhin was a CIA agent. But there were more twists and turns in just this one small corner of the counterintelligence maze, for among the names that Aldrich Ames had passed to the KGB was the name of Boris Yuzhin. The name was gratefully received by the KGB, although it had already learned about Yuzhin a year earlier from Edward Lee Howard. But now the KGB knew from not one, but two, sources that Boris Yuzhin was an American spy. In due course, it would act on that knowledge. Small wonder that James Angleton, the CIA's first counterintelligence chief, became lost in what he called "a wilderness of mirrors."[7]

Aside from the Howard and Pelton cases and the contents of the key telegram from Vienna, Yurchenko provided the CIA with information about many other cases and KGB technical operations. He warned the CIA, for example, that the KGB was using "spy dust," invisible tracking chemicals to monitor the movements and contacts of the agency's case officers in Moscow.

Although it was not publicized at the time—not all of Yurchenko's information leaked to the press—Yurchenko informed the CIA about two other technical developments employed by the KGB. He told in detail of a laboratory in Moscow where KGB scientists developed poisons for operational use. Yurchenko said it was called Special Lab 100, also known as SL 100. It was there, he said, that the KGB developed and tested exotic poisons of the sort used on an umbrella tip to murder a Bulgarian exile in London in 1978.

After the collapse of communism, the new government of Bulgaria admitted that its spy agency had been responsible for the famed "poison umbrella" attack on Georgi I. Markov, a Bulgarian exile. Markov died after he was jabbed in the back of his right thigh with the umbrella. The umbrella tip implanted a tiny pellet under his skin containing ricin, a deadly poison derived from the seeds of the castor-oil plant. General Oleg Kalugin, the former chief of counterintelligence for the KGB, has admitted that Gen. Sergei Mikhailovich Golubev, of the KGB's Directorate K, was dispatched to Sofia, along with a second officer, to advise the Durzhavna Sigurnost (DS), the Bulgarian secret service, on the hit. Later, the KGB also provided the umbrella and the poison pellet that were used to kill Markov.

A CIA officer familiar with the Yurchenko case said that the defector described the location of the laboratory. "He gave us an

---

[7]It was in a British television interview that Angleton referred to "a wilderness of mirrors," a phrase taken from T. S. Eliot's poem "Gerontion." Author (and later CBS correspondent) David Martin used it as the title of his book about Angleton's futile search for KGB spies in the CIA. David C. Martin, *Wilderness of Mirrors* (New York: Harper & Row, 1980).

address and through analysis of satellite photos of Moscow, we were able to pinpoint the installation. We could confirm there was a building at that location that fit the description. We couldn't prove they made poisons there. But we had reporting from other, low-level sources that Special Laboratory 100 existed.

"Yurchenko also told us about an installation in the Moscow main post office, a machine that could detect the presence of secret writing of any kind. It was a chemical detector." Secret writing, or SW, uses inks that are invisible to the naked eye. Typically the words are read by treatment with a second chemical that renders them visible.[8]

Yurchenko also provided new details about the mystery surrounding the disappearance in Vienna in 1975 of Nicholas G. Shadrin, an American double agent for the CIA. Yurchenko said Shadrin was accidentally chloroformed and killed while struggling in the backseat of a car in which Soviet agents were trying to abduct him. Shadrin, whose real name was Nikolai F. Artamonov, was the youngest destroyer commander in the Soviet navy when he defected with his Polish fiancée by sailing across the Baltic Sea to Sweden in a motor launch. After the couple moved to the United States, Shadrin was contacted by the KGB but agreed to become a double agent for U.S. intelligence. He disappeared in 1975 when the CIA sent him to Vienna to meet with the KGB.

Right after Labor Day, there were major changes in the CI Group and in the arrangements for handling Yurchenko. Rod Carlson, the chief of the CI Group, the official who earned his place in the agency's history as Oleg Penkovsky's case officer, retired after twenty-seven years. And Rick Ames began preparing for a new assignment.

Sometime in 1984, before Ames is believed to have begun spy-

---

[8]The CIA officer who told the author about the postal machine was a Yurchenko skeptic who doubted that the defector was genuine. "The installation in the post office was considered hot stuff," the officer said, "but about a month later I ran across a misfiled piece of paper dated in the 1970s. It was a report from a low-level defector whose wife had worked in this installation and it gave almost verbatim the same information. In fact the defector had given us a better description of it."

ing for the KGB, he applied for a slot as Soviet branch chief in the Rome station. Everyone knew the job was open; and Carlson, his boss, suggested that Ames apply. Now, in September 1985, Ames was told the Rome job was his.

Normally, Ames would have welcomed the assignment to a prestigious overseas post. But the news created a dilemma for him; leaving the Soviet counterintelligence branch would reduce his access to sensitive secrets. On the other hand, it would have seemed suspicious for Ames to turn down a desirable post for which he had already applied. The KGB did not suggest that Ames maneuver to remain in Langley. The Soviets, after all, had already received a huge number of names and a great deal of other information from Ames. It would take time to digest the enormous haul, especially since only a very small group of KGB officers were allowed to handle his material. Moreover, whatever the KGB would lose in access by Ames's transfer to Rome would be offset by the greater ease with which its agents could meet with him. There would be no FBI looking over their shoulders.

It is of passing interest that Rosario Ames met Vitaly Yurchenko. In a repeat of his performance in New York the previous year, Ames, again in violation of the rules, brought Rosario to the safe house in northern Virginia where he had been debriefing Yurchenko. Burton Gerber was unhappy when he heard about it, but once again, nothing happened.

By now, Ames had met with Yurchenko some twenty times. Sometimes they were alone; Colin Thompson and the FBI agents did not sit in on every session. What the two men might have said to each other on these occasions is not known; but Ames has denied that Yurchenko knew he was a KGB mole or that he ever told his secret to the defector.

So, in September, Ames went off to language school to learn Italian. Paul Redmond replaced Carlson as chief of the CI Group, and Colin Thompson became chief of the Yurchenko task force. He continued to debrief Yurchenko, assisted by a new case officer, Frederick L. Walters.

At the same time, the CIA moved Yurchenko to an elegant, two-story safe house in Coventry, a development in the Virginia countryside forty miles southwest of Washington near Fredericks-burg. Later that month, Yurchenko made his disappointing trip to Montreal to see Valentina Yereskovsky.

In the meantime, the FBI had finally been told by the CIA that ROBERT was Edward Lee Howard. The bureau moved a team of agents to Santa Fe and placed the former CIA officer under sur-veillance. It was not easy; Howard lived out in the desert in El Dorado, a development twelve miles south of the city. The houses were spaced far apart, and it was the sort of neighborhood where strangers are noticed immediately. The FBI finally moved a trailer into place in a field several hundred feet from Howard's house. A video camera was trained on the house, with monitor screens in the trailer. The FBI also tapped Howard's home telephone.

The bureau confronted Howard on September 19, but he admitted nothing. Two days later, on the afternoon of September 21, with his wife Mary at the wheel, Howard drove from the house. The young FBI agent in the trailer failed to see him leave, although it was broad daylight. The Howards drove to a restau-rant. After dinner, when it was dark, Howard jumped from the car as it went around a sharp bend, just as the CIA had trained him to do. Mary Howard popped up a dummy that her husband had rigged, a homemade version of the dummy that the CIA taught Howard to use to escape pursuers.[9]

Had the FBI been following the Howards, it would have appeared that Howard was still riding in the passenger seat. As it turned out, Howard's jump from the moving car was unnecessary. No one was following them, since the FBI had not seen them leave the house. The dummy ruse was successful, however, because it fooled the FBI when Mary Howard drove back home—

[9]The CIA dummy that Howard used in training was spring-loaded and car-ried inside an attaché case that is placed on the front seat of a car. When the attaché is unlatched, the dummy pops up. The device is known as a "jib," because it operates on the same principle as a child's jack-in-the-box. During his dummy training, Howard told me, he found the device useful to com-mute to CIA headquarters on Route I-66, which has restrictions that ban sin-gle-passenger cars during rush hours. "A couple of times when we were doing training, I used the dummy on I-66," he said.

this time the agent in the trailer saw the car with the "Howards" enter the garage. The deception gave Howard a crucial, twenty-five-hour head start. Using his TWA "Getaway Card," he flew to New York and then to Helsinki. Eleven months later, the Soviets announced that Howard was in Moscow and had been granted asylum. He remained there, guarded by the KGB and its successor agency, the SVR.

Vitaly Yurchenko, whose disclosures to the CIA had led Howard to flee, spent Saturday, November 2, in the Washington area. He was taken on a shopping trip to a department store in Manassas, Virginia, by his young CIA guard, Thomas Hannah. That evening, Yurchenko persuaded his CIA keeper to take him to Georgetown, where they dined at Au Pied de Cochon, a restaurant only a little over a mile from the Soviet compound on upper Wisconsin Avenue. Yurchenko simply walked out.

"I'll be back in fifteen or twenty minutes," he told the CIA man. And with that, Vitaly Yurchenko, prize KGB defector, disappeared into the crowded Saturday-night sidewalks of Georgetown. He hailed a taxi, and within a few minutes was at the gates of the Soviet embassy compound. After identifying himself, he was let inside.

Two days later, on November 4, Yurchenko surfaced at a press conference in the compound. He spoke in English, then in Russian. He told a story, which no one believed, of being drugged and kidnapped by the CIA in Rome. He complained about the conditions under which he was held by the CIA and about the news leaks from the agency. He said he knew nothing about Edward Lee Howard except what he had read in the newspapers. Most of what he said was patently untrue. But the most interesting aspect of the Yurchenko press conference was his demeanor. He appeared to be highly agitated, nervous, and hyperactive, and he seemed to want to keep talking; Soviet embassy officials had trouble shutting him up when they decided the press conference had run long enough. If Yurchenko was not a genuine defector, he was the greatest actor since Sir Laurence Olivier.

On November 6, three months after Aldrich Ames had met him at Andrews Air Force Base, Yurchenko boarded an Aeroflot jet at

Dulles airport and headed home. Stanislav Androsov, the KGB resident in Washington, instructed Lt. Col. Valery F. Martynov to accompany Yurchenko on the plane. Martynov's wife, Natalya, thought it odd, since her husband's job was to collect scientific and technical information. He would normally not have been assigned to special flight duty. Martynov was unconcerned; he kissed his wife and two children good-bye that morning and assured them he would return soon.

The CIA was aware, of course, that GTGENTILE/PIMENTA was on the plane with its lost defector. What it did not know was that Rick Ames had betrayed Martynov at lunch with Sergei Chuvakhin five months earlier. It did not know that GTGENTILE was flying home to a firing squad.

12

"I ALWAYS WANTED A JAGUAR"

Spring is the most beautiful time of year in Washington. First the forsythia bloom, covering the hillsides in gold, the daffodils appear, then the cherry trees, the pink dogwoods, and finally the early pale green leaves of the oaks and maples announce that winter is truly over.

But Rick Ames was not enjoying the spring of 1986. On paper, everything looked fine. The KGB money was flowing, more than he had ever dreamed of, and Rome, a vibrant and exciting city, awaited him and Rosario, his new bride. His CIA career, which had looked so dismal in Mexico only three years before, was on the upswing.

There were, however, some frightening problems. Beginning in the fall of 1985 and continuing into early 1986, the CIA was losing its agents in the Soviet Union at a startling rate. Some twenty agents simply disappeared, vanishing off the agency's screen.

It was clear that something was terribly wrong. Although Ames had been assigned to language school to prepare for Rome, he was still based in the Soviet division, and he knew about the agent losses. Ames was horrified because the KGB, by rolling up all the names he had sold to it, was acting in a totally unexpected and unorthodox manner and placing him in great danger.

Ames had assumed that the KGB, following time-honored procedures, would arrest the CIA assets gradually, over a long period of time, going to great lengths to disguise the reasons why, salting the trail with false leads to make it appear that some reason other than a mole had caused each compromise. In that way, the CIA might have been lulled into thinking that sloppy tradecraft by a Soviet agent, or a communications intercept, or plain bad luck had caused agents to lose contact with Langley.

Instead of proceeding cautiously, using a scalpel, Yasnevo had unleashed a blunderbuss. As Ames later said, "It was as if neon lights and searchlights lit up all over the Kremlin. . . shone all the way across the Atlantic Ocean, saying, 'There is a penetration.'"[1]

Moreover, because Ames no longer headed the Soviet division's counterintelligence branch, he was not in a position to know if a source inside the KGB, perhaps a new recruitment, was reporting clues to Langley about the identity of a mole in the CIA. "Had I stayed in the SE counterintelligence branch I would have had a very good chance at sort of early warning," Ames said. "But after I left and went to the language school, absolutely not."[2]

Almost equally scary to Ames was the lie detector test that he faced on May 2. The polygraph is an imperfect instrument, at best. It does not detect lies. What it does is measure physiological changes in breathing, blood pressure, heartbeat, and sweat. The theory of the polygraph is that when people knowingly lie, the stress will cause physiological changes that can be measured.[3] There is a great deal of mumbo jumbo in all this, because liars can

[1]Tim Weiner, "Jailed, Turncoat at C.I.A. Tells of a Long Betrayal," *New York Times,* July 27, 1994, p. B10.

[2]Senate Interview, p. 45.

[3]Ancient cultures have also thought that guilt can be detected by physical changes. In Europe and Asia, the authorities believed that a guilty man had a dry mouth. A suspect's mouth would be stuffed with bread or rice; if he could swallow, he was judged to be innocent. If not, he was put to death.

and do pass polygraph tests, and the machine frequently registers deception when someone is telling the truth.

Although the CIA theoretically required its officers to take a polygraph test every five years, the operators, struggling under a huge workload, fell hopelessly behind; some officers were not polygraphed for decades. Ames had not faced the black box since 1976, but because he was about to go overseas again, he was scheduled for another test.

As the date approached, Ames, who had now been selling secrets to the KGB for more than a year, admitted feeling "tremendous apprehension." Most DO officers facing the polygraph are nervous, but Ames had real reason to be.

He had heard that the KGB had developed certain techniques to foil the polygraph. It was widely known inside the CIA that some drugs may affect the results of a lie detector test. Scientific studies have shown that a person who before being tested takes four hundred milligrams of meprobamate, a common tranquilizer sold under the name of Miltown, will probably be able to lie successfully in a polygraph examination.[4] Other, less reliable, methods of "beating the machine" have also been suggested, ranging from physical actions, such as biting the tongue or squeezing the toes against the floor, to mental conditioning.

Ames was able to get a note to Sergei Chuvakhin, his Soviet embassy contact, warning that he faced a lie detector test and asking for the KGB's advice. Ames's faith in the KGB was initially shaken by the reply. "I had no idea of what kind of advice I would get. . . . You know, wiggle a toe, take a certain drug. But what I got were two or three points. . . . Get a real good night's sleep. Be fresh and rested. Be cooperative. Develop rapport with the examiner. . . . And try to remain as calm and easy as you can. And my first impulse on seeing that advice was, is this the answer?"

Although disappointed, Ames said he knew that the KGB had spent a lot of time studying the polygraph, although it did not share the CIA's faith in the device. "They had studied it very, very

[4]A 1981 study at the University of Pennsylvania reported that of volunteers who took meprobamate and lied, the polygraph was able to detect only 27.2 percent; nearly three-quarters of those lying were undetected.

carefully," Ames said. "I also thought that there probably isn't anyone that the KGB wants to help pass a polygraph more than myself. So, what I am getting is serious advice. Simple though it looks, it's got to be the best advice there is." Ames said he took the KGB's advice "very, very seriously and implemented it. . . I think fairly well, and, indeed, I passed."[5] Ames said he was surprised he had passed, and felt great "relief, relief washed everything out."[6]

In fact, he should not have passed. Ames was asked about unauthorized contacts with a foreign intelligence service and unauthorized disclosure of classified information. He sailed right by, but stumbled when asked if he had been "pitched" by a foreign spy agency. Ames double-talked his way out of it, saying, among other explanations, that he was worried that he *might* be pitched in Rome by the KGB. The polygraph operator ran through the questions again and decided that Ames was "bright. . . direct" and truthful.

But in June 1993, when the FBI finally focused on Aldrich Ames, it reviewed the CIA's 1986 polygraph test and concluded that the deception Ames had shown about being "pitched" had never been resolved. The FBI also concluded that Ames had shown significant deceptive responses when asked about unauthorized disclosure of classified material.

In addition to the polygraph, before Ames left for Rome the CIA's Office of Medical Services gave him a second blood test to try to detect any signs of alcohol abuse. The results showed slight elevations of two liver enzymes. There was no follow-up by the CIA, and the agency's medical staff concluded that no further action was warranted.

On Saturday, May 17, two weeks after Rick had passed his polygraph test, his mother, Rachel, arrived at Rick and Rosario's apartment in Falls Church to attend the graduation of her oldest grandson, Stephen Everly, from the United States Naval Academy at Annapolis. Rachel stayed in the guest bedroom of the Ames's apartment in the Idylwood Towers. On Sunday evening, she went to bed and died of an apparent heart attack during the night.

[5]House Interview, p. 20.
[6]Senate Interview, p. 61.

There is no evidence she knew or suspected that her son was a Russian spy.

Sometime that spring, Ames purchased his first computer and arranged to take it with him to Rome. He also acquired WordPerfect word-processing software. He planned to use the computer to communicate with the KGB in Rome.

Rick and Rosario Ames arrived in Rome on July 22, 1986, and Ames took up his duties as Soviet branch chief in the CIA station. His cover title was "first secretary" of the American embassy in the Palazzo Margherita on the Via Veneto. For several months, he and Rosario lived in the Velabro, a fashionable residence near the Roman Forum.

When Ames came to Rome, the ambassador was Maxwell M. Rabb, a former assistant to President Eisenhower, who presided over an embassy of some two hundred Americans and several hundred Italians. The chief of the large CIA station, then located on the second floor, was Alan D. Wolfe, a fifty-eight-year-old native New Yorker and graduate of Columbia College, where he had studied chemical engineering. He earned a master of arts degree at Columbia in 1950 and then joined the CIA. Wolfe was first sent to Pakistan, but he spent much of his long career in the Middle East, in Jordan, Iraq, and Afghanistan.

A white-haired man with a florid complexion, Wolfe, like his close friend Dewey Clarridge, liked to pepper his speech with four-letter words.[7] Among friends, however, he could also drop the tough-guy pose and quote Shakespeare and the English poets, and he was known as a connoisseur of fine wines. But Wolfe's personal style was dyspeptic and combative; he had a short fuse, which did not endear him to many of his colleagues. Behind his back, they called him "Camel Shit," in mock recognition of his many years in the sands of the Middle East.

Wolfe had been the COS when Vitaly Yurchenko defected in Rome the previous August, an event that was a feather in the cap

---

[7]As it happened, it fell to Clarridge, the chief of the CIA's European division (EUR) in 1986, to approve Ames's assignment in Rome. As Ames's supervisor in Ankara in 1972, it was Clarridge who had suggested that Ames was better suited for headquarters work where he would not have to recruit agents.

of the station chief. Wolfe was serving out his last overseas tour in Rome before retiring, and he left much of the day-to-day work of running the Rome station to the deputy chief of station, John P. "Jack" Gower, fifty, a crew-cut CIA veteran with a reputation as a true-blue company man who followed orders unquestioningly.

Although Langley had assured Alan Wolfe that Ames was "highly regarded" by the Soviet division, the Rome station chief soon discovered that his new officer was nothing but trouble. In Rome, Ames would go out for long lunches and return to the office too drunk to work.

His colleagues noticed, of course. In the culture of the Directorate of Operations, hard drinking is considered macho and acceptable. But three women in the station complained to their superiors about Ames's long absences in the afternoons and failure to do his job. One of Ames's supervisors in Rome later admitted that Rick was drunk "about three times a week" between 1986 and 1988.[8]

Some of the drinking episodes could not be ignored. Ames would get well oiled before and during his meetings with the KGB. Once, Ames returned from a meeting with his KGB cutout too drunk to write a cable that he had been instructed to send to Langley. Then, at a July 4 reception in the garden of Ambassador Rabb's residence in 1987, Ames got drunk again and fell into a loud argument with another guest. Rosario was visiting her mother in Bogotá at the time and was not at the reception. Ames left and passed out in the street. The Italian *carabinieri* picked him up out of the gutter and took him to the hospital. He had no memory of how he got there.

The next day, by Ames's account, Wolfe saw him in the hall and said, "You should be more careful." As Ames recalled it, "I gave him a kind of a. . . hangdog and apologetic look and said. . . that was really something, to that effect. And that was that."[9]

Wolfe told CIA investigators, however, that he had warned Ames that he would be sent back to Washington if there was

[8]Senate Report, p. 40.
[9]Senate Interview, pp. 77–78.

another such episode. After Ames's arrest Wolfe was so outraged at his former subordinate's spying for the KGB that he broke the agency's traditional code of *omerta* and, briefly, went public. He described Ames as "a lackluster officer and a drunk." Wolfe added: "I had to counsel him on the extent to which he was drinking his lunch."

Ames's drinking was placing strains on his marriage as well. Rosario told the CIA after her guilty plea that Rick's alcoholism had damaged their relationship. "She said her marriage had fallen to pieces during their Rome tour and they had numerous fights."[10]

In Rome, Ames began meeting openly with his new intermediary for the KGB, Aleksei Khrenkov, code-named SAM II. Khrenkov, a diplomat in the Soviet Ministry of Foreign Affairs, played the same role that Sergei Chuvakhin, SAM I, had filled in Washington. The Rome station was aware that Ames was meeting regularly with Khrenkov. But to Wolfe, Gower, and the CIA station, Khrenkov was a "developmental," a Soviet target that Ames was bringing along as a possible recruit for the agency. Ames was careful to downplay Khrenkov's potential—it would not do at all for Langley to get too interested and start asking when Khrenkov might become operational and begin to pass information to the CIA.

As he had done at headquarters, Ames simply strolled out of the Rome station with classified cables and documents inside envelopes in a shopping bag. No one leaving the embassy was searched.

And there was enough to transmit to the KGB, even though Ames was no longer at the center of the CIA's Soviet counterintelligence operations. In Rome, Ames still had access to the identities of CIA agents and copies of their reports. At weekly staff meetings, he would learn about CIA assets and potential recruitments. He received sensitive CIA intelligence reports from all over the world, not just from Italy; Langley headquarters regularly sends copies of an enormous number of documents to all stations. In Rome, Ames

[10]Senate Report, p. 41, citing the classified version of the CIA inspector general's report on the Ames case.

coordinated double-agent operations of the U.S. military. He responded to the KGB's questions about past CIA penetrations of Soviet intelligence, and he passed along the identities of numerous agents working for the CIA in Eastern European countries.

Both in Rome and in Washington, Ames gave the KGB original CIA documents that crossed his desk in the normal course of his work. He seldom bothered to Xerox anything, which might have attracted attention to him in any event. He did not need to make copies to keep for himself because he usually received more than one copy of a document. Although TOP SECRET documents were controlled and numbered, with access to them restricted to certain officials, most of the documents circulating in the Directorate of Operations were classified SECRET, with no special controls. Ames simply put them in his shopping bag and walked out.[11]

When Ames met with Khrenkov, usually in the early evening, he would hand over the shopping bags full of documents and receive cash in return. Ames would also pass along notes to the KGB that he had written on his computer at home. And at the meetings, Khrenkov would give him new instructions from the KGB.

Three times while Ames was in Rome, his KGB handler, VLAD, flew into Rome to meet with Ames. Much later, from a description provided by Ames after he had pleaded guilty, the FBI concluded that VLAD was Vladimir Mechulayev, a senior officer of Directorate K, the KGB's counterintelligence directorate. The two men had first met in Bogotá at Christmas of 1985. Ames and his wife had flown to Colombia to visit Rosario's mother, Cecilia. While there, Ames slipped into the Soviet embassy in Bogotá and met for an hour and a half with VLAD. It was Ames's first face-to-face meeting with his KGB control, who was to remain his handler for the next several years.

[11]It was not only the KGB that was astounded at how easy it was for Ames to collect documents and walk out with them unhindered; Senator DeConcini was equally amazed. "I just took the originals," Ames explained to the chairman of the Senate Intelligence Committee. "Paper is basically unaccountable. . . . Every time they would inventory TOP SECRET documents, you know. . . hundreds and thousands would turn up missing." Senate Interview, pp. 30, 84.

The initial meeting of Ames and VLAD in Rome took place at a café in October 1986. At the meeting, Ames said he had planned to raise the question of why the KGB had rolled up all the CIA agents whose names Ames had passed to Chuvakhin in Washington in 1985. "But he brought it up first. And essentially he apologized for it. . . . He said. . . you know we would never have done what we did. He said, but we were forced to. It went up to the highest levels and we argued against it and we lost. . . . I think the shock effect of the mass of information that I gave them in June and then that summer was such a shock at the highest level. . . that a political decision was made that this had to be wiped out. . . . And I believed VLAD. . . . And he said never again would we be in that position."[12]

If Ames's account is credible and the explanation he received was accurate, then the clear implication was that the Politburo, then headed by Mikhail Gorbachev, had overruled the KGB and ordered the CIA agents rolled up all at once, regardless of the risk to the source. Ames understood it this way; he said that VLAD implied that the decision "was maybe even outside the KGB."[13]

Ames had fortified himself by arriving at the café an hour early and drinking in advance of the meeting. The drinking continued during the lengthy session, so much so that Ames forgot that he was to meet VLAD at the same café the next night to receive a large cash payment. Ames never showed up. Several months later, in 1987, when he next met with VLAD, Ames apologized for missing the meeting and blamed it on alcohol and on the fact that he had been frightened to discover blood in his urine that night, the result of an infection. But the KGB officer, Ames recalled, accepted his excuses and said, "I simply had too much to drink. . . . And he dismissed it. Just like an agency manager."[14]

When VLAD visited Rome, on most occasions Khrenkov would pick Ames up in his car and drive him to the Villa Abamelek, the Soviet ambassador's residence on the western edge of Rome, just south of the Vatican. Ames would crouch low in the car with a

[12]Senate Interview, pp. 39–40.
[13]House Interview, p. 32.
[14]Senate Interview, p. 79.

baseball cap pulled down over his face as they drove through the streets of Rome and into the gates of the Soviet compound.

In the attic of the ambassador's residence, in a room swept for bugs by the KGB, Ames would meet with VLAD for two or three hours as the vodka flowed. "I respected him and trusted him," Ames said. "It was businesslike."[15]

At the meetings with VLAD and his regular encounters with Khrenkov, Ames received cash payments that typically ranged between $20,000 and $50,000 each time. Once, Khrenkov gave him a box of Cuban cigars. The box was lined with currency. Ames thought the cigars were not top quality; he had no complaints about the cash.

The problem was what to do with all that money. In December Ames opened the first of two Swiss bank accounts at the Credit Suisse bank in Zurich, one in his name and the other in the name of his mother-in-law, Cecilia, with himself as trustee. These were not small Christmas-club savings accounts; while in Rome, Ames deposited just under $1 million in the two Swiss accounts, which eventually reached a total of $1,810,189.

Ames did not have any numbered accounts in Switzerland; he believed, correctly, that the Swiss were fussy about opening numbered accounts, and he relied on the general secrecy of Swiss banking laws to protect him. To avoid electronic transfers, which might have been noticed, Ames flew to Zurich several times with large amounts of cash. One deposit was for $300,000.

Meanwhile, the Ameses were doing their best to spend a great deal of the money. Rosario sometimes accompanied Rick on his trips to Switzerland, and the Ameses also traveled to London and Germany. Their telephone bills in Rome were running $5,000 a month, and the couple were buying expensive clothes.

Rosario was not stupid—indeed her Colombian friends all attest to her remarkable brilliance—and it is possible that she might have displayed just a teeny bit of curiosity about the origins of their newfound wealth. Only months before their marriage, Ames complained he was broke; suddenly they were flying around the

[15]Senate Interview, p. 32.

continent, opening banks accounts in Zurich, shopping in the most expensive stores on the Via Condotti, and dining in Rome's best restaurants.

Ames could hardly tell Rosario that the money was coming from her family; she *knew* that was not true. Whatever others might think, the Casas clan, while well connected politically, and respected, was not at all wealthy. She also knew that Ames worked in sensitive positions for the CIA and seemed to spend a great deal of time with the Russians. Be that as it may, both Ames and his wife later claimed that Rosario suspected nothing; in order to explain his fabulous new wealth to her, he said, he invented a character he called "Robert from Chicago."

To account for the first $50,000 that he had received in Washington, Ames said he told Rosario that he had an old college friend in Chicago for whom he had once done a big favor. He had arranged an abortion for the man's girlfriend. He would ask the generous "Robert," who never seemed to acquire a last name, for a loan.

But even before the Ameses went to Rome, the $50,000 had been long spent, and Ames said he needed another story for Rosario. "And what I told her was that this friend of mine, I only identified him to her as Robert, and his associates were interested in investing money in Europe. And that while I was in Rome, I would look after some of their investments and manage them. . . . And I would get a commission. . . . I gave Rosario to understand that I was making a lot of money at this. And we were on the way to becoming, if not exactly wealthy, quite well off. And I began to encourage, I wouldn't say necessarily an extravagant, but a, but a lifestyle that gradually sort of went up and up. We started buying expensive clothing and generally people understood, I think, that we had extra money."[16] At the same time, Ames allowed the word to spread among his CIA colleagues that Rosario came from a wealthy family in Colombia.

The embassy's security officer noticed Ames's lavish spending habits as well as his drinking and reported it to the CIA's Rome

---

[16]Senate Interview, pp. 46–47.

station chief. Nothing happened.[17] Everyone knew that Rosario was wealthy.

In Rome, meanwhile, Ames was passing so much information to the KGB that VLAD gently suggested it was sometimes too much—the CIA secrets were beginning to clog the KGB's files. It had come up at one meeting when Ames asked his handler if he would like to see some CIA traffic on a particular subject. "And he said, 'No, I think not,' and he said, 'You know, there's an awful lot of the information that you give us, even though it is very valuable and very interesting, we simply can't handle.'" As VLAD explained it, the KGB had "a very small group of people working on my case." Ames was providing perhaps a thousand documents a year in Rome, and each one had to be handled carefully within the KGB to protect the source, and "that's a lot of work for a very small group of people. . . . So, in a sense, they had a lot more than they could use and they weren't eager for more."[18]

In December 1986, one week after Ames opened his first Swiss bank account, William Casey, the director of the CIA, suffered a seizure in his office. His deputy, Robert M. Gates, became acting director. Casey never returned to Langley; he died of a malignant brain tumor on May 6, 1987. President Reagan nominated Gates to be director, but Gates, along with Casey, had been tarred by the Iran-contra scandal. He withdrew, and Reagan nominated FBI director William H. Webster as the new CIA chief. Webster became the CIA director on May 26.

Early in 1987 reports surfaced that the KGB had penetrated the marine guards at the American embassy in Moscow and supposedly gained access to the code room. That allegation was later dropped. In the end, the overblown "marine spy scandal" resulted in the espionage conviction, on August 24, 1987, of only a single embassy guard, Marine Sergeant Clayton J. Lonetree, who had fallen into a "honey trap"—he was compromised by an attractive young woman under KGB control who worked as an embassy translator. Lonetree's sentence of thirty years was reduced to fifteen years after he cooperated with the damage assessment.

[17]Senate Interview, pp. 46–47.
[18]House Interview, pp. 52–53.

The following month, Ames wrote a message to the KGB on his home computer. Suspicions that CIA agent losses were due to other persons such as Clayton Lonetree, Ames wrote, "get me off the hook." In his letter, Ames emphasized his commitment to the KGB. He discussed planned meetings with the Soviet intelligence agency in Rome and Vienna and identified more names of Soviet agents working for the CIA.

Up to now Ames and Rosario had been tooling around Rome in an Alfa Romeo. In the past few months alone, Rick had deposited $165,000 from the KGB in the account in Zurich in his name. Clearly, it was time to move up to a more expensive car.

As it happened, that same month of September, the British deputy chief of mission in Rome, Giles Eden FitzHerbert, was about to leave Rome to become Her Majesty's ambassador to Venezuela. He was looking to sell his silver-gray Jaguar. He would have an official car in Caracas, so he didn't need the Jag any longer. Giles, an Oxford man and a member of White's, who had served as an officer in the King's Royal Irish Hussars before joining the Foreign Office, did not advertise, of course. There was no need; everyone in the close-knit diplomatic corps knew that the car was available.

The Jaguar fit Giles FitzHerbert, who was something of a dandy, although he liked to walk around his office at the British embassy in carpet slippers. He was the son-in-law of Evelyn Waugh, or had been until his wife, Margaret, was tragically struck down and killed by an automobile a year earlier.[19]

Giles was delighted when a chap from the American embassy contacted him about the Jaguar. "He came to the embassy and took it out for a spin," FitzHerbert recalled. "He said he liked it and would buy it. Just before I left he came by the embassy and

[19]Waugh was infatuated with his daughter Margaret and admitted a strong physical attraction to her when she was ten. He bitterly resented her marriage to Giles FitzHerbert, whom he considered a rival for her affection. "She has fallen head over heels for an Irishman[. . .]raffish, penniless," he wrote to Lady Diana Cooper. "I would forbid the marriage if I had any other cause than jealousy & snobbery." Quoted in Martin Stannard, *Evelyn Waugh: The Later Years, 1939–1966* (New York: W. W. Norton & Co., 1992), pp. 458–59.

picked up the car. He gave me a check, there was no cash involved. And I remember he said, 'I always wanted to own a Jaguar.'"[20]

In November 1987, while Rick was in Rome, his sister Alison died of breast cancer at age forty-one. She had been in and out of the hospital for a long time; in the summer of 1986, before Rick and Rosario went to Rome, they went down to see her in the hospital in Charlotte, North Carolina. Alison was very angry with Rosario because she wanted to speak privately to her brother and Rosario would not leave them alone. When Alison died, Rick did not return from Rome for her funeral. Later, he had difficulty talking about her death, or why he did not come back to see her at the end or to attend the service.

Early in 1988, Rosario had exciting news for her husband. She was pregnant. And Ames, despite his nonstellar performance in Rome—he received only lukewarm performance reports—won a one-year extension of his normal two-year tour to three years. There was more good news in September when Alan Wolfe, who had not headed the Ames fan club in the Eternal City, departed as station chief.

His replacement was Jack Devine, a huge man, over six foot five, who had been chief of the CIA task force that supervised the agency's covert operation against the Soviet-backed government of Afghanistan. Wolfe and Devine overlapped briefly in Rome.

---

[20]In October of 1994, I located Giles FitzHerbert, retired by now from the diplomatic service, milking a cow in County Carlow, Ireland. His wife asked me to ring back in twenty minutes when he was through milking. I did. He came inside the house to the phone, and he confirmed the details of the sale of the Jaguar, but had difficulty remembering the name of the American who bought it. "But why are you asking about this Ames chap?" he said. I replied that Ames had worked for the CIA, and was a big spy who had sold secrets to the Russians, and had been arrested eight months earlier and sent to prison for life. "Oh my, I didn't know that," FitzHerbert exclaimed. "I don't much read the papers anymore. Find I don't need them here, you know." After examining a photograph of Ames that I sent to him, FitzHerbert wrote back that "it seems more than probable that he was the man" who bought the Jaguar. In addition, a CIA colleague remembered that Ames had purchased his car from a British diplomat in Rome.

Within the CIA station, word circulated that Wolfe, who had no great admiration for his successor, refused to surrender his office or home for a time, forcing Devine to camp out in a tiny office and a hotel.

Meanwhile, Ames was the only American embassy employee driving a Jaguar to work each day—a fact that was noticed. When one CIA colleague in Rome bluntly asked Ames at a party how he could afford to live so well, Ames replied: "I'm an expert on the market." As the colleague pressed for some pointers, it became obvious that Ames actually knew very little about investments. Finally, Ames said it wasn't his own knowledge, it was a friend who handled his account. Ames's colleague said that he talked to Jack Devine, the new station chief, about Ames's claim to have made huge amounts of money in the stock market. Devine, according to the CIA man, replied, "Yes, he's got a fantastic broker." No one, either in Rome or in Washington, seemed to connect Ames's sudden and ostentatious display of new wealth with the inexplicable and disastrous loss of virtually all of the CIA's agents inside the Soviet Union.

On November 11, a son was born to Rick and Rosario. They named him Paul, but within the family he was known by the affectionate Spanish diminutive Pablito.

In the spring of 1989, as Ames's tour in Rome was winding down, he betrayed to the KGB yet another CIA agent, code-named GTMOTORBOAT. On May 16 Ames revealed the identity of the agent, who was an officer in the Bulgarian internal intelligence service. Ames had met the agent in Rome a couple of times, and the officer had passed documents to him. After Ames transmitted the name to the Soviets, GTMOTORBOAT disappeared. He was not executed, however, because some years later, after Ames's arrest in 1994, the CIA learned that he was alive. Although it is not known how he escaped the fate of others whom Ames betrayed, most of whom were executed or imprisoned, the agency's counterintelligence officials speculated that the KGB had not wanted to risk their prime source, Aldrich Ames, to retaliate against an agent of a sister service in Sofia. The KGB may also have worried that

Ames might come under suspicion if it arrested an agent he had handled personally.[21]

In June, Ames received an extraordinary "Dear Friend" letter from the KGB. "This is your balance sheet as on the May 1, 1989," it began. "All in all you have been appropriated [$]2,705,000. . . we have delivered to You [$]1,881,811.51. On the above date You have on Your account (including 250,000$ in bonds) [$]1,535,077.28."[22]

Enclosed with the letter were five color photographs of land on a riverbank somewhere in the Soviet Union, where, the KGB promised, Ames's country dacha would one day be built. The sylvan scenes featured tall trees and a heavily wooded area along a peaceful river. Ames dreamed one day of retiring and sailing a boat. Perhaps the KGB knew that, which is why it selected land on the water.

At the end of the financial accounting, the KGB wrote: "P.S. We believe that these pictures would give You some idea about the beautiful piece of land on the river bank, which from now belongs to You forever. We decided not to take pictures of housing in this area with the understanding that You have much better idea of how Your country house (dacha) should look like. Good luck."

It was clear from the letter and the photographs that the KGB was looking ahead to the day that its premier spy might retire to the Soviet Union, as Kim Philby had done when he fled Beirut in 1963. From the wording of the letter it was also clear that VLAD

---

[21]The CIA has not said what happened to GTMOTORBOAT, and may not know, but he vanished without a trace for a time. At a hearing before Magistrate Poretz in federal court in Alexandria on March 1, 1994, the FBI's Les Wiser noted: "The CIA has made many attempts to locate him and has failed." Later, however, GTMOTORBOAT crossed the agency's screen again.

[22]Exactly how much Ames was paid and promised by the KGB is a slippery business, and probably no one, including Ames, knows the precise totals. The 1989 KGB "accounting" seemed to say that almost $1.9 million had been "delivered" to Ames and another $800,000 was being held in his Moscow "account," making a total of $2.7 million. As will be seen, later payments and guarantees raised the total amount paid or promised to Ames by the KGB to $4.6 million.

and Ames had already discussed the possibility and that Ames seemed to have some architectural ideas of his own about the design of the dacha. There is no reason to think that the KGB was stringing Ames along with the promise of a country retreat and a dacha; they were paying him millions of dollars as it was.[23] Land and a house in the Soviet Union would have cost much less than the precious hard currency payments the KGB had already expended on Ames.

Around the same time, the KGB passed a nine-page letter to Ames. It amounted to a tasking list, questions the KGB wanted Ames to answer when he returned to CIA headquarters. Topping the list was a request for the identities of any CIA penetrations of the KGB and the GRU, the Soviet military intelligence service. Moscow sought "info about the Soviet agents of the Agency and other [security services] of your country, first of all from KGB, GRU. . . [and] other state, party, scientific and military organizations." In other words, Ames, the KGB's mole, was to try to ferret out any additional CIA moles inside Soviet intelligence. Yasnevo also tasked Ames to provide information about double-agent operations.

In addition, the letter asked Ames to provide leads on other possible moles who might be recruited inside the CIA by the KGB. It requested that Ames act as a spotter, or talent scout, to be on the lookout for CIA colleagues who, for one reason or another, might be vulnerable to recruitment by the KGB.[24]

---

[23]Edward Lee Howard, whose Swiss bank account contained less than $150,000 in KGB money, lives in a substantial brick dacha outside Moscow, with a caretaker couple who provide cooking and gardening, in addition to his round-the-clock KGB guards.

[24]After Ames pleaded guilty to espionage, he told government debriefers that he had turned over to Moscow some names of CIA officers who were being transferred, at least in one instance because the person had performed poorly. Ames claimed he did not turn over the names of colleagues who might be targeted for recruitment because of personal vulnerabilities. In interviews, Ames has said he knows of no other moles in the agency, but assumes that they "probably" exist. (Senate Interview, p. 99, and CNN interview, December 27, 1994.)

In the letter, the KGB also detailed new arrangements for making cash payments to Ames upon his return to Washington. The Soviets provided a new plan to allow Ames to communicate with the KGB. An elaborate system of dead drops and signal sites in the Washington area was to replace the more convenient exchanges of shopping bags. Presumably, the KGB opted for the traditional system of dealing with its agents because it could not be sure that Ames would return to a position at CIA where he would have reason to meet openly with Soviet diplomats. Also, since a dead drop, or hiding place, is visited separately by an agent and his handler to secrete or retrieve money or documents, the risks inherent in face-to-face meetings are greatly reduced.

The communications plan also provided that Ames would have personal meetings with the KGB at least once a year at locations outside the United States. The nine-page letter also established an "iron site" in Bogotá for meetings with Ames on the first Tuesday of every December. "Iron site" is a KGB term for a fixed location (i.e., one made of iron) that never changes. The concept behind it is that if all other means of communication should fail, the agent knows he can always make recontact at the iron site. Finally, the communication plan provided that additional personal meetings could be held in other cities, including Vienna, Austria—an all-time KGB favorite—if needed.

The KGB's tasking letter assured Ames that his personal security was its paramount concern, and it warned him to be on the alert for traps that the CIA sets to try to catch moles. In particular, the KGB warned Ames to be careful of computer traps.

Finally, the KGB assured Ames that in the next two meetings prior to his leaving Rome, he would receive a total of $300,000. Apparently, the KGB was good to its word, because at the end of June, Ames deposited $450,000 in his two Zurich accounts.

Before leaving Rome, Ames tried to sell his Jaguar to another CIA case officer, the same one he had told about his investment adviser who was a wizard in the stock market.

Since most CIA employees cannot afford Jaguars, there was no sale. Ames found another buyer.

On July 20, 1989, Rick, Rosario, and little Paul returned to

Washington. The fear Ames had felt three years earlier when the KGB had rolled up the agents he had betrayed had long since dissipated. An apartment in Falls Church was no longer suitable for a millionaire.

Ames decided to buy a large house for his growing family.

And he would need another luxury car. He decided a new white Jaguar would do nicely this time.

13

MOLE HUNT

She was a short, gray-haired woman with glasses, so plain looking, so mousy and nondescript that she would never stand out in a crowd, which suited her. She might be taken for a librarian or a schoolteacher, or somebody's grandmother, although she was none of these.

She had never married, as far as anyone knew. The CIA was her life. She lived alone in a condo in McLean, so close to Langley headquarters that she walked to work each day. If a co-worker stopped to offer her a lift, she would not accept, unless it was raining hard.

Jeanne R. Vertefeuille might have seemed, at first glance, an unlikely choice to hunt down the most damaging, dangerous mole in the history of the Central Intelligence Agency. In fact, she was almost preordained for the task.

For years, she had toiled quietly in the research section of the Soviet division and the Counterintelligence Staff. There was hardly an important, or even an unimportant, case involving the KGB or the GRU that she did not know. Jeanne Vertefeuille could follow the gossamer threads, sometimes so tangled and difficult to comprehend, that might link a case in Kuala Lumpur ten years ago to one in Vienna today. If a KGB colonel had appeared in Copenhagen under one name and turned up a decade later in New Delhi with another identity, give it to Jeanne, she would sort it out. Unlike the Bourbon kings, she learned everything and forgot nothing.

She liked to work in quiet obscurity. She preferred the anonymity that went with her job. Within the agency, there were some who compared her to John le Carré's fictional Connie Sachs, the brilliant woman researcher who knew all the Soviet cases and embodied the institutional memory of the Circus. But Vertefeuille did not encourage such talk; it veered entirely too close to a kind of celebrity, even though she was being equated with a woman who did not exist.

What eventually became the hunt for the mole had begun haltingly, in fits and starts, late in 1985. At first, the Soviet division's counterintelligence officers suspected a KGB penetration of CIA communications, either an electronic intercept or perhaps the compromise of a code clerk. To try to verify this possibility, the CIA ran a series of probes and tests designed to elicit a response from the KGB. The agency might, for example, have sent a cable falsely suggesting that a known KGB officer in Istanbul had been recruited as an asset and given a CIA code name. If the officer went about his normal business and was not recalled to Moscow, it might indicate that the KGB was not, after all, reading the CIA's traffic.

The fact that the Soviet division's first assumption was a communications breach in itself tells something about the deeply ingrained culture of the DO. The Operations Directorate, the agency's clandestine arm, was like a fraternity. Its members were loath to think even for a moment that one of their own might be working for the opposition. There was a presumption that no colleague, once initiated into their secret world, could be a traitor. To the officers of the DO, the thought that someone they knew, who reported to his desk in the Soviet division each day, sat with his co-workers in the cafeteria, and then commuted home to Falls Church, or Oakton, or Woodbridge, or one of the other bedroom communities in northern Virginia, who coached his kids at soccer or Little League—the thought that such an ordinary, familiar colleague might be a bewhiskered mole for the KGB was not easily accepted. The British might have their Philby, or their Guy Burgess or Donald MacLean, but this, after all, was Langley, not London.

Late in 1985, as the CIA was attempting to discover if its communications had been penetrated, CIA director William Casey ordered Clair George, the deputy director for operations (DDO), to try to find out why the agency's Soviet sources were disappearing. The possibility of a mole, however unattractive, could not be totally discounted, and the agency decided at least to hedge its bets. In January 1986, the Soviet division tightened access to its Soviet operations. It reduced the number of officers who could read incoming cable traffic from the field and narrowed the list of those who had access to the files of new Soviet or East European agents.

In the same month, Casey and Clair George met with John H. Stein, who had just left his post as the CIA's inspector general to prepare to go overseas again as station chief in Korea. Stein had preceded Clair George as the chief of the agency's clandestine operations.

Tall and graying, with an easy, pleasant manner, Stein fit the traditional Ivy League image of the agency's covert operators. A fifty-three-year-old Yale graduate from New England, he had joined the agency in the 1950s and spent much of his career in Africa, in Zaire, Cameroon, and Libya. He was a senior operations official in the Soviet division, then chief of station in Brussels, where he impressed President Carter's CIA director, Adm. Stansfield Turner, who brought him back to headquarters as assistant DDO. William Casey promoted him to DDO in 1981.

Three years later he was replaced by Clair George in a bureaucratic shuffle of four top CIA officials.

"We have a problem," Casey told Stein. "Sources we have aren't heard from when they get back to Moscow. We've lost some agents."

Casey asked Stein to review the compromised cases and analyze the possible reasons. Stein spent three or four months studying fifteen to twenty cases. He produced a ten-page memo that concluded that the KGB's detection of the Soviet agents could be explained by various problems evident in each case. Like any espionage operation, he wrote, each case contained to some degree "the seeds of its own destruction." Stein did not completely rule out the possibility of a human penetration, perhaps in Moscow, or a compromise of the agency's codes.[1]

Stein had labored in good faith, but his central conclusion that agents were lost for operational reasons was, of course, entirely wrong. Nevertheless, his analysis had a considerable impact inside Langley, where senior officials seized on the concept that each case had contained "the seeds of its own destruction." It was a comforting explanation in the paneled offices on the seventh floor, the CIA's executive suite, where pipes were smoked and deep thoughts conceived, because it discounted the possibility of a traitor inside Langley headquarters. Operational problems, a communications glitch, these were the risks of the great game; they went with the territory. Even the best Soviet asset could slip up, make a mistake in tradecraft that might prove fatal. These things happened, after all.

Clair George, the deputy director for operations, didn't think so. To George, it seemed entirely too coincidental that ten or fifteen or twenty cases had all self-destructed on their own.

---

[1]Stein gave the only copy of his report to Casey. Eight years later, when the CIA's inspector general investigated the Ames case, the Stein report apparently could not be found. The inspector general's report, in describing the contents of Stein's study, seemed to rely on the recollections of those who had read it. There was an operational reason that Stein had leaned toward thinking that the problem, if human, might be in the Moscow station rather than in Langley. When the agency recruited a Soviet source in another country, Moscow station normally would not be told of the recruitment until the source returned home and the Moscow station would have to take over the case. Since the CIA's Soviet agents were disappearing after they got back to Moscow, Stein reasoned that the leak, if any, was more likely to be in the Moscow station than in Langley.

He went to see Bill Casey.

I think we've been penetrated, he told the CIA director.

Casey reacted by calling in his senior managers for what apparently was the first meeting held in the Directorate of Operations to ponder the agent losses. John N. MacMahon, a handsome, silver-haired Irishman, the CIA deputy director, was there, along with Clair George; Gus Hathaway, the head of the CIA's Counterintelligence Staff; Burton Gerber, the chief of the Soviet division; and Jim Lynch, the stocky, mustached new director of the CIA's Office of Security.

Clair George, who was known, if not always loved, for his aggressive style, proposed that every CIA officer who had access to the compromised cases immediately be interrogated and polygraphed. His idea was shot down as too sweeping; CIA employees had rights, it was argued. The blanket approach was rejected.

Casey was assured that the Soviet division was reviewing the files. It was looking at the compromised cases and exploring the possibility of a technical penetration. Various ideas were tossed around. But as is so often the case in staff meetings in large organizations, afterward nothing happened.

About the same time, both the CIA inspector general and the President's Foreign Intelligence Advisory Board weighed in with reports on the Edward Lee Howard case. The report of the president's board was blunt. It noted, accurately, that "senior CIA officers [had] continued to misread or ignore signs that Howard was a major CIA problem." The report blamed "a fundamental inability of anyone in the SE division to think the unthinkable—that a DO employee could engage in espionage."[2]

Casey fired off a strong memo to Clair George roasting the DDO and Burton Gerber, the chief of the Soviet division, for the agency's unwillingness to consider that a mole might have burrowed into Langley. The CIA director held George personally responsible for the Howard disaster. Casey had a quick temper, but he was directing his ire at the handling of the Howard case, closing the barn door after the horse had escaped. There is no evidence that his

[2]Senate Report, p. 27.

anger had any effect on the search for the cause of the 1985 compromises, the more immediate and pressing problem.

All the while that spring, Rick Ames was continuing to lunch with Sergei Chuvakhin and hand over his shopping bags full of CIA secrets. He was receiving advice from the KGB, through Chuvakhin, on how to pass his polygraph test and getting ready to go to Rome.

There was one other little detail that Ames and his wife had to take care of that April. Rick and Rosario signed the first of what would be eight years of false federal income tax returns. They failed to report any of the money that Rick knew had come from the KGB during 1985.

As the CIA began, slowly, to try to figure out why its agents were disappearing, a branch chief in the Soviet division at headquarters came across a routine bit of information that greatly aroused her curiosity. Sandra Jan Jackson, the chief of the SE/X/FR branch,[3] learned from a woman colleague that a senior KGB officer, previously stationed in Mexico, had applied for a visa to come to the United States for a tour in the Soviet consulate in San Francisco. His name was Igor Shurygin.

Although Shurygin was masquerading as a Soviet diplomat, Jackson knew him to be an American targets officer in the KGB. In the 1970s Jackson had been branch chief of SE/Bio, handling name traces of every Soviet diplomat in the world. In the early 1980s, she had worked on the CIA's Counterintelligence Staff, and Mexico was one of the stations she had monitored.

One of the CIA's tasks is to study visa applications to see if there is some reason that a diplomat or intelligence officer should be turned down and barred from entering the country. Checking the agency's file on Shurygin, Jackson discovered he was GTPOTATO. She began reading the reports Rick Ames had sent from Mexico between 1981 and 1983. She was astonished to see their volume and to realize that Ames and the KGB counterintelligence chief in Mexico City were spending whole days together drinking.

As Jackson read the reports, she concluded that Ames had not

[3]The designation stood for Soviet East European division, External Operations Group, Foreign Resources. Translated, it meant a branch of the Soviet division for operations against the Soviets in the United States.

been getting anywhere in developing Shurygin, whom she knew was closely involved with the Cuban mission in Mexico. To Jackson, it looked more like Shurygin was developing Ames rather than the other way around.

There was no reason then to suspect Ames, but it was clear to Jackson that Shurygin had tied up a CIA officer in Mexico City for two years with no result. If the Russian came to San Francisco, the pattern might be repeated; Shurygin would lead the agency and the FBI on a merry chase, taking up the time of officers who might better be used on other cases.

Jackson and her colleague decided to write an SPR, or "spravka," on Igor Shurygin.[4] The KGB man had wasted the time of a CIA case officer for two years in Mexico, Jackson noted. Citing Ames's reports from Mexico, she suggested that the State Department and the FBI bar Shurygin.

Before Jackson's report ever got out of the CIA, however, Shurygin's visa was approved. The KGB man arrived in San Francisco in December 1985, which is interesting since Ames had begun spying for Moscow only eight months earlier. It raised the possibility that the KGB wanted Shurygin in place in the United States to serve as a backup for the operation. There is no record that Ames was in contact with Shurygin, however. After ten months, Shurygin was declared persona non grata by the State Department and expelled during a round-robin of expulsions by both sides. He departed the United States on October 7.[5]

[4]The term "spravka" is a Russian word that, in its broadest sense, means an official document that certifies or attests to something. As used more narrowly by KGB counterintelligence, it meant a report or inquiry. The CIA adopted the same term and meaning. The letters SPR are simply agency shorthand for spravka.

[5]The expulsions of Shurygin and the other Soviets was code-named FAMISH by the FBI. The round of retaliations began after the arrest for espionage on August 23, 1986, in New York of Gennadi F. Zakharov, a Soviet intelligence agent working at the United Nations. A week later, the American reporter Nicholas Daniloff was arrested in Moscow. On September 17, 1986, twenty-five Russians were expelled from the United States. On October 19, Moscow expelled five Americans, and two days later, Washington expelled fifty-five Soviet diplomats.

In that same month of October 1986, almost a year after the CIA began to realize it had a serious problem on its hands, it finally acted to try to pinpoint the source of the trouble. With Clair George's approval, Gus Hathaway, the counterintelligence chief, moved to appoint a mole-hunt unit.

A veteran officer of the Directorate of Operations, Hathaway, then sixty-one, had occupied the counterintelligence post for only a little over a year. He was a wiry, intensely energetic man with a thin, patrician face who favored Ivy League, three-button suits and striped ties. He usually wore an acerbic, skeptical expression.

Born in Danville, Virginia, deep in the southern part of the state, he had graduated from the University of Virginia in 1950 and joined the CIA. Within the agency, Hathaway was universally described as FFV—the initials stand for First Families of Virginia.[6] Hathaway had been assigned to the the Soviet division from the start. In the 1950s, he ran operations against the Poles out of Berlin base. In the 1960s, Hathaway was posted to Rio de Janeiro and Buenos Aires, and by 1973 he was in Montevideo as chief of station. Along the way, he divorced and remarried. Although serving in Latin America, he was still targeting Soviet-bloc diplomats and installations. He earned a good reputation as a case officer and did a tour of duty as chief of station in Moscow. In the spring of 1985 he was tapped to head CIA counterintelligence.

It was not a popular job. Everyone remembered the havoc wreaked by James Angleton, who had headed CIA counterintelligence for two decades and ruined the careers of several loyal officers whom he suspected of being possible Soviet moles. In the agency's hierarchy, counterintelligence was seen as only a notch above the Office of Security. Within the CIA those who toiled in OS were regarded as little better than house dicks, bothersome cops looking for minor infractions, lost badges, or orange peels in the burn bag. The Counterintelligence Staff was regarded with somewhat more respect; everyone knew that CI was necessary,

---

[6]Hathaway's colleagues may have simply meant that he seemed like a Virginia gentleman; the Order of the First Families of Virginia did not list him in its registry of members, who must prove that an ancestor arrived before 1625.

but assignment to counterintelligence work was not seen as enhancing one's career.

It was Hathaway and Burton Gerber who had bungled the Howard case by hiding—there is no other word for it—from the FBI their knowledge that Howard was a potential spy for Moscow. Despite this, Hathaway enjoyed generally good relations with the bureau and had earned the respect of its counterintelligence officials. From Langley's viewpoint, however, the puzzling loss of CIA agents in 1985 was not primarily a bureau affair, and with any luck, it could be kept that way.[7]

But something had to be done. Hathaway called in Jeanne Vertefeuille. He told her he was creating a Special Task Force (STF), to analyze the compromised cases and try to find their cause. He assigned her to head what, in time, became known as the mole-hunt unit.

There was a belief among the agency's senior male executives, outrageously sexist though it was, that "little gray-haired old ladies," as one case officer put it, were best suited to perform the painstaking work of catching a mole. Computers might help, the prevailing wisdom went, but only the women had the patience and the skills to go through mountains of files and extract the clues that might lead to the mole's burrow, the traitor's lair.

And Vertefeuille fit this vision of a mole-catcher's profile better than anyone else. She was little, and gray-haired, and at age fifty-four certainly not getting any younger. And she was known for her patient, analytical counterintelligence skills.

Jeanne Vertefeuille was of French extraction; she sometimes mentioned that. She was fluent in French, a language in which her name meant "green leaf." She seldom talked about herself, but it was known she had grown up in the Northeast. She had been posted to Ethiopia in the late 1950s and served in the CIA station in Finland in the early 1960s and in The Hague in the mid-1960s. In the early 1970s, she had found her métier, counterintelligence.

---

[7]The FBI had, of course, lost the two KGB sources in the Soviet embassy in Washington that it shared with the agency, Valery Martynov, PIMENTA (the CIA's GTGENTILE) and Sergei Motorin, MEGAS (the CIA's GTGAUZE), but the great majority of the lost agents were exclusively the CIA's.

She was appointed head of the research section in the Soviet division's CI Group, then chief of the division's SE/Bio branch. When a new KGB officer popped up in Bangkok, or the agency was targeting a GRU colonel in Prague as a possible recruit, the field would ask headquarters to run name traces on these individuals to see what the CIA's computers might hold. Vertefeuille was in charge of that process. She knew where the bodies were buried, or might be.

By the early 1980s, she was working in the agency's Counterintelligence Staff. In 1984, she was rewarded by being named chief of station in Gabon, in French-speaking West Africa. Even today, in the male-dominated CIA, there are relatively few women station chiefs, and her appointment more than a decade ago was an unusual recognition of her talents.

Never mind that Gabon had not even had a station chief until 1981, that Vertefeuille ran a one-woman station, in charge only of herself, an assistant, and a code clerk, and that it was not London or Paris. The point was, she was a COS.

Gabon was a fairly sleepy post. The oil-rich country, about the size of Colorado, with a population barely over a million, was politically stable and pro-Western. President Omar Bongo was always reelected, but then, he was the only candidate. President Bongo put a lot of money into making Libreville, the capital, a relatively modern town. There were nice beaches, but Gabon exports tropical hardwood, and large logs tended to float downriver into the ocean and onto the sand; swimming was dangerous and the surf rough. A battalion of French marines was stationed just down the street from the American embassy, which was comforting; Gabon was one of a few former French colonies that by treaty permitted Paris to keep troops in its country.

Vertefeuille, whose cover was that of a State Department political officer, got on well with the career ambassador, Larry C. Williamson. In Gabon, embassy staff meetings tended to be rather informal; once a week the ambassador and the station chief would get together for a beer. Williamson wanted to make sure that Vertefeuille hadn't learned anything that he might have missed.

From an intelligence viewpoint, Gabon was a French playground, dominated by the the French external service, the Direction Générale de la Sécurité Extérieure (DGSE), better known as "la Piscine," or the swimming pool, the nickname for its headquarters in northeast Paris.[8] If a Soviet KGB officer chose to defect in Gabon, the DGSE would be much more likely to get him than the CIA. But Vertefeuille would have handled any assets previously recruited by the CIA in an Eastern European embassy in Libreville, for example.

Late in 1986, after two and a half years in Gabon, it was time to come home. It was then that Gus Hathaway assigned Vertefeuille to head the mole-hunt unit. To help her, she enlisted Fran Smith, a short, stout, gray-haired woman veteran in the Soviet division, and two retirees, who were called back in to Langley to serve on the Special Task Force. Later, Sandy Grimes, a tall, blond woman, like Vertefeuille an experienced officer in the Soviet division, joined the team.

One of the retirees was a fifty-six-year-old longtime Soviet division officer, the well-respected Benjamin Franklin Pepper. A handsome, six-foot, athletic-looking Princeton man with graying brown hair, Pepper came from a moneyed Philadelphia background. He had served in Berlin in the mid-1950s and in Mexico City in the early 1960s. A decade later, he went to London under a CIA program to send experienced Soviet case officers to assist MI5, the British security service, in working against the KGB.

Pepper had spent much of his career in the Soviet division at headquarters, working in counterintelligence. He was known as a leading opponent within the agency of the convoluted theories of James Angleton, long the chief of the CIA's Counterintelligence Staff. In 1968, Pepper had participated in a CIA study that concluded that Yuri I. Nosenko, the controversial KGB defector, was genuine.[9] Later, Pepper had conducted a similar study that found

---

[8]The DGSE acquired that name under President François Mitterand in 1981. It is located in a ten-story office building at 141 Boulevard Mortier, adjacent to a public swimming pool, which explains its aquatic nickname.

[9]See Tom Mangold, *Cold Warrior: James Jesus Angleton the CIA's Master Spy Hunter* (New York: Simon & Schuster, 1991), pp. 201, 400.

that FEDORA, the FBI source in New York, was bona fide. Based on Pepper's study, the CIA had acknowledged FEDORA as a true source in 1975, a year after the departure of Angleton, who had never accepted either FEDORA, TOPHAT, or Nosenko as authentic.

Aside from Pepper's obvious credentials to serve on the mole-hunt unit, he had one other qualification: He was a very close friend and admirer of Gus Hathaway, to whom the Special Task Force reported. Pepper and Hathaway had joined the agency right out of college and met as trainees at the Farm. They had been friends ever since. CIA officers often form a close bond with their fellow trainees, and it is common for members of the same class at the Farm to remain in touch for years, even as their careers may take them to different corners of the world. Or sometimes even to the same places; Pepper had replaced Hathaway in Berlin in the 1950s.

So it had been natural for Gus Hathaway to think of Ben Pepper when he was putting together the task force. The two men had met for lunch.

Hathaway, always serious, even driven about his work, looked particularly unhappy that day. "Jesus Christ," he said, "I know we've been penetrated."

Pepper volunteered on the spot to come back in and help. Hathaway never had to ask.

The other CIA veteran called in to join Vertefeuille on the task force was Daniel R. Niesciur[10], then sixty, a New York native who had served in the Army in World War II, graduated from Canisius College in Buffalo, New York, and then joined the CIA in its early years. Niesciur was a Far East hand who had worked in Rangoon and Bangkok as a CIA case officer before gravitating to counterintelligence work. With his background as an Asian specialist, he had been chosen to conduct a comprehensive study of an earlier CIA mole, Larry Wu-Tai Chin, who had spied for Communist China for thirty years.

Chin was arrested in November 1985 four years after he had retired from the agency. Born in Peking, Chin had worked as an analyst for the Foreign Broadcast Information Service, an arm of the CIA. Using the code name "Mr. Yang," he was paid $140,000

[10]His name was pronounced "knee-sher."

to spy for China. He was convicted of espionage in February 1986, and two weeks later, facing life in prison, committed suicide in his jail cell. He was found with a plastic bag over his head, tied with laces from his sneakers.[11]

Niesciur's still-classified study traced the origins of the case, described how Chin had managed to spy for three decades, and assessed the damage the spy had done. Aside from hunting for moles, Niesciur's other passion was tennis; a slender, bespectacled man, he kept in shape on the courts and on at least one occasion flew to England to join the spectators at Wimbledon.

The Special Task Force was discreetly housed on the second floor at Langley headquarters, just another office among the several of the Counterintelligence Staff. The CI Staff had occupied offices in the C and D corridors of the original headquarters building from the start.[12] Hathaway's office was only two doors down from the task force.

The existence of the special unit and the work it was performing were tightly held secrets. Even close friends of Ben Pepper, who knew he had retired and come back to Langley, did not know why.

It was not, at first, known as the mole-hunt unit, although it came to be called that in time. For more than two years, the Special Task Force focused in part on the possibility of a communications penetration. If the KGB had intercepted CIA traffic, it would be of marginal use unless the Soviets could also break the U.S. code. But what if the KGB had recruited a code clerk and code keys? Then it might gain access to the cable traffic and be able to read it as well.

Nor could Vertefeuille's unit overlook the possibility of another sort of technical penetration. In 1964, the U.S. embassy in Moscow had discovered a network of microphones in the wall, and it was assumed that the KGB had managed to plant other

[11]In an ironic foreshadowing of the Ames case, Chin said it was "easy" to walk out of the CIA with reams of classified documents. "They do not search your body when you go out." *New York Times*, February 11, 1986, p. A29.

[12]When James Angleton, the CIA's most controversial mole hunter, was chief of counterintelligence more than a decade earlier, his office was room 2C43, which meant office number 43 in the C corridor on the second floor.

bugs to replace them. The embassy had been bombarded with mysterious microwaves, which may also have been linked to eavesdropping devices. In 1985, work was halted on construction of the new American embassy in Moscow after it was found to be honeycombed with tiny transmitters embedded in the steel beams, bugs that had turned the building into one large microphone.[13]

Since all of the CIA's agents had vanished in Moscow, Ben Pepper in particular was intrigued by the possibility of a technical penetration of the agency's Moscow station. That possibility assumed even greater importance in December 1986 when Marine Sergeant Clayton Lonetree, who had been stationed in Moscow, approached a CIA officer at an embassy Christmas party in Vienna and blurted out the confession of his dealings with the KGB. It was more than a year before the agency and the FBI concluded that none of the marines had allowed the KGB into the CIA's code room in Moscow.

But even as it explored the possibility of a technical penetration, the task force had also begun to focus on the possibility of a human penetration. In part for that reason, Vertefeuille insisted on keeping the size of the mole-hunt team small. Expanding its membership to include other officers with experience in Soviet operations might very well mean that the mole himself, or herself, might end up on the mole-hunt unit, which would be a total disaster.

One good reason for bringing in the two officers who had retired—they were known as "annuitants"—was that neither could be the mole, since they had left headquarters before the Soviet cases began to go bad.

Enlarging the size of the mole-hunt team would also have certainly increased the risk of alerting the mole, and others, to the fact that an intensive search was under way for a penetration. As one counterintelligence officer put it, "You can't do it with a hundred people, word gets around; you have to be discreet. Adding

[13]In 1990, after years of debate in the government and in Congress, the State Department hired a St. Louis architectural firm to redesign the bugged embassy. Plans called for demolition of the building down to the floor slab of the sixth floor and construction of five new floors above it, plus a penthouse, at a cost of $240 million.

ten more bodies does not necessarily make you more efficient."

Jeanne Vertefeuille, Pepper, and the two other mole hunters on the team had their work cut out for them; on October 22, 1986, the same month that the unit was established, the Soviets announced that Adolf G. Tolkachev, the CIA agent in Moscow, a defense researcher and expert on stealth aircraft technology, had been executed.

Tolkachev, GTSPHERE, had been caught on June 13, 1985, it will be recalled, the same day that Ames turned over his identity to the KGB in Washington. But the CIA concluded that the KGB had already learned of Tolkachev's identity from Edward Lee Howard.

On October 31, only nine days after the announcement of Tolkachev's execution, the CIA learned that KGB Lt. Col. Valery Martynov, the CIA's GTGENTILE, and Sergei Motorin, whom the CIA called GTGAUZE, were both to be executed. Unknown to the mole-hunt unit, of course, both had been betrayed by Rick Ames.

In November, as Ames was settling into his Rome assignment, Paul Redmond, the chief of the Soviet division's CI Group, wrote a memo concluding that as many as "forty-five Soviet and East European cases" had been compromised or had developed problems. In January 1987, Redmond fired off another internal memo warning, "We have suffered very serious losses. . . . In fact I am not aware of any Soviet case we have left that is producing anything worthwhile."[14]

Vertefeuille's task was to look at all the compromised cases and to discover, first, which CIA offices had handled or known of the cases and which officers had access to the files. She was asked to find any common threads among the cases that might provide clues to what had happened and to untangle how many cases might have been known to, and compromised by, Edward Lee Howard. Of the cases Howard had not known about, Vertefeuille was asked to determine how many might be explained by other factors, such as sloppy tradecraft either on the part of the agent or the CIA case officer.

One of those familiar with the work of the task force disputed a

[14]Senate Report, p. 47.

later finding of the CIA's inspector general that the unit had not drawn up a list of suspects or investigated particular persons. "That is categorically not true," the officer said. "Perhaps there was no printed list. But we had a computer, a stand-alone computer, not linked to any network, with every name anyone could think of. Ames's name was in the computer. He was on the list."

Had the task force confined itself simply to analyzing cases? "No way," the CIA officer replied. "This was not an academic exercise. We were looking for the mole."

So, as it turned out, was the FBI. When the CIA and the FBI learned in October 1986, the same month the mole-hunt unit began work, that Martynov and Motorin, the two sources in the Washington embassy, had been arrested and were to be executed, the FBI formed its own six-person team to try to find out how the two KGB assets had been caught.

Tim Caruso, a counterintelligence supervisor at FBI headquarters, was given the job. A tall, trim New Yorker, with thinning red hair, Caruso named the task force ANLACE, after a tapered medieval dagger. He chose the code name deliberately. "I wanted to get something that spoke to the ancient and nasty profession espionage is," Caruso recalled.

Caruso assigned Jim Holt, the FBI agent who had handled Martynov, to the new task force, along with two other agents from the field office and two from headquarters. But ANLACE was created to analyze how the two Russians had been detected; it was not investigating the reasons that dozens of other agents had been lost to the CIA.

However, in December the two agencies held the first of a series of eight meetings that were to take place over the next two years in a gingerly, sometimes strained effort at cooperation.[15] The rivalry between the CIA and the FBI had existed from the agency's creation in 1947, rooted partly in the fear of J. Edgar Hoover, the

---

[15]In September 1987, the FBI's ANLACE task force issued a final report. It concluded that Edward Lee Howard would have had access to the files on Martynov, GTGENTILE, but would not have known about Sergei Motorin, GTGAUZE.

FBI chief, that the new, upstart intelligence agency would threaten the bureau's power. The turf wars were legendary; in 1970 Hoover, piqued, cut off all liaison with the CIA.[16]

The friction over the Howard case, when the CIA had sat on the problem for two years, still rankled. But the difficulty went much deeper than a particular case. In its counterintelligence role, the FBI, a law enforcement agency, was primarily interested in catching spies. The CIA, in the business of collecting intelligence, was more interested in letting cases run to see where they might lead. The agency was not particularly anxious to put Soviet spies in jail, although of course it wanted to root out any moles in its own ranks. The competing goals of the two agencies often led to conflicts between the attorney general and the director of the CIA over the prosecution of particular espionage cases.

Moreover, in addition to the difference in their missions, the CIA and the FBI were often caught up in the normal bureaucratic rivalries that exist between any two government agencies with overlapping responsibilities and common turf. The bureau and the agency were somewhat like lovers in a long-running and contentious relationship. They could not live without each other, but the years had been marked by arguments, brawls, suspicion, and mutual distrust.

It was also characterized, particularly at the working level, by respect, camaraderie, and sometimes, mutual admiration. In sum, the CIA-FBI relationship was a complicated one, not easily portrayed by shorthand descriptions.

The complexity of that relationship was illustrated by what happened after the first meeting between the two agencies on the compromised cases. One of the CIA officers present expressed his concern to Burton Gerber, the chief of the Soviet division, over the FBI's inquisitiveness about the CIA's organization and operations.

Although the FBI had exposed some of its own "dirty linen" at the meeting, the CIA man wrote in a memo, "A conscious decision

---

[16]Contacts at the working level continued, but formal liaison was not restored between the FBI and the CIA until after Hoover's death in 1972.

has to be made here concerning the degree to which we are going to cooperate with, and open ourselves up to, the FBI."[17] The answer was not long in coming.

A KGB mole might be destroying the CIA from within, killing agents and crippling the agency's ability to spy on the Soviet Union—at the time its main reason for existence—but there were limits to how far Langley would go to cooperate with outsiders.

For the next two years, as the joint meetings continued, the agency gave the bureau information about the two doomed former Washington sources, and it provided sanitized summaries of its own compromised cases. But the CIA would not open up its files to the FBI.

[17]Senate Report, p. 45.

14

THE MILLIONAIRES

Even before he and Rosario had returned from Rome in July 1989, Rick Ames had gotten in touch with a northern Virginia real estate broker who specialized in selling houses to foreign service officers.

Anne Gomez, an associate at M. B. Kirn Real Estate, had several houses ready for the Ameses to look at. The couple thought that the spacious two-story residence on North Randolph Street in Arlington would be adequate for their needs. It had five bedrooms, built-in closets, and a family room with a fireplace. The split-level brick home belonged to a prosperous lawyer. The price was $540,000.

It was obvious from their clothes and their demeanor that the couple had money, which became even clearer when Ames announced that he would pay the entire amount in cash. Still, a real estate transaction of that size with no mortgage was unusual. "We do get cash sales," said Mary B. Kirn, the company's owner. "It does happen. But it doesn't happen every day."

Why Ames chose to pay cash when a conventional mortgage

would have aroused less curiosity is something of a mystery. But cash it was, and to launder the KGB money, Rick moved the funds from his mother-in-law's account in Switzerland, of which he was the trustee, to his bank in northern Virginia. As part of the scam surrounding the house purchase, and to avoid paying taxes on the money, Ames disguised the transaction to look like a gift from his mother-in-law. Soon after their return from Rome, Rick and Rosario flew to Colombia. Ames accompanied Rosario's mother, Cecilia, to the U.S. embassy in Bogotá where she executed a gift letter so that it would appear that the cash for the house was a present from her.

Ames had liked tooling around Rome in the silver-gray Jaguar he bought from Giles FitzHerbert, so one of his first orders of business back in Washington was to buy another. This time the Jaguar was new, white, and cost around $49,500.

Not long after Rick and Rosario moved into the house in Arlington, their good friend David Samson paid them a visit. He was back from a two-year tour in the American embassy in Manila, where he had been posted after Mexico City.

In Mexico, Rick had lived modestly and complained about being broke. And Samson knew that Rosario's family, while minor aristocrats, were not wealthy. He remembered Rosario's nondescript car in Mexico. It had been stolen; the Colombian ambassador had raised hell about it with Los Piños, the presidential palace, and the car mysteriously had been recovered.

"That's why it came as a great shock to me when I saw Rick's house for the first time," Samson recalled. "It was obvious it was a very expensive house. I said. 'Rick, how did you get this house?' And he smiled and said, 'Not only did I get it, I paid cash for it. It cost over half a million. Cecilia paid for it.'"

Samson was flabbergasted. "I said, 'What are the agency's security people going to think of this?' He said, 'You know, this was all done legitimately. Cecilia took this money to the embassy in Bogotá and declared it.'"

"Don't you have to pay taxes?" Samson asked.

"No," Ames replied. "As long as it comes into the country and is declared, we don't have to pay taxes on it."

GOOD TIMES AND BAD TIMES:

Acapulco, April 1983: Aldrich Ames (*left*) reclining, and Rosario Casas relax on the beach at the Mexican resort. At the time, Ames worked in the CIA station in Mexico City and Rosario was on the CIA's payroll.

Alexandria, Virginia, March 1994: Manacled and chained, Rick and Rosario are escorted from the federal courthouse two weeks after their arrest by the FBI.

Wedding photograph of Ames's parents, Carleton and Rachel Aldrich Ames. They were married in New Richmond, Wisconsin, December 1, 1938. Carleton later went to work for the CIA in Burma.

The Ames family: Rick (*center*) standing, his sisters Nancy (*left*) and Alison, with their parents. Photo was taken about 1958–59 during Rick's senior year in high school.

At McLean High School, Ames was voted "wittiest" by his senior class. Here he hams it up in this photograph from the 1959 yearbook.

Shortly before leaving Washington for Burma in 1953, Rick (*left*) poses proudly in his scout's uniform with his uncle, Frank LaBrash, a West Point cadet.

". . . his first taste of the good life." In Rangoon, Rick Ames lived in this large oriental-style house with servants.

Rangoon, Burma, 1954: Aldrich Ames, age thirteen, won second place in the men's long distance race at the Kokine Swim Club.

Aldrich Ames, as Cassius (*standing facing camera*) washes his hands in the blood of Caesar in a play at McLean High School, spring 1958.

Ames, just after his twenty-sixth birthday, chopped wood on a weekend outing with friends in Sugar Grove, West Virginia.

Rick Ames, sporting a handlebar mustache, celebrates Christmas 1979 with his sisters Alison (*left*) and Nancy (*center*).

LANGLEY'S MAN:

Rick Ames (*left*) and his best friend in Mexico, David Samson, and their dates enjoying a weekend in Acapulco about November of 1982. About a month later, Ames started dating Rosario, his future wife.

The first published photograph of Igor I. Shurygin, the mysterious KGB counterintelligence chief in Mexico City. Ames developed a close relationship with the KGB man, code-named GTPOTATO by the CIA, in long drinking sessions in Mexico—three years before Ames himself became a KGB spy.

August 9, 1985: Rick Ames relaxes with sisters Alison (*left*) and Nancy, and his mother, Rachel (*far right*), at the rehearsal dinner in Merrifield, Virginia, on the eve of Rick and Rosario's wedding. Ames had a secret—he was already a spy for the KGB.

At the CIA, Ames, despite a serious alcohol problem, was appointed chief of the Soviet counterintelligence branch at the agency's Langley headquarters, a job that gave him access to the innermost secrets of the CIA.

The electrifying news that the KGB had a mole at the heart of the CIA was tightly held at the headquarters of the KGB's First Chief Directorate, its foreign intelligence arm, in Yasnevo, on the ring road along the southern outskirts of Moscow. Ironically, the modern buildings in Yasnevo resemble the CIA's own headquarters in Langley, Virginia.

In April 1985, Ames boldly walked into the Soviet embassy in Washington offering the first three names of agents to the KGB in exchange for $50,000.

June 13, 1985: It was here during lunch at Chadwick's, a Washington restaurant along the Georgetown waterfront, that Ames handed over a plastic bag containing the identities of every major CIA source inside the Soviet Union. Ten agents were shot as a result. The KGB, in gratitude, promised Ames his first $2 million. Ames gave the names to...

... this man, Sergei D. Chuvakhin, a Soviet diplomat designated by the KGB as Ames's bag man. Ames and Chuvakhin lunched regularly, and the Russian handed over cash in amounts ranging from $20,000 to $50,000 for the CIA's secrets.

Ames debriefed Soviet defector Vitaly Yurchenko in 1985, reporting to the KGB everything the Russian said. After three months, Yurchenko went back to the Soviet Union.

Aldrich Ames and son, Paul, Rome, early 1989.

> Dear Friend,
> this is Your balance sheet as on the May 1, 1989.
>
> * All in all You have been appropriated ---- 2,705,000 $
> * Keam the time of openning of Your
> account in our Bank (December 26,
> 1986) Your profit is -------------------- 385,077$ 28c
> (including 14,468$ 94c as profit on bonds, which we
> bought for You on the sum of 250,000$)
> * Since December 1989 Your salary is ------ 300,000$
> * All in all we have delivered to You ----- 1,881,811$ 51c
> * On the above date You have on Your
> account (including 250,000$ in bonds) --- 1,535,077$ 28c
>
> N.N. We believe that these pictures would give You some
> idea about the beautiful piece of land on the river bank,
> which from now belongs to You forever. We decided not to take
> pictures of housing in this area with the understanding that
> You have much better idea of how Your country-house (dacha)
> should look like.
>
> Good luck,

In Rome in June of 1989, Ames received this "balance sheet" from the KGB, indicating that he had been paid more than $1.8 million. The "Dear Friend" letter also enclosed pictures (*right*) of sylvan land along a river where Ames could build a dacha, presumably when he retired from his life as a mole.

". . . the beautiful piece of land on the river bank, which from now belongs to You forever."

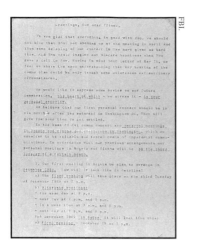

June 1989: While still in Rome for the CIA, Ames received this nine-page letter from the KGB that included a list of tasks. In the letter the Soviets went on to say that Ames's top priority was to uncover CIA moles inside Soviet intelligence. The FBI recovered the letter from a closet in Ames's home after his arrest on February 21, 1994.

It's a wonderful life: Rick and Rosario, millionaires now, are a picture of happiness as they dine with friends at a Chinese restaurant in northern Virginia in August 1990.

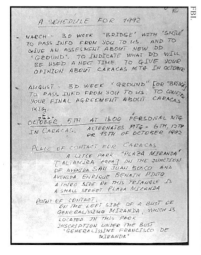

The KGB and its successor, the SVR, gave Ames a communications schedule each year, detailing signal sites, dead drops, and meeting places. This schedule for 1992 tells Ames exactly when and where to meet his KGB contact, at a statue in a park in Caracas.

Mailbox, signal site SMILE, on the corner of 37th and R Streets in Georgetown with chalk mark that Ames made on October 13, 1993, to signal that he would meet the KGB in Bogotá in November.

My dear friends,

All is well with me and I have recovered somewhat from my earlier period of pessimism and anxiety. My security situation is unchanged -- that is to say, I have no indications of any problems. My family is well and my wife has accomodated herself to understanding what I am doing, in a very supportive way. I will come to Caracas for the meeting as planned...

Rosario knows. In this August 1992 message to the KGB, Ames claims that his wife is "very supportive" of his spying. The FBI reconstructed the note from a printer ribbon it recovered from the Ameses' trash in October 1993.

© David Wise.

THE SEARCH BEGINS:

Edward Lee Howard relaxes on the deck of his dacha near Moscow. At first, the CIA thought Howard was responsible for betraying all of the agents it was losing. Then it realized there had to be another source as well. The author took this photo in October 1991.

Diego Goldberg/Sygma.

Under CIA director William J. Casey the CIA in October of 1986 created a small, supersecret task force to try to discover why Langley was losing all of its agents in Moscow. The mole-hunt team was headed by a veteran Soviet specialist, Jeanne R. Vertefeuille.

John Maguire.

"No one ever told us we had a mole. . . " William H. Webster, the former FBI director who succeeded Casey at the CIA, said he was never told the full extent of the agent losses.

Agence France-Presse.

". . . my God, I would have told the president." Robert M. Gates, Webster's successor as CIA director, says he was unaware that Ames was under suspicion.

THE HUNTERS:

Special Agent Leslie G. Wiser, Jr., led the FBI team that placed the Ameses under surveillance, wiretapped and bugged their home, and gathered the evidence to arrest Ames and his wife.

Assistant U. S. Attorney Mark J. Hulkower successfully prosecuted Ames and his wife for conspiracy to commit espionage.

Robert M. "Bear" Bryant, the FBI assistant director in charge of the National Security Division, had overall responsibility for the Ames investigation.

"We knew we were dealing with a live penetration." John F. Lewis, Jr., the FBI's number-two counterintelligence official, supervised the ten-month investigation that ended with the arrest of the Ameses.

THE QUARRY:

Rosario Ames is caught by an FBI surveillance camera.

Rick Ames in Bogotá, November 1993. The FBI secretly videotaped the CIA mole as he strolled through a shopping mall to meet his Russian contact.

Ames paid $540,000 in cash for this five-bedroom, split-level house in Arlington, Virginia.

I AM READY TO MEET AT B ON 1 OCT.
I CANNOT READ NORTH 13-19 SEPT.
IF YOU WILL MEET AT B ON 1 OCT. PLS SIGNAL NORTH u OF 20 SEPT TO CONFI. NO MESSAGE AT PIPE.
IF YOU CANNOT MEE. 1 OCT, SIGNAL NORTH AFTER 27 SEPT WITH MESSAGE AT PIPE.

On September 15, 1993, the FBI recovered this draft note from Ames's trash, confirming that he was ready to meet his Russian contact in Bogotá. It was the first concrete evidence that Ames was a spy.

TOPHAT in a tophat. Soviet General Dimitri F. Polyakov (*far right*) was the highest-ranking and most important Soviet source executed as a result of Aldrich Ames's treachery. TOPHAT was recruited by the FBI in January 1962, and later turned over to the CIA. This previously unpublished photo of Polyakov and two unidentified Soviet companions was taken aboard the *Queen Elizabeth* in June 1962, as TOPHAT was returning to Moscow.

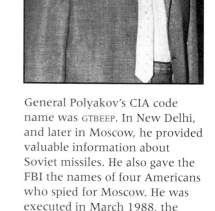

FBI counterintelligence agent John F. Mabey recruited Polyakov in 1962 in a midnight rendezvous at the deserted Grant's Tomb in New York. It was Mabey who gave him the code name TOPHAT.

General Polyakov's CIA code name was GTBEEP. In New Delhi, and later in Moscow, he provided valuable information about Soviet missiles. He also gave the FBI the names of four Americans who spied for Moscow. He was executed in March 1988, the Russians later announced.

MOODY—Donald F., please write as promised. Uncle Charles and sister Clara are well and would like to hear from you. Don't forget address Dave, Doug and spouses. Travelling? When? Where? We hope for family reunion soon. Regards and best wishes, brothers, Edward H. and John F. Closter, N.J.

The FBI used this ad in the *New York Times* in May of 1964 to communicate with TOPHAT in Moscow. The men's names were signal sites in the Soviet capital, and the women's names were dead drops.

KGB Lt. Colonel Valery F. Martynov, code-named GTGENTILE by the CIA and PIMENTA by the FBI, was jointly recruited by the two agencies in Washington in 1982 under the COURTSHIP program. After Ames betrayed Martynov, the KGB sent him back to Moscow on a pretext. He was executed by a firing squad in May 1987.

KGB Major Sergei M. Motorin, CIA code name GTGAUZE, FBI code name MEGAS. Like Martynov, Motorin was stationed in Washington. Six months after Motorin went back to Moscow, Ames gave him away, and he was executed.

Adolf G. Tolkachev is arrested by agents of the KGB in 1985. Tolkachev, a Soviet defense researcher working for the CIA, was betrayed to the KGB by both Edward Lee Howard and Aldrich Ames. He was executed in September 1986.

Courtesy of U.S. Congressman Chris Smith.

CIA agent Vladimir V. Potashov (*far left*) photographed in the brutal Perm-35 prison in the Ural mountains during a visit by an American congressional delegation in 1990. One of many agents imprisoned because of Ames, Potashov was released by President Boris Yeltsin of Russia in 1992 and now lives in the United States.

NYT Pictures.

Michael Trevillion.

The KGB's Boris Yuzhin, CIA code name CKTWINE, served five years in a Soviet prison after Ames betrayed him. He now lives in California.

The KGB's Oleg Gordievsky worked for MI6, British intelligence, for eleven years when he was suddenly recalled to Moscow in 1985. Ames gave Gordievsky's name to the Russians, but the KGB may already have suspected him. MI6 got Gordievsky out of Russia in a daring rescue operation. He now lives in England.

Ames had personally handled Sergei
Fedorenko for the CIA in New York in the
mid-1970s but betrayed him to the KGB
anyway. The CIA was suspicious that
Fedorenko was never arrested, but the FBI
backed Fedorenko, who now lives in New
England.

Col. Sergei Bokhan of the GRU,
Soviet military intelligence, was a
CIA agent code-named GTBLIZZARD.
He narrowly escaped from Athens in
1985 after Ames turned him in to
the KGB.

February 21, 1994, the moment of truth. "There must be some mistake," Ames kept saying as he was handcuffed by FBI agents. "Espionage, me?" he asked.

In the wake of the Ames case, the CIA became the butt of cartoonists.

". . . the eleventh victim of Aldrich Ames." CIA director R. James Woolsey abruptly resigned at the end of 1994.

Ames said something else that Samson remembered long afterward. "He made a very strange comment. He said, 'I've decided I'm going to live as well as I possibly can for the duration of my stay in Washington.'"

Samson did not know what to make of his friend's new affluence. It was not only the house. Equally surprising was the fact that Ames seemed to have acquired property in South America. "He and Rosario had decided once they retired they would go off to live in Colombia," Samson said.

"He told me that a friend of Cecilia's owned beach property near Santa Marta. They had shown me pictures. They said this guy had a big estate and it was important it not be bought by Club Med or a hotel, and he was pleased to sell portions to his lifetime friends."

The oceanfront land that Rick described to Samson was one of three properties that the Ameses acquired in Colombia.[1] The beach property was located in Guajira, a picturesque peninsula that juts into the Caribbean in Colombia's far north.

"I said, 'Gee, maybe I'd like to buy some of that.'" Rick said, 'Don't worry, Dave, there will always be a place for you on our property.' Which I took to mean room for me to build a house."

Samson was delighted with his friend's good fortune, but still a little puzzled by it. "My first reaction was, well, that's a surprise, I had the impression Rosario's family had no money. But on the other hand her father had been a senator and a governor and I knew she knew President Turbay because I was in her apartment once when he telephoned her.[2] Anyone in politics has the possibility of amassing terrific wealth, particularly if the president of the country is your buddy. Maybe there was money salted away somewhere."

Rich Thurman, the foreign service officer who had become a close friend of Ames in Mexico City, had a similar experience. Thurman had been posted to Brazil and then lectured at the war

---

[1] At the time of their arrest, the Ameses also owned an apartment in Bogotá and a condo in Cartegena, a fashionable seaside resort.

[2] The apartment, of course, was the flat in Mexico City that the CIA was paying Rosario $200 a month to use as a safe house.

college at Maxwell Air Force Base in Alabama. On a visit to Washington to put his daughter in college, he stayed with Rick and Rosario for a couple of days in their new house in Arlington. When he arrived, Thurman's eyes popped. There was a Jaguar out front, and Rosario's Honda Accord LX-i, a large hot tub on the back deck.

"Rick, this is unbelievable, this is fabulous, how can you do this?" Thurman asked.

It's all from an inheritance from Rosario's father, Ames replied.

There were other signs of his friend's newfound wealth. Rick and Rosario had begun remodeling the kitchen; the Ameses and Thurman ate out each night.

At the CIA, colleagues noticed a much snappier-looking Rick Ames, with capped teeth and expensive Italian suits and shoes. They also noticed that he drove a Jaguar into the CIA parking lot each day. A few who knew Ames well were aware that he had Filipino servants whom he had flown to and from the Philippines. Varying the lies that he told David Samson and Rich Thurman, Rick explained to other friends that Rosario's uncle bought him the house because he was so pleased at Paul's birth.

As he settled back into Langley headquarters, Ames did run into a problem. The problem was Milton A. Bearden, the new chief of the Soviet division. Six foot one, with light brown hair and glasses, Bearden wore cowboy boots and a western belt. Although he was thought of as a Texan, since he had grown up in Houston, he was born in Oklahoma and spent his early childhood during World War II in Washington State, where his father had helped to build the atom bomb as a manager on the Manhattan Project.

Bearden had graduated from Yale, like so many senior DO officers, and was enrolled in a Ph.D. program at the University of Texas when the CIA offered him a job. He had served in Germany, Hong Kong, Switzerland, and Africa, then returned to headquarters in July 1985 as deputy chief of the Soviet division under Burton Gerber.

There he met Ames for the first time; it was three months after Rick had begun spying for the KGB. Then in 1986, Bearden had been sent to Pakistan to run the covert war against the Soviet-backed regime in Afghanistan. The mujahedin rebels, aided by the CIA, had prevailed; the last Soviet troops walked over the Friendship Bridge and out of Afghanistan in February 1989.

Five months later, Bearden was back at headquarters, replacing Gerber as the new chief of the Soviet division. The communist regimes of Eastern Europe had already begun to crumble; the Berlin Wall toppled that November. Trying to adapt the division to these new conditions, Bearden moved twenty to twenty-five midlevel officers out of FE; they were officers whom he felt had been shaped by the past. Rick Ames, whom Bearden considered lazy, was in the group slated to go.

Somehow, Ames slipped through the net. Instead of being forced out of the division as Bearden wanted, Ames that summer ended up as European branch chief of the Soviet division's External Operations Group. When that job was eliminated by a reorganization in December, Ames managed to land on his feet and remain in SE as branch chief for Czechoslovak operations. All this was very good for Ames and the KGB, since it meant he was still in a position to acquire, and pass on, useful secrets to Moscow.

He did so through personal meetings abroad and dead drops around Washington. The system of signal sites and dead drops followed classic KGB tradecraft. First, Ames would place a signal, such as a chalk mark on a mailbox, to alert the KGB that he was ready to load a drop, to place classified information or a message in a preselected hiding place. It worked the same way in reverse; the KGB would mark a signal site and use a dead drop to pass money and instructions to Ames.

In Washington, the Ames operation was now under the supervision of Ivan Semyonovich Gromakov, who had replaced Stanislav Androsov as the KGB resident in Washington in November 1986. Gromakov looked like a KGB *apparatchik* right out of central casting. Short and bald, with thick glasses, Gromakov spoke good English but better German; he had been previously stationed in Bonn and was in Berlin for eight years in the 1950s. He was a shrewd veteran of the KGB's First Chief Directorate. For Gromakov, supervising Ames was the crown jewel in his long career.

And the KGB kept the money coming. Ames hardly knew where to stash it all. In addition to his Swiss bank accounts in Zurich, Ames had opened an account in Geneva, one in Bogotá at the Banco Internacional de Colombia, and another in Rome in the notorious Banca Nazionale del Lavoro, or BNL. Ames also maintained accounts in eight banks or investment companies in the United States, including two accounts at the Dominion Bank of Virginia, and accounts at the Riggs National Bank of Washington and Citibank and Morgan Stanley and Company in New York. Millions of dollars flowed through the accounts.

Although Ames's position in the Soviet division's Czech branch was of interest in Yasnevo, both Ames and his Soviet handlers must have thirsted for the days when he was in the very center of CIA operations against the KGB. And so in 1990, Ames asked to handle sensitive Soviet cases again. Turned down, he put in for the job of deputy chief of station in Moscow. Again, Ames was rejected.

But there was some solace for the KGB. Although in his performance evaluations Ames ranked in the bottom 10 percent of GS-14 officers in the Directorate of Operations, he was put on a promotion panel giving him access to the records of all the younger officers in the DO. Passing on their names and details of their backgrounds would make it that much easier for the KGB to spot them when they were sent overseas and possibly to target for recruitment any who, for one reason or another, were considered vulnerable.

In November 1989, just before Ames landed in his job as branch chief for Czechoslovak operations, the CIA received the very first tip pointing to Aldrich Ames. A woman employee of the agency who knew Ames well reported that he had bought an expensive house and was living beyond his means. The informant also knew that Ames had access to the compromised Soviet cases in which agents had disappeared. And she knew Ames well enough to know that Rosario's family was not wealthy. Based on this information, Dan Payne, a thin, bespectacled young CIA investigator assigned to the mole-hunt unit, began a financial inquiry into Ames's lavish spending.

Payne, a native of East Chicago, Indiana, had joined the agency in 1984 after graduating from Ball State University in Muncie. At age twenty-nine, more or less self-trained as an investigator, he suddenly found himself a key figure in the search for the most destructive mole in the history of the CIA.

CIA director William Webster, responding to the Howard case and the 1985 agent losses, had created a new Counterintelligence Center on April 1, 1988. It replaced the Counterintelligence Staff. As part of the effort to upgrade the importance of CI, Webster also provided that the director of the new center would simultaneously have the title of assistant deputy director for counterintelligence, or ADDO/CI. Webster named Gus Hathaway, who was director of the CI Staff, to head the new center. The mole-hunt unit that was trying to find the cause of the agent losses was folded into the center.

In June 1990, Ames flew to Vienna for a personal meeting with Vladimir Mechulayev, the KGB handler whom Ames knew as VLAD and who had met with Ames three times in Rome. After Ames returned from his tour in Italy, he had no face-to-face meetings with the KGB in the United States; given the close FBI surveillance of Soviet intelligence officers, it was considered too risky. Ames was supposed to meet VLAD in Vienna again in October. Confused, he flew to Zurich instead and missed the meeting. Since Ames drank heavily before and during his meetings with his KGB handlers, often leaving these encounters in an alcoholic fog, it is not entirely surprising that he forgot his instructions and flew to Switzerland instead of Austria.

In the same month of October, a full year after the woman CIA employee had warned that Ames was spending lavishly, an astonishing development occurred. Ames was assigned to the CIA Counterintelligence Center. Milton Bearden, the Soviet division chief, had finally succeeded in pushing Ames out the door, in part because of the security questions that had been raised about him, in addition to his uneven work record. Bearden maneuvered Ames out of the division by selecting another officer as chief of the Czech branch. That forced Ames to look for a job elsewhere in the DO. And what better spot than the Counterintelligence Center?

Rick Ames, master mole, was now working in the very CIA component designed to protect the agency against penetration.

The center was supposed to find moles. Ames was given this mystifying, mind-boggling assignment even though he was under investigation. By this time Gus Hathaway had retired. In March 1990 his deputy, Hugh E. "Ted" Price, had moved up to be director of the CI Center.

Ames was not, fortunately, assigned to the mole-hunt unit itself. He was given a position in the USSR branch of the center's Analysis Group. Amazingly, both Price and Ames's supervisor, the head of the group, were aware that Ames was considered a security risk. But the Analysis Group needed a DO case officer, and Rick Ames was welcomed aboard. Once again, bureaucratic needs took precedence over common sense.

Price, then fifty-three, was a short, sandy-haired man who favored tweeds and fiddled constantly with a pipe.[3] He was a New Yorker, a Yale graduate, and an ex-marine who joined the CIA 1965. A Far East hand who spoke Mandarin Chinese, Price ran the Counterintelligence Center for ten months, until December, and then switched over to the job of assistant deputy director for operations.

Early in December 1990, two months after Ames went to work in the Counterintelligence Center, he flew to Bogotá. He was following the instructions he had received in Rome, the KGB arrangement to meet Ames on the first Tuesday of every December at an "iron site" in Bogotá. There he was introduced to his second KGB case officer, ANDRE. Later, when Ames cooperated after his plea bargain with federal prosecutors, the FBI, based on Ames's description, was able to identify ANDRE as Yuri Karetkin, a KGB officer. A few months after the encounter in Bogotá, Ames was supposed to meet ANDRE again, in Vienna. Ames flew there, but for the second time he was confused about the site and the meeting never took place.

[3]In September 1990, CIA director William Webster banned smoking inside Langley headquarters, effective January 1, 1991. After that, presumably, Price's pipe was unlit. Smoking at CIA was allowed only outside the building or in the courtyard. Aldrich Ames would go outside to smoke, and sometimes, by gossiping with fellow smokers from different offices, picked up information that he passed on to the KGB.

Despite these problems, the KGB was pleased, and probably amused, that Ames had landed a job in the CI Center, for several reasons. First, it must have reassured the First Chief Directorate in Yasnevo that Ames was not under any serious suspicion—surely if it were otherwise he would never have been assigned to counter-intelligence. Second, Ames was preparing analyses of KGB operations, which was truly placing the fox in charge of the chicken coop. The KGB was now in a position to influence, and read, the content of the CIA's studies about the KGB. The black mirrors were nicely in place.

And finally, in the CI Center, Ames had access to extremely sensitive double-agent operations. Intelligence agencies at times dangle double agents in front of the opposition. If a CIA double-agent operation was successful, the KGB would recruit an agent who was really under the control of Langley. The agency would then be in a position to feed misleading information to the KGB through the double agent. It could also learn of gaps in the KGB's knowledge by what the Soviets asked the double agent to find out.

With Ames inside the CI Center, the KGB knew which "dangles" and walk-ins were really under CIA control. It could turn them away or manipulate them to its own advantage. It could allow an operation to run, for example; it could let the CIA think it was planting misleading information, all the while knowing the truth. The puppets would dance, but Yasnevo would be holding the strings.

The Analysis Group of the CI Center was housed in what is known as a "vaulted area," which could be entered only after punching in a code on an electronic lock. Inside were large shelves that pulled out, containing files on all of the CIA's most important cases, from Penkovsky and Popov to more recent ones. Since the vault itself was in effect a large safe, the files were unlocked and easily accessible.

Ames worked alongside a dozen or more people who spent much of their time analyzing old cases, including some that had failed, to detect what went wrong. It meant that Ames could look at old cases and learn the names of CIA and FBI assets, some of whom had returned undetected to the Soviet Union.

Ames was not limited to the dusty files of the past. He could tap into the CIA's computers as well. Ames had known nothing about computers in Mexico. But he had become computer literate in Rome; he had worked hard at becoming proficient. He had taught himself the intricacies of DOS and WordPerfect and knew how to navigate smoothly through a database. And in the Counterintelligence Center, Ames now had access to highly sensitive databases that contained the details, among other subjects, of the double-agent cases. He could and did browse at leisure through the secret electronic files. For the KGB, it was rather like subscribing to a new and highly classified database called CIA Online, with the First Chief Directorate of the KGB as its sole, albeit unknown, client.

The CIA's computers in the Directorate of Operations do not have floppy drives; they are deliberately designed that way to prevent anyone from downloading data onto floppy disks. But many other agency computers did have floppy disk drives. Ames was not at this point downloading data onto floppies—that came later—but he did use a computer to pass some information to the Soviets. In Rome, Ames wrote messages to the KGB on his home computer, printed them out, and gave his handlers the hard copies.

Back in Washington, Ames began passing computer disks to the KGB. Ames himself devised a system to use floppy disks, which were password protected. That meant that only someone with access to the password— in this case Rick Ames and the KGB— could read the disks if they fell into the wrong hands. Ames used his computer to write one- or two-page messages to the KGB, which he transferred to floppy disks. He would then leave the floppies in a dead drop, and the same disks would later be returned to him at another drop site. The bulk of the information that Ames passed, however, continued to be in the form of actual CIA documents.

Ames described the CIA's computer systems to the KGB but was surprised to discover that, at least at the field level, his Soviet case officers knew little about computers. They were quite proud of themselves when they figured out how to boot up their computers into WordPerfect and read the latest messages from their most valuable mole.

In December 1990, the same month that Ames flew to Bogotá to keep his rendezvous at the "iron site" with ANDRE, his backup KGB handler, Ames betrayed yet another CIA source in Moscow. Ames had earlier passed along information about an agency asset in the KGB's Second Chief Directorate, which was responsible for counterintelligence inside the Soviet Union.[4] But Ames did not, at first, know the man's CIA crypt.

Around December 17, Ames wrote a message to the KGB: "I did learn that GTPROLOGUE is the cryptonym for the SCD officer I provided you information about earlier."[5] If the CIA learned the fate of GTPROLOGUE, it did not disclose it, but after these messages from Ames, his life expectancy could not have been high.

Like a cat, Ames seemed to have nine lives. He did his damage in the Counterintelligence Center for one year. Then, in September 1991, he wormed his way back into the Soviet division as chief of the KGB Working Group. Somehow, Ames managed to gain the approval of Milton Bearden, the same division chief who had eased him out a year earlier.

Although Ames, as head of the KGB Working Group, did not have access to current operations against the Soviets, he did once again have access to the files and personnel of the division.

In December, after only three months as chief of the working group, Ames was transferred to the CIA's Counternarcotics Center (CNC), his fifth job in a little more than two years. Later, after Ames and his wife were arrested, the CIA implied that the transfer to the CNC was a clever stratagem designed to maneuver an officer under suspicion out of the Soviet division and into a part of CIA where he could do less damage. In fact, there is some reason to think that the transfer was fairly routine, just another lateral move for Ames, a place to put him. If anyone thought about the possible security implications of the fact that Ames's wife, Rosario,

---

[4]The Second Chief Directorate had functions roughly equivalent to the intelligence division of the FBI; the First Chief Directorate, a foreign intelligence service, paralleled the CIA.

[5]FBI affidavit, February 21, 1994, p. 17.

was from Colombia—a country that was the epicenter of the world's cocaine cartels—it did not affect his assignment to counternarcotics work.

William Webster and his deputy, Richard J. Kerr, had established the Counternarcotics Center a year earlier. As the cold war was winding down, the CIA was seeking new directions to justify its existence. Fighting the international drug traffic was one obvious target.

Ames's supervisors in the Counternarcotics Center were not told at first that he was the subject of a security investigation, however. And Ames, with his background in Soviet operations, was assigned to the branch of the center that monitored drug trafficking in the Soviet Union.

The very month that Ames began work in the CNC, the Soviet Union collapsed. That cataclysmic event alarmed Ames, since it could have endangered his cash flow from Moscow. The Gucci shoes might become history. In the event, there was no need to worry; the KGB was split up and its various functions farmed out to other units of the Russian Federation. But the First Chief Directorate, the foreign intelligence arm, remained intact, metamorphosing into the SVR, the Sluzhba Vneshnei Razvedki, or Foreign Intelligence Service.[6] It stayed in its modern headquarters in Yasnevo and continued to run Aldrich Ames as its agent inside the CIA.

The SVR, sensitive to Ames's worries about a Russia under new management, was quick to reassure its man in Langley. His handlers told him that the political changes in Moscow would make no difference; the same officers would continue to run him.

But Ames was apprehensive that the collapse of communism might increase the likelihood that a defector who knew something about him might come over and provide information that would lead to his downfall. He discussed his fears of betrayal with the

---

[6]In September 1991, even before the collapse of the Soviet Union, Mikhail Gorbachev had designated the First Chief Directorate as an independent agency and named Yevgeny M. Primakov, a veteran diplomat who was his closest foreign policy adviser, to head it. President Boris Yeltsin of Russia named Primakov chief of the new SVR.

KGB. "I talked about this with my handlers and they agreed in general but they said, you know, we're still, the few of us working on the case, we're still here."[7]

After the breakup of the KGB, there was talk in Langley of actual cooperation between the SVR and the CIA. In time, CIA directors Robert M. Gates and R. James Woolsey would journey to Moscow and meet with Yevgeny Primakov, the head of the SVR. But the idea that the CIA and the successor to the KGB might cooperate "got kind of a horselaugh inside the agency," according to Ames.[8] He did not worry that even the assignment of a few SVR officers to Langley, if it ever got that far, would lead to his unmasking.

Ames's bank accounts were proof enough that the collapse of the Soviet Union had no effect on his payments from the KGB. His cash deposits in three Washington-area banks during 1992, the first year he was working for the SVR, actually more than doubled over the previous year. In 1991, Ames deposited $91,100; in 1992, his deposits were $187,000. All were "structured," that is, in amounts of $10,000 or less. Ames did this to try to circumvent the law requiring banks to file Currency Transaction Reports (CTRs) with the Treasury Department when they receive amounts larger than $10,000. Such "structuring" to evade the law is itself a crime.

Ames and his wife managed to spend almost $1.4 million, including the purchase of their house, between 1985 and 1993, racking up credit card bills totaling $455,000 during this period, or an average of about $50,000 a year. The couple spent just under $100,000 on home improvements and $25,000 on tuition for Rosario, who was pursuing her graduate studies in philosophy at Georgetown University. They paid Paul's Salvadoran nanny, Maria Trinidad Chirino, $14,300 a year. All of this on an annual CIA salary that at the time of Ames's arrest was $69,843.

In the years after Ames returned from Rome, he frequently met his friend Rich Thurman for lunch. The routine seldom varied. Ames would drive in from Langley, pick up his friend at the State Department, and proceed to Mr. Eagan's, an old-fashioned saloon

[7] House Interview, pp. 66–67.
[8] Ibid., p. 67.

and restaurant on Connecticut Avenue just below Dupont Circle. It is the sort of place where the gravel-voiced proprietress, Jackie Eagan, jokes with the customers and knows everybody.

At the lunches, Rick would drink, sometimes doze off for a few minutes, and then come awake. Yet he would be able to drive Thurman back to the State Department, drop him off, and return to the CIA. After these liquid lunches, he would caution Thurman, "Don't tell Rosario."

It was fun, though, just like the old days in Mexico. Thurman could not help but notice and wonder, however, at one small detail that was new. When they drove to Mr. Eagan's, Rick would park anywhere. Once, he parked in front of a fire hydrant. He got a ticket, but he didn't seem to care if he got tickets.

Thurman was puzzled by his friend's behavior; it was really strange. Rick Ames, Thurman realized, did not pay any attention to parking meters. He didn't bother to put quarters in.

15

IT'S NOT EASY HUNTING MOLES

We have never found a real 'mole' in CIA," Gus Hathaway, the agency's chief of counterintelligence, assured the Senate Intelligence Committee in November 1985.

"We have not found any full-time staff officers who were recruited by the Soviets and served them while they worked for CIA. . . . There has never been an agent of the Soviets in the center of the CIA itself. We may have failed to find such an agent, but I doubt it."

Hathaway's bland assurances to the senators were carefully phrased, because Edward Lee Howard had escaped into the New Mexico desert only two months earlier. But Howard was not working in Langley at the time he vanished—he had been dismissed in 1983—so Hathaway was able to say, accurately, that the agency had never found a "real 'mole'" as he defined the term.

At the time that he testified, however, Aldrich Ames, a deeply entrenched mole by any definition, had been burrowing away at headquarters for more than six months. The Soviets were already beginning to roll up all of the CIA's agents in Moscow. The early signs of that were visible in Langley; a few agents had already, inexplicably, disappeared.

A whole year would pass before Hathaway, with the approval of Clair George, the deputy director for operations, formed the mole-hunt unit and appointed Jeanne Vertefeuille to head it. The task force was already at work in late May 1987 when William Webster succeeded William Casey, who had died three weeks earlier, as head of the CIA.

Webster, a handsome, affable native of St. Louis, had been a U.S. attorney in Missouri and was a federal appeals court judge when President Carter selected him to head the FBI in 1978. His reputation for integrity followed him into the bureau, and when President Reagan needed a new CIA director to restore the agency's tarnished image in the wake of the Iran-contra scandal, he turned to Webster.[1] It was the first time the CIA had ever been headed by a former director of the rival FBI.

Webster's first job was to clear away the underbrush of Iran-contra. In November, Clair George, who had misled Congress about the CIA's role, resigned. At the end of the year, Webster disciplined seven CIA officers in the scandal, dismissing two, demoting Dewey Clarridge, and reprimanding Alan Fiers.

To replace George, Webster brought back Richard F. Stolz, Jr., then sixty-one, who had retired from his last post as the CIA's London station chief six years earlier and was thus untouched by the Iran-contra scandal. A short, bright, compact man with brown hair, glasses, and a square face, Stolz was two years behind Webster at Amherst College. In 1964 he had been the second person in the CIA to hold the job of Moscow station chief, and a decade later he ran the Soviet division. Stolz had joined the CIA in 1950, a year after college, and had served as a DO officer in Turkey, Germany, Bulgaria, Italy, and Yugoslavia. He had been in

---

[1]To replace Casey, Reagan had first nominated Robert Gates, the CIA's deputy director, but Gates withdrew after questions were raised in Congress about his knowledge of Iran-contra.

line for the job of DDO but left the agency when Casey instead appointed a political crony, Max Hugel, a New Hampshire businessman who quit under fire two months later after the *Washington Post* accused him of improper stock market dealings.

Having been retired, Stolz did not know when he took over the Directorate of Operations that the CIA's Soviet operations had been devastated. He found out fairly soon. Early in 1988, about a month after he had returned to Langley, Stolz was briefed by Hathaway and Burton Gerber, the head of the Soviet division, about the agent losses.

Soon after, Jeanne Vertefeuille, the head of the mole-hunt unit, briefed Stolz in more detail about the problem. Stolz realized that Webster would also have to be told.

"I had brought Dick Stolz back as DDO," Webster said in an interview in his law office in downtown Washington. "In the course of his [Stolz's] getting briefed they introduced him to this team. Very few people in the agency knew about this. The team was a small group, very tight. It had to be small so as not to call attention to itself. Dick learned about this and said, 'I think you ought to brief the director.' We had a meeting in early in 1988.

"The first assumption when the agents were lost was that either Howard or Lonetree were responsible. Then they found some things that Howard and Lonetree couldn't have known about. The team was to investigate the problem of agent losses that could not be blamed on Howard. Gus had picked the people.

"They started off with zero information, other than the losses. They didn't know whether it was a human penetration, a communications penetration—had they broken a code, was it good surveillance work by the KGB in Moscow? They [the KGB] dedicate an enormous number of people to keep track of every American embassy person over there. So the mole team was starting from scratch. They began this analytical process. Who knows? Who had access? It wasn't even certain that the problem was with the agency. It could be another U.S. agency. They knew we had unexplainable losses but they really didn't know why.

"So I was briefed by the team; Jeanne did the briefing. Stolz was there, probably Hathaway. I knew Gus in the FBI; we attended some highly classified meetings in various parts of the world. We played tennis together. The first thing I asked Gus was whether they were working with the FBI and I was assured that they were working closely."

Later, after Ames's arrest, CIA inspector general Frederick P. Hitz criticized Webster for not giving the mole hunt top priority. But Webster said that even later on, during his entire time as CIA director, he was never told the magnitude of the problem—that dozens of agents had been lost. At the briefing, he said, "My best recollection, I think I was told that four to six people were lost. We didn't know there was a mole. There was nothing to suggest a mole."

The new CIA director and his chief of clandestine operations were now aware that there had been at least some agent losses and that an effort was under way to track down the cause. But the agency's concern over the problem appeared to diminish with each passing day. The disaster had occurred three years earlier, in 1985.

In a bureaucracy, be it the navy, the Department of Agriculture, or the CIA, there is a prevailing mind-set, and a nautical phrase, that is universally invoked to avoid responsibility for a problem: "It didn't happen on my watch." Casey was dead, and the CIA and the DO had new leadership, although Webster had kept on the controversial Robert Gates as the CIA's deputy director.

Richard Stolz, the new DDO, was dealing with the agency's current problems and operations in 1988. He was not inclined to look backward. "There was nothing we knew of in 1988," said one former CIA man, a senior official of the agency's clandestine arm at the time. "We weren't losing more agents. These were three-year-old problems. We were not even sure we were looking for a mole."

The comment illustrated the ostrichlike, head-in-the-sand attitude all too pervasive at the higher echelons of the DO. Moreover, the problems were not three years old; in the fall of 1987, only a few months earlier, the agency had learned that three more Soviet agents, all recruited before 1985, had been arrested and that one had been executed.

Meanwhile, Jean Vertefeuille and her task force were not having an easy time. It was not only the lack of support from above, the atmosphere of languid unconcern that permeated the agency's executive suite. The KGB made its own contribution. From the start, the KGB assumed that the CIA would start looking for a penetration after it swooped down on the CIA's agents in a short period of time toward the end of 1985. Moscow therefore did everything it could to deflect the attention of the mole hunters and, if possible, send them down blind alleys.

Inside the headquarters of the First Chief Directorate in Yasnevo, word was deliberately spread that Edward Lee Howard was responsible for the KGB's sudden success against the CIA. The assumption was that if thousands of employees in Yasnevo and abroad believed this fable, it might eventually reach the ears of the CIA.

In addition, the KGB held back and did not, at first, arrest some CIA assets whose identities it knew from Rick Ames. It planted misinformation with these CIA assets to explain why other American agents had been uncovered and arrested. Later, the sources who passed along this information to the CIA, having served their purpose, were themselves arrested.

The KGB also forced some of the agents already arrested and imprisoned to take part in various schemes to mislead the CIA mole hunters. For example, one source arrested by the KGB was made to contact a person in the United States in an effort to convince the FBI that his life was normal and he was having no problems. Finally, Soviet officials, prodded by the KGB, suggested to CIA officers that agents had been lost because of sloppy tradecraft.

This game continued for several years. As early as 1986, Hathaway's Counterintelligence Staff and the mole-hunt unit realized that something was going on, but they did not know exactly what. Vertefeuille and her people met with the FBI's parallel ANLACE task force and shared information about the odd noises coming from Moscow. The investigators recognized that some of the information flowing into the CIA was designed to mislead it. But they assumed that much of this was just the KGB blowing clouds of smoke at Langley; they did not perceive that it was all part of a scheme to divert attention from a mole in the CIA.

Attempting to fight fire with fire, the CIA and the FBI agreed in 1987 to try to recruit new Soviet intelligence sources to see if they could shed light on why agents were vanishing. This effort went on for seven years, until the arrest of the Ameses, with little or no result.

Starting in the spring of 1988, the CIA followed a false trail for a year after it received a tip that an agency employee—not Rick Ames—who had in the past had great difficulty passing his lie detector tests was spending large amounts of money.

Dan Payne, the young investigator who later checked into Ames's finances, was assigned to the yearlong probe of the CIA man who was reported to be spending excessively. In the end, in a weird foreshadowing of the Ames case and Rick's spurious claims, Payne established that the money had indeed come from an inheritance received by the CIA man's wife. It was a dead end.

But the mole-hunt team, starting with nothing, had to investigate every lead that seemed at all promising. It chased another wild goose when information was received that the KGB might have penetrated a CIA office. Because the office did not handle Soviet operations, no one who worked there could have known the identities of the lost agents. But the fear was that someone in the office had later moved into the Soviet division and betrayed the names.

Dan Payne was the only investigator assigned to help Vertefeuille. He was again diverted to follow the latest false trail. He checked on ninety employees who had worked in the suspect office and came up with no fewer than ten suspects. But, the frustrated investigator noted in his report, "There are so many problem personalities. . . that no one stands out."

It was in April 1988, a couple of months after Webster had been briefed about the 1985 compromised cases, that he established the CI Center and put Gus Hathaway in charge. Jean Vertefeuille and her tiny band of mole hunters were caught up in the reorganization. "There was no physical move," one of them recalled. "We were on the second floor, in the old CI area. The only change was

Gus moved upstairs to the seventh floor to be ADDO for counter-intelligence."[2]

But there were bureaucratic changes, and they further slowed the hunt for the mole. Vertefeuille was suddenly no longer head of the Special Task Force, which was absorbed into a new Investigations Branch of the Security Group of the CI Center. She was appointed deputy director of the Security Group and simultaneously served as director of the Investigations Branch.

The branch had responsibility for investigating all cases involving possible human penetration of the CIA. The mole-hunt unit, which had been concentrating on why virtually all of the CIA's agents had been caught inside the Soviet Union, now had somewhat broader responsibilities.

An official CIA inquiry into the Ames case in 1994 concluded that the mole-hunt effort "diminished significantly in 1988 as its participants became caught up in the creation of the Counterintelligence Center (CIC). Between 1988 and 1990, the CIA mole hunt came to a low ebb as the officers involved concentrated on other CI matters that were believed to have higher priority."[3]

In June 1988, two months after the creation of the center and the bureaucratic reshuffle of the mole-hunt unit, the KGB launched its most elaborate operation designed to distract and confuse the CIA.

A KGB officer gave information to the CIA about five of the cases that Ames had betrayed to Moscow, suggesting that each had been blown by poor tradecraft either by the CIA asset or his case officer. Although the agency was not sure whether the information was genuine, it spent two years analyzing the five cases and trying to determine whether they had indeed unraveled because of operational mistakes.

As these events were taking place, William Webster was work-

---

[2]Later, the mole-hunt team moved to the fourth floor of the modern steel-and-green-glass addition to the CIA headquarters that opened in June 1988 and connected to the west facade of the original building.

[3]IG Report, p. 4.

ing to try to repair the agency's relations with the FBI, which had become badly frayed in the Edward Lee Howard case. Webster was particularly sensitive to the problem because he had headed the FBI for more than nine years and was its director during the Howard affair. He knew that the CIA had concealed information about the case from the FBI for two years.

Webster approached William S. Sessions, another former federal judge, who had succeeded him as FBI chief. He proposed that the two agencies draw up a formal agreement pledging that, in the future, the CIA would notify the FBI when there was reason to believe that an agency employee might be engaged in espionage or might compromise classified information.

"I had been using the Howard case as an example of how not to work together," Webster said. "I wanted the agency to alert the FBI of any problem in sufficient time to act." Howard had escaped in September 1985 when the young FBI agent assigned to watch his house near Santa Fe failed to see him leave. "That aspect was egg on the FBI's face. The egg on the agency's face was they were so slow in telling the bureau that Howard was sitting on a park bench thinking about going into the Soviet embassy. I was very determined in the agency and in talking to Bill Sessions that we did everything possible to make sure each side understood its obligations."

On June 7, Webster and Sessions signed a formal "Memorandum of Understanding" spelling out the agreement between the two agencies. The secret agreement—a direct result of Howard's escape—required that Langley provide "timely notification" to the FBI whenever it had a "reasonable belief" that a CIA employee or even a former employee might be thinking about "espionage, defection, or other compromise of classified information" or had an "unauthorized contact" with a foreign intelligence service.[4]

The agreement did not require proof that a CIA mole or former

[4]"Memorandum of Understanding Between the Central Intelligence Agency (CIA) and the Federal Bureau of Investigation (FBI) Regarding Activities of Present or Former CIA Officers or Employees That Are of Counterintelligence Concern," June 7, 1988. Excerpts quoted here and that follow are all from the unpublished text obtained by the author.

employee had already spied for a foreign power; its purpose was "the prevention of such violations." Thus, the agency was required to notify the bureau even in cases of "ambiguous circumstances or questionable activities" by an employee.

The agreement also required that the FBI "notify the CIA Director of Security when the FBI independently develops information concerning a CIA officer or employee that may be of counterintelligence. . . significance to the agency." Under the secret agreement, the CIA pledged to step out of the investigation of a possible mole once it had referred the case to the FBI, but promised to pass along any additional information it learned "such as the emotional condition of an individual, e.g., his or her proclivity to engage in vindictive behavior. . . ."

Although the Memorandum of Understanding might be read to suggest that the CIA would have to notify the FBI only when a specific "present or former CIA officer or employee" fell under suspicion, it also contains broad language about "other facts or circumstances" that might equally require notification—when a series of unexplained agent losses occurred, for example.[5]

Yet, it was three years after the agreement was signed before the CIA formally joined forces with the FBI to track down the mole who was betraying and killing its agents, and who turned out to be Rick Ames. And it was not until 1993—eight years after the agency began losing its assets in Moscow—that the CIA formally notified the bureau about Ames and the FBI took over the case. As in the past, the two agencies had continued their wary, arm's-length relationship. Despite this, the picture was not as bleak as the noncooperation during the Howard case, since Vertefeuille's mole hunters and the FBI task force had been meeting on the working level to try to find out what had gone wrong. Informally, at least, the FBI's intelligence division knew that the agency might have been penetrated.

[5]The broad catch-all language in the memorandum required the CIA to notify the FBI of "any other facts or circumstances which reasonably indicate that a present or former CIA officer or employee has engaged or may engage in espionage or a related offense, or conspire with others to commit such an offense." Ibid., p. 2.

On July 1, 1988, Jeanne Vertefeuille briefed Robert Gates, then the deputy director of the CIA, on the 1985 agent losses. Gates was a bureaucratic eel, a smart, smooth, ambitious operator who had moved easily back and forth between the CIA and the White House as he climbed the ladder of power. He was not the sort to go near a briar patch like the agent losses; if Gates left any footprints during the search for the mole, they are hard to find.

But Gates insisted he, too, was told very little about the compromised cases or the mole hunt, either as deputy director, or later as director. He thought he had been briefed earlier that year. "I think I probably sat in on the briefing of Webster," Gates said. "Our general understanding was there had been a handful of compromises. We, Bill and I, walked away with the feeling there had been four to five compromises. Their greatest worry was a technical penetration. Second, a mole. The third had been Lonetree and [Marine Corporal Arnold] Bracy because at first Bracy said that he let people into all the closed spaces in the Moscow embassy. But we had concluded by the end of 1987 that Lonetree and Bracy had not given access to the KGB.

"By the time Jeanne briefed me in July of 1988 they had pretty well concluded there was a mole, but they had no idea who it was. They were just beginning the investigative process to winnow down the numbers. We were told that about two hundred people [at CIA] had some sort of access."

When the mole-hunt unit and the FBI task force met three weeks later, the CIA estimated that it had up to then lost sixteen agents. Edward Lee Howard, the agency concluded, knew of only three of the identities for sure and might have known something about seven others. That meant that six of the losses could not be attributed to Howard.

Even with this knowledge, it was almost a year and a half before the CIA focused for the first time on Aldrich Ames, when it received the tip from the woman employee that Ames was living way over his head. Dan Payne, the same overworked investigator assigned to Vertefeuille's unit, began a routine inquiry into Ames's finances.

Payne examined real estate records in Arlington County and

found that Ames had paid $540,000 for his house. There was no record of a mortgage. He asked the Treasury Department about whether Ames's name had shown up on any Currency Transaction Reports, which require banks and merchants to notify the government of payments larger than $10,000. Payne got three hits.[6]

The CIA now knew that Ames had bought a house worth more than half a million dollars in cash, that he was putting large chunks of cash in the bank, and that he was an officer with access to the blown Soviet cases. It also knew from the woman informant that his wife's family was not wealthy. Yet no flashing red lights and alarm bells went off in Langley.

Instead, in January 1990, Payne was assigned to begin a two-month training course. No one was brought in to replace him. When he returned in March, he was pulled off the Ames investigation and sent overseas to interview a source who was believed to have information about the supposed penetration of a CIA office, the case that he had investigated earlier. That goose chase redux kept him busy through May.

In June, Payne was sent to Berlin to check out the newly opened East German intelligence files. His mission was to determine what the Stasi knew about CIA operations and whether the East German intelligence service had recruited a CIA officer who might have had access to the 1985 Soviet cases that had been compromised.

In August, the mole-hunt unit was diverted by yet another red herring when a KGB defector claimed that Moscow had recruited an unidentified CIA officer in the Soviet division back in the 1970s, an officer known for his carousing and free-spending ways. For more than a year, the mole hunters tried to match the information to any current or retired CIA officer. In the end, the lead was deemed unreliable.

In September, Payne briefly returned to the Ames inquiry. He requested a routine credit check of Rick and Rosario. But of course

---

[6]In January 1990, Treasury told CIA that Ames had deposited $13,000 in cash into a local bank account in 1985, $15,000 into the account in 1986, and had converted Italian lira into $22,107 after he got back from Rome.

Ames's credit was excellent, since he had no great difficulty paying his bills, enormous though they were. Finally, in the fall of 1990—one full year after the tip on Ames had come in—the mole hunters decided that Ames should be the subject of a background investigation and another polygraph.

But Ames had last been polygraphed in 1986 and would be due for another after five years, in 1991. It was decided to wait until then, to make the polygraph appear to be routine so as not to alert Ames.

On December 5, 1990, Payne sent a memo to the CIA's Office of Security asking that OS open an investigation of Ames based on his "lavish spending habits over the past five years." The memo noted that Ames was working in the Counterintelligence Center itself.

The memo went on to observe that Ames and his wife had purchased the Arlington house for $540,000 with no mortgage, that he was renovating the kitchen, "sparing no expense," and had bought a $49,500 Jaguar.

The investigator said there might be a "logical explanation for Ames's spending habits." Ames's mother had died, and he might have inherited money or property. Her last residence was not known, so Payne said he could not find out from public records whether she had left anything to her son. Or the money could have come from his in-laws, who "were well connected politically in Colombia." In Mexico, Payne noted, Rosario had been "directly appointed" to her embassy job "by the president of Colombia." The deposits into Ames's checking account could have come from loans from the Federal Credit Union. These wishful rationalizations—one can almost hear the young investigator yearning for innocent explanations, anything but the awful truth—were balanced by a cautious concern that Ames might indeed be earning his money in some less pleasant manner.

"There is a degree of urgency involved in our request," Payne wrote. "Since Ames has been assigned to CIC, his access has been limited to a degree. Unfortunately, we are quickly running out of things for him to do without granting him greater access. It is our hope to at least get Ames through polygraph before we are forced to take such action."[7]

The mole hunt crept along at an appallingly slow pace at least in part because of the legacy of James Jesus Angleton. As an institution, the CIA was wary of repeating the mistakes of the past. For twenty years, from 1954 to 1974, Angleton had headed the Counterintelligence Staff, and such was the depth of his suspicion of KGB intrigue that he virtually paralyzed the ability of the Soviet division to run operations against the Soviets at the height of the cold war. To Angleton, all Soviet sources and defectors save one, Anatoly Golitsin, were bad, under Moscow's control. In the search for the mole he never found, he destroyed or damaged the careers of dozens of loyal CIA officers. Years later, three were compensated under a special law passed by Congress and known inside Langley as "the Mole Relief Act."[8]

CIA director William E. Colby tried to ease Angleton out and finally fired him in 1974. But Angleton's departure left the agency wounded and, remembering the past, reluctant to move too quickly against suspected moles. Moreover, much of Angleton's empire had been dismantled along with his dismissal, and CI was, ironically, left in a weakened state. Beyond that, it was an area of the CIA generally shunned by case officers as a sort of purgatory not likely to enhance their careers. It did not attract the best and the brightest.

Much later, Senator DeConcini asked Ames himself, who was certainly an authority on moles, why the agency had so much trouble unearthing him. The CIA did not devote enough resources to the task, Ames said. Was the culture such, DeConcini asked,

[7]Memo to Office of Security, December 5, 1990, Senate Report, Appendix 2.

[8]The officers compensated were S. Peter Karlow, who lost his left leg on a PT boat mission for the Office of Strategic Services in World War II, was forced out of the CIA in 1963, and—after fighting for twenty-six years to clear his name—received $500,000; Paul Garbler, the first Moscow station chief; and Richard Kovich, both of whom received compensation in the $100,000 range. All had, groundlessly, come under suspicion by James Angleton.

that the agency's officials did not "want to admit" there could be a mole?

"The culture and the difficulty. . . in allocating resources," Ames replied. "They are busy with Irangate, they are busy with this, they are busy with that. . . . The sort of feeling that it is not the biggest thing to do."

"Was it different under. . . Angleton?" the senator asked hopefully.

"No," said Rick Ames. "No, that's—Angleton, that's a great fallacy. Angleton wouldn't have known what to do with a mole if it bit him in the leg."

16

CLOSING IN

On April 12, 1991, Ames reported in for his lie detector test at CIA headquarters. Unlike his experience in 1986, Ames was not panicked this time by the prospect of facing the polygraph. He had some apprehension, of course; no CIA officer enjoys being "fluttered," the agency jargon for the polygraph test. And Ames had a great deal to conceal.

He had passed his polygraph test in 1986, although he was already a KGB spy. As far as he knew, the upcoming test was routine; CIA employees are supposed to be tested every five years. Moreover, in 1986, Ames had benefited from the advice of the KGB on how to beat the machine. He had done it, and that experience gave him confidence.

Ames had no reason to think that his colleagues in the Counterintelligence Center were already investigating him. He would, of course, have been extremely alarmed if the polygraph operators had questioned him about his finances or asked why he had paid cash for his house. That would have meant that he had become a specific target of inquiry.

On the same day that Ames was wired into the lie detector machine, the CIA's Office of Security had completed its background investigation of him. The report was devastating. It found that Ames had been assigned to the CI Center "under a cloud," that the Soviet division did not trust him, that in Rome, Ames had spent a lot of time with Soviet and Eastern-bloc assets and drank during his lunch hour, that he lived high and had paid cash for a house worth half a million dollars. The report quoted one colleague as saying he would not be entirely surprised if Ames was a spy, although the co-worker backpedaled when questioned further about his remark.[1] Unfavorable as the report was, the December 5, 1990, memo from Vertefeuille's investigator, Dan Payne, was even more alarming.

But Aldrich Ames need not have worried about these two documents, as damning as they were. The two polygraphers who tested Ames were aware that there was some question about his unexplained wealth, but they were never shown the background investigation. Both denied having seen the December 5 memo or knowing of its contents. Once again, the lack of coordination in the sprawling bureaucracy at Langley had unwittingly come to the rescue of Rick Ames. The polygraph operators were out of the loop.

There are two parts to a polygraph test. First comes the interview, which takes place before the subject is actually strapped to the machine. Many CIA officers, fearful of what may show up on the polygraph, often confess all kinds of guilty secrets and personal misdeeds in this interview phase. After that, they are wired to the polygraph, which registers their physical reactions on a roll of moving graph paper, much like an electrocardiogram.

During the interview phase, Ames shrewdly volunteered information about his finances. Most of the money, he said, had come from his mother-in-law in Colombia, where he also owned property, and he claimed he had made a number of lucrative invest-

[1]The witless Office of Security supervisor who reviewed the report of the Ames background investigation concluded that it "had no CI implications," according to the inspector general's report on the Ames case. Senate Report, p. 71.

ments as well. This was a sort of blend of Ames's wealthy in-laws and "Robert from Chicago" stories.

When the second phase began, with the polygraph turned on, Ames was asked whether he was concealing any financial difficulties from the CIA. He answered no, and of course showed no signs of deception, since the last thing Rick Ames had was financial difficulties. No one at CIA ever asked Ames, on the polygraph test or at any other time, to explain the source of his wealth.

Ames showed no reaction when asked by the polygraphers whether he was working for a foreign intelligence service. He said no, and again displayed no signs of deception. So much for the ability of the polygraph to detect lies.

But Ames had trouble when asked if he was hiding contacts with foreign nationals. When the polygraph operator told him he was reacting to the question, Ames explained that his wife received money from her mother in Colombia, and he had thought about going into the export-import business there after he retired; perhaps that was spooking the machine. After several hours of testing, however, he continued to show deception on the question. Following standard practice, the examiner broke off the test and asked Ames to come back in four days to complete it.

When Ames did, he must have been relieved to find another polygraph operator administering the test. This time he answered every question, including the one about foreign contacts, without showing deception. The examiner dismissed Ames and wrote that he had passed.[2]

Much later, after Ames was finally caught, several former and current polygraph operators were asked to review the results of the 1986 and 1991 tests. The problem, they surmised, was that the examiners in each case had failed to establish the proper psychological atmosphere of fear and intimidation. Unless the subject is afraid of detection, the experts said, the needle won't jump. The tests, they concluded, were invalid because the examiners were too friendly.

[2]The first examiner was a bit more skeptical, however. In a note to the files, he wrote: "I don't think he is a spy, but I am not 100 percent convinced because of the money situation." Senate Report, p. 73.

Be that as it may, Ames had passed his lie detector test, and the result was that the mole-hunt unit was now less suspicious of him. In a culture that believed in witch doctors, Ames, for the moment at least, had caused the right gourds and rattles to be shaken.

Still, there was a nagging question about the source of all that money. And so in July, a CIA officer flew to Bogotá to check on whether Rosario's family was really wealthy. The CIA man reported that the Casas family was well known, had political clout, and that a company owned by the family owned ice cream parlors and was engaged in a number of business ventures. He had even heard that Rosario's family had donated land worth millions of dollars for a soccer field several years back. But it was Rosario's uncle, her father's brother, who had prospered in business. Her father, an academic and political appointee, had followed a different, humbler path. Rick Ames's in-laws owned no ice cream parlors.

Presumably, the CIA officer relayed his rosy and reassuring, but entirely misleading, report to Langley by a telephone in his shoe, in the great tradition of television's Maxwell Smart. In the event, the report from Bogotá, combined with Ames's successful lie detector test, had one predictable result: In the fall of 1991, the Ames investigation was put on a hold button. Ames had been within the agency's grasp and wriggled away.

About two days after Ames had reported in to take his polygraph test, and before he returned to complete it, he and Rosario signed another false income tax return, reporting total income for 1990 of a little over $60,000. Less than two weeks later, Ames flew to Vienna—the trip on which, for the second time, he was confused about the meeting place and failed to link up with his KGB control.

Some time in 1991, Rosario Ames was later to claim, she made a startling discovery. She needed a small wallet to fit in her purse and recalled that Rick had a little red one that he did not use. Rummaging in a drawer, she told the FBI on the day of her arrest, she found the wallet and inside a mysterious typed note. It referred to a meeting in an embassy in "the city where your mother-in-law lives."

Alarmed at the cryptic reference to her mother, Rosario said, she asked Rick for an explanation. He put her off, according to her version, but two weeks later took her to Germaine's, a popular Vietnamese restaurant on upper Wisconsin Avenue above Georgetown. Over dinner, Rosario maintained, Rick confessed: "I'm working for the Russians."[3] Later, during plea-bargain negotiations with federal prosecutors, Rosario Ames changed her story and said she believed she had found the wallet in 1992, not 1991.

In any event, by Rosario's own admission, she became aware at some point that her husband was a spy for Moscow, that the source of all those millions, the clothes, the jewels, the house, the Jaguars, the trips to Bogotá, the nannies, was not, after all, either the tooth fairy or a benevolent investment adviser known to her only by his first name, "Robert."

Rick Ames did not realize it, but in April 1991, the same month that he got through his lie detector test, wheels were beginning to turn that would finally, if very slowly, trap him. Paul Redmond and another CIA official went to the FBI and met with Raymond A. Mislock, Jr., chief of the Soviet section of the intelligence division, and Robert B. Wade, the assistant section chief. Redmond told the two FBI men that the agency was reviving the mole hunt. The FBI officials suggested that the two agencies join forces, and the CIA agreed. Now, for the first time, the agency and the bureau formed a joint mole-hunt team. Moreover, the search for the mole moved from its emphasis on the analysis of failed cases to a sharper focus on the hunt for individual suspects. By this time, Jeanne Vertefeuille's mole-hunt unit had moved from its original office to the fourth floor of the CIA's modern new headquarters, which is adjacent to the original building.

Paul Redmond, the CIA official credited with resuscitating the mole hunt at this critical juncture, was the same counterintelligence official who had estimated back in 1986 that forty-five CIA operations had been compromised. As chief of the Yurchenko task

---

[3]Rosario Ames told the story of the wallet and the dinner at Germaine's to the FBI, and to interviewers. See Sally Quinn, "The Terrible Secret of Rosario Ames," *Washington Post*, October 19, 1994.

force in 1985, Redmond had supervised Aldrich Ames during the debriefings of the Soviet defector.

Redmond disliked Ames. In 1989, when Ames had returned from Rome, Redmond, then deputy chief of the Soviet division, was again his superior. Redmond confronted Ames over Sergei Fedorenko, GTPYRRHIC, who had been Ames's agent in New York. Fedorenko returned to Moscow, and more than a decade later surfaced again in Washington, where he met with Ames in the fall of 1989. Redmond wondered why Fedorenko was still walking around, since virtually all of the CIA's other agents in Moscow had been arrested. Milton Bearden, who had recently taken over the Soviet division, shared Redmond's suspicions that Fedorenko was a double agent. They later arranged to have Fedorenko subjected to a hostile polygraph. Fedorenko was told that he had failed the test, and the CIA dropped him. The Fedorenko case, as will be seen, remains one of the more intriguing aspects of the Ames story.

Early in 1991, Redmond became deputy chief of the Counterintelligence Center.[4] Ames had gone to work there a few months before. Once again, Redmond was Ames's boss, and they clashed frequently.

In May, a month after the CIA and the FBI finally joined forces, Webster retired as CIA chief, and President Bush, himself a former director of the agency, nominated Robert Gates to succeed him. After protracted hearings and much controversy, this time the Gates nomination survived and the Senate confirmed him on November 5.[5]

As the joint CIA-FBI mole-hunt team began work, the bureau assigned two FBI men, James P. Milburn and James Holt, to work with the CIA officers. The FBI considered Milburn the best analyst of KGB operations in the bureau. Jeanne Vertefeuille remained in charge of the CIA half of the team.

---

[4]At the same time, Ted Price left his job as chief of the CI Center to become assistant deputy director for operations (ADDO). He was replaced in the counterintelligence post by James Olson, a six-foot, slender, blond Iowan who had served in the Moscow station several years earlier.

[5]Gates served as director for a little over a year, until January 1993, when President Clinton replaced him with R. James Woolsey.

By August, the combined unit had drawn up a list of 198 CIA employees who had access to the failed cases. From these names, the mole hunters compiled a priority list of 29 persons to be investigated first. Aldrich Ames was at the top of the list.

Despite this, some members of the joint team were more suspicious of CIA employees on the short list other than Ames. But one CIA mole hunter began compiling a detailed chronology of Ames's career and activities. The CIA-FBI team did not develop a similar chronology on any other suspect.

In October a CIA officer overseas reported that he had learned from a KGB source that the Soviet intelligence agency had, years before, penetrated the agency with a Russian-born employee who had provided details of the CIA's operations in Moscow to the KGB. Worse yet, the mole was reported to be still active.

It sounded like another KGB red herring, but this time the origin of the report was shocking. The CIA officer who had provided the lead was recalled so that he could be questioned further. The agency concluded that the officer had fabricated the story, either to enhance his career or perhaps to win a promotion and more money. Confronted, the officer resigned. The CIA referred his case to the Justice Department for possible criminal prosecution.

Although diverted for a time by the phony story, the joint team in November began interviewing the CIA employees on the list of suspects. The mole hunters were careful not to suggest to those called in that they were suspects. The questions were kept low key and dealt with housekeeping details: who attended what meetings, how were documents handled, and so on. But the officers who were interviewed, unless they were unusually dim-witted, must have understood that the team was trying to unearth a mole.

On November 12, the joint team interviewed Rick Ames. He had no doubt about what was going on. Twice, he volunteered that he had received a security violation while in the Soviet division for leaving a safe open. The safe, Ames added helpfully, had contained chronologies of Soviet cases and the combinations to other safes. It seems clear, in retrospect, that Ames was trying to explain a possible cause of the 1985 agent losses while deflecting suspicion that he was himself the mole.

The mole hunters did not buy it. They ran a computer search of all DO records for all traces on Aldrich Ames, something that was not done on any other suspect. The search turned up the reports that Ames had written about his meetings with Sergei Chuvakhin back in 1985 and 1986, the very encounters where Ames had turned over most of the names of the CIA agents. The computer also found the FBI inquiry about why Ames was not reporting all of his contacts with Chuvakhin.[6]

Let the hunters hunt, a mole must enjoy life to the hilt while he can. In January 1992 Ames bought his third Jaguar. He traded in his two-and-a-half-year-old white one for his famous red XJ6 Jaguar. As he had done all along, Ames blithely drove the Jaguar, Virginia license plate ZZU-7277, into the CIA parking lot every workday.[7]

That spring, the joint mole-hunt unit decided to take another look at Ames's wealth. Paul Redmond ordered Dan Payne, the investigator who had begun the financial inquiry three years earlier, but who had been pulled off it to explore various side tracks and dead ends, to complete the job. Once again, Ames was the only suspect singled out for a financial investigation.

Under a federal law, the Right to Financial Privacy Act, if a government agency, under ordinary circumstances, snoops into a citizen's bank account or financial records, the banks or companies must notify the person that the records have been made available to investigators. This might seem an awkward problem if one were looking for a mole.

In fact, the law provides for scrutiny of bank accounts and other financial records without notification in cases involving foreign

[6]It was not until several months later, in 1992, that the FBI reviewed the records of its Washington field office and discovered that Ames and Chuvakhin had a great many contacts that had gone unreported.

[7]According to William Webster, the Jaguar might have raised eyebrows but was not enough in itself to lead the mole hunters to Ames; other CIA employees owned expensive cars. "A lot of people in the agency had family money," he said. "My driver owned a Corvette, with double-oh-seven plates." The James Bond license was on his driver's private car, Webster explained, not the one that was used to drive the CIA director.

counterintelligence.[8] The government agency must certify in writing to the financial institution that it is invoking this provision of the law. The CIA had the authority all along to check Ames's bank accounts without his knowledge. It could have done so three years earlier when it received the tip from the woman employee and began the investigation of his wealth.

Better late than never, and the agency, invoking these secrecy provisions of the law, queried banks and credit card companies. In June, the responses began to flow in, and the CIA learned for the first time that Rick and Rosario were spending at least $30,000 a month on credit cards and that Ames had traveled overseas without reporting it some of the time, as CIA rules required.

By August, the CIA knew that hundreds of thousands of dollars had been deposited in Ames's accounts in the Dominion Bank of Virginia, much of the money from wire transfers of undetermined origin. Now the CIA was inching toward the truth, albeit at a snaillike pace. As it dug further into Ames's bank accounts that fall of 1992, it discovered that by this time, wire transfers of about $1 million and cash deposits of more than $500,000 had found their way into his bank accounts.

In 1992, as the mole hunters drew closer to their target, Jeanne Vertefeuille turned sixty, and, under CIA rules, she had to take mandatory retirement. She had searched for the traitor for almost six years and could have gone off to the Sun Belt to enjoy life, like so many of her colleagues. But Vertefeuille was not about to give up the chase, especially now. She returned to the CIA on contract with no break in her employment.

So far, the mole hunters believed that Ames's affluence might be explained "by legitimate family wealth or even illegal activities in Colombia such as narcotics or emerald smuggling."[9] While smuggling emeralds from South America can be a lucrative profession, presumably few of those engaged in it also have access to the identities of the CIA's Soviet agents.

---

[8]Section 3414 of the Act specifically exempts from the disclosure provisions the FBI and other unnamed government agencies authorized to conduct foreign counterintelligence or to gather intelligence—such as the CIA.

[9]Senate Report, p. 80.

At this point, the joint mole-hunt team finally began to hear the faint sound of digging below ground. It was Sandy Grimes, a member of Vertefeuille's unit, who made the breakthrough. She carefully analyzed the dates of Ames's meetings with Chuvakhin in 1985 and 1986 and correlated the meetings with the dates of his bank deposits. She found that many of the cash deposits came right after the luncheons.

Now, in October 1992, the mole hunters were reasonably sure that they had their quarry, and that it was Rick Ames. Even so, a few other CIA officers remained under suspicion. But the focus was, finally, on Aldrich Ames.

President Clinton was elected in November and named the new CIA director, R. James Woolsey, in December. As 1993 rolled around, the mole-hunt unit in January began briefing FBI officials and others on its findings.

The Central Intelligence Agency is not responsible for catching spies. It has no power to arrest them. It was time, the CIA decided, to turn the case over to the FBI.

17

NIGHTMOVER

In the third week of March 1992, as spring came to Washington, Aldrich Ames strolled past a mailbox at the corner of Thirty-seventh and R Streets in a quiet residential neighborhood a block from Georgetown University. As he walked by, he surreptitiously made a chalk mark on the mailbox.

To any passerby, the chalk mark meant nothing, probably if noticed at all, something a child had done. To the SVR, which had replaced the KGB as Russia's intelligence agency, the chalk line meant that Ames had activated signal site SMILE. It also meant that dead drop BRIDGE would be ready to be unloaded.[1]

Before he drove to Georgetown to lay down the signal, Ames, unaware that the mole hunters were finally on his trail, wrote a message on his home computer to the SVR. He said he would be transmitting more CIA secrets along with his note and asked that he be promptly paid through a dead drop.

[1]BRIDGE, one of several dead drops in the Washington area used by Ames, was beneath a pedestrian footbridge in a wooded area at Massachusetts Avenue and Little Falls Parkway in suburban Maryland.

Even with the millions flowing in to Rick and Rosario, it wasn't enough. Although Ames had successfully assured his polygraph operator that he had no financial problems, that was a year ago, and this was now. A few months later, Ames dunned the SVR in rather sharp language:

My most immediate need, as I pointed out in March, is money. As I have mentioned several times, I do my best to invest a good part of the cash I received, but keep part of it out for ordinary expenses. Now, I am faced with the need to cash in investments to meet current needs—a very tight and unpleasant situation! I have had to sell a certificate of deposit in Zurich and some stock here to help make up the gap. Therefore, I will need as much cash delivered in PIPE[2] as you think can be accomodated [sic]—it seems to me that it could accomodate [sic] up to $100,000.[3]

As he had done in March, Ames sent the letter by marking the mailbox in Georgetown. After activating the signal site, he then hid his message in dead drop BRIDGE.

In May, Rick Ames—a Russian spy—dined at the White House. That accomplishment could only have increased his prestige in the

---

[2]PIPE was a dead drop in a drainpipe along a horse path in Wheaton Regional Park in Maryland. Only Ames, never the Russians, would retrieve material from PIPE, on Sundays.

[3]At the time that Ames wrote this message, on June 8, he was not yet under surveillance by the FBI. More than a year later, on October 9, 1993, the FBI, acting on the written authority of Attorney General Janet Reno, clandestinely entered his house and copied this message and others from his computer and from diskettes discovered in his home. Under executive order 12333 issued by President Reagan on December 4, 1981, the attorney general at the time of the entry into Ames's house could approve searches without a warrant when the target was "a foreign power or an agent of a foreign power." Whether the provision violated the constitutional protections of the Fourth Amendment had not been tested in the Supreme Court, however. In the wake of the Ames case, Congress in 1994 enacted a law requiring that a warrant be issued by the special Foreign Intelligence Surveillance Court for counterintelligence searches of this type. The messages quoted in this chapter are from the FBI affidavit of February 21, 1994, and related court documents.

eyes of his handlers in Moscow. In Mexico, Ames's cover had been that of an officer in the political section, and there he had come to know Roman Popadiuk, then a junior foreign service officer in the embassy. Once, Popadiuk held a chess tournament at his apartment for Soviet diplomats in Mexico; Rick had brought the soda and chips.[4] A decade later, Popadiuk was serving in the Bush administration as the deputy White House press secretary under Marlin Fitzwater and spokesman for Brent Scowcroft, the president's national security adviser. Popadiuk's family background was Ukrainian, and he spoke the language, so he was a natural choice for President Bush to select as the first ambassador to Ukraine, which became an independent country following the breakup of the Soviet Union.

Soon after Popadiuk had been confirmed by the Senate on May 7, Ames telephoned his friend Rich Thurman, whom Popadiuk had also known in Mexico, and suggested they all get together before the ambassador left to take up his duties in Kiev. Popadiuk invited his friends to join him for lunch in the prestigious senior White House mess. Although a social occasion, it was also more than that, since Popadiuk knew that Ames was a CIA Soviet specialist who might have some valuable insights to contribute.

In the wake of the collapse of the Soviet Union, there was considerable tension between Russia and Ukraine over the control of the Black Sea fleet and a host of other bilateral issues. At lunch, Ames was constantly asking questions. Popadiuk said that in his view, the fleet would have to be split, but it would be no easy task. He talked about his goals as ambassador and his efforts to increase the size of the embassy staff, which he felt was too small. He also wanted a marine detachment for the embassy. Popadiuk was circumspect, since he was not yet serving as ambassador, but he said a lot that must have been of interest to Rick Ames and the SVR. After all, as far as Popadiuk knew, he was speaking to a fellow foreign service officer, Rich Thurman, and Rick Ames, a trusted CIA case officer. Through Ames, the luncheon would have given Yasnevo a valuable window into the mind of the new U.S. ambassador to the rival Ukraine.

[4]The Russians won.

Nor was it the first time that Ames had lunch in the White House. In June 1991, his friend David Samson was staying with him on a visit to Washington. Samson made a lunch date with Popadiuk and suggested that Rick come along. "Before lunch, Roman trotted us in to meet Fitzwater, and gave us a personal tour of the White House offices," Samson recalled. "It was a tour of the offices in the West Wing, and we went down into the Situation Room in the basement. I remember how Rick was just delighted to have met Fitzwater and to have a personal tour of the White House. Later, looking back, I thought he was delighted because it would impress the people in Moscow. That he was in the White House and in the Situation Room!"[5]

At the FBI, Tim Caruso, who had run the ANLACE task force, had been assigned to the Washington field office and ordered to assemble a team of agents. They were to be ready to move when the report of the joint CIA-FBI mole-hunt task force, originally expected in the spring of 1992, was complete. In the meantime, Caruso and his team reviewed unresolved past allegations of penetrations of American intelligence.

The most serious of these had begun in the 1970s when the FBI had received information suggesting that an unidentified CIA officer had volunteered information to the Russians. The bureau gave the case the code name TRAPDOOR. "We were attempting to resolve TRAPDOOR," Caruso said. "It had been closed and reopened several times. It had been a thorn in the side for some time."

As the FBI reopened its investigation of TRAPDOOR, Ames continued passing CIA secrets to the Russians. On August 19, 1992, he wrote another letter to the SVR. He confirmed that he would keep a scheduled meeting with his handler in Caracas the first week in October.

Ames put the note in with a package of CIA documents to be placed in a dead drop. He hoped, he wrote, that his message "will cause the people here"—by which he meant the Washington resi-

---

[5]The White House Situation Room is the very nerve center of the national security apparatus. During the Cuban missile crisis and other foreign policy emergencies, presidents have relied on the information flowing into the Situation Room to stay abreast of developments minute by minute.

dency of the SVR—to cable Moscow confirming "my intent to make our scheduled meeting on 5/6 October."

For years, Ames had been pressing the Russians to pay him by electronic transfers into his Zurich accounts, or by some other banking mode. Although Ames had optimistically thought that dead drop PIPE would hold $100,000 in cash, some drops were too small to hold very much cash, and there was always the risk that a curious dog, or children playing, might come upon the cache. And cash was bulky; it meant walking around with plastic bags full of money or carrying conspicuous packages onto airplanes. But the Russians, wary of traceable wire transfers, preferred to deal in cash. It was a constant bone of contention between Ames and his handlers.

He expected cash in Caracas, Ames wrote, but he reminded the SVR "how little I like this method, though it is acceptable" but "I still hope that you will have decided on some safer, paper transfer of some sort of a large amount."

Having been stuck in the Counternarcotics Center for nine months, Ames was also chafing at the difficulties of getting his hands on valuable secrets for Moscow. "My lack of access frustrates me," he wrote, "since I would need to work harder to get what I can to you. It was easier to simply hand over cables! Documents are enclosed in this package which should be of interest."

The documents would certainly have been of interest; they included information on CIA operations in Moscow, the CIA's conclusions about Russian technical penetration of the American embassy in Moscow, and the agency's plans to recruit Russian officials.

Finally, Ames wrote a significant sentence about Rosario. "My wife has accomodated [sic] herself to understanding what I am doing in a very supportive way."

Ames closed this letter with, "Until we meet in Caracas. . . K 18/19 August."[6] Ames signed the message "K" as shorthand for

---

[6]The FBI obtained this year-old message from Ames's trash on October 6, 1993, three days before it entered his house and downloaded his computer. The message was on a printer ribbon from which the FBI was able to reconstruct this and other documents.

KOLOKOL, the code name he had chosen for himself.

Not everything in the spy world goes according to plan. The next morning, Ames left a pencil mark at signal site HILL, indicating that the package and letter would be loaded into dead drop GROUND, where he placed them at 4:00 P.M. that day.[7] The next morning, Ames checked the signal site and saw that the pencil mark had not been erased, which meant that the pickup had not taken place. Ames retrieved the package. On September 1, he wrote another note to the SVR, explaining that he had recovered the package and would place the material back in GROUND two days later.

In his letter, Ames made reference to an intriguing trip he had taken. As the CIA officer in charge of monitoring drug traffic in the Black Sea area of the former Soviet Union, Ames—although already under suspicion—had been permitted by the CIA to travel to Moscow earlier that year. In some ways, that fact is one of the more startling aspects of the Ames case. It was almost as though Ames was traveling under a unique CIA "send a mole to Moscow" program.

Ames could have stayed in Russia if either he or the SVR had learned that he was under investigation. And Ames would then have been beyond reach forever. There was ample precedent. Kim Philby, the British master mole, had escaped from Beirut to Moscow in 1963 as MI6 closed in on him. In Ames's case, it would have been much easier—the CIA *sent* him to Moscow on official business. And it was not the only trip that Ames took to Russia and other former Soviet republics. In 1993 he visited former Soviet Georgia and Almaty in Kazakhstan, as well as Turkey.

In his letter, referring to the Moscow trip, Ames wrote: "You have probably heard a bit about me by this time from your (and now my) colleagues in the MBRF."[8]

---

[7]HILL was a guardrail on Massachusetts Avenue at Whitehaven Street in northwest Washington. GROUND was a dead drop under a pedestrian footbridge in Washington's Rock Creek Park near Beach Drive.

[8]At the time, the initials stood for the Russian Federal Ministry for Security, the Russian counterintelligence arm, formerly the Second Chief Directorate of the KGB. The agency later changed its name; in January 1994, the month before Ames was arrested, it became the Federal Service for Counterintelligence, or FSK.

The reference to "and now my. . . colleagues" was revealing. It meant that Ames was not only selling secrets for money, he had mentally switched loyalties and was fully identifying with the SVR. He considered himself one of them, and their colleagues in the Russian counterintelligence service were also his.

In that same month of September 1992, Ames became so drunk at a liaison meeting with foreign officials that he started talking out of turn about CIA operations and officers and passed out cold at the table. As usual, nothing happened.

On September 18, as required by CIA rules, Ames informed the agency that he planned to travel to Bogotá to see his mother-in-law.[9] Although all foreign travel must be reported, Ames with good reason did not say that he was going on to Caracas.

Ames arrived in the Venezuelan capital about October 4. He met with his Soviet handler, turned over more classified information, and received a whopping $150,000 in cash. The SVR also provided Ames with his communications plan for 1993.[10]

After he returned to Washington through Miami, Ames deposited a little more than half of the money, $85,000, in bank accounts that he and Rosario controlled in northern Virginia. Each deposit was less than $10,000 to avoid any Currency Transaction Reports to the Treasury.

In January 1993, the CIA mole hunters, persuaded now that Ames was their man, began briefing the FBI so that the bureau could take over the case; the CIA has no power to arrest spies. But another delay developed when the FBI decided to await the final report of the joint CIA-FBI mole-hunt team before moving. That report, slow in coming, was not completed until March 15. According to Jim Holt, one of the two FBI agents on the joint team, there was good reason the report had taken two years to

[9]The reason Ames gave to the CIA was entirely bogus; Rosario's mother, Cecilia Casas, was in the United States while Ames was in Bogotá.

[10]The plan called for Ames to transmit information and messages via dead drops in the Washington area in January, April, July, and October, and to retrieve cash and instructions the same way in March, June, and September. In addition, Ames was to meet the SVR in Bogotá again in November and December.

produce. "We didn't want to miss anyone in case Ames wasn't the only one," he said.

Code-named PLAYACTOR/SKYLIGHT, the report estimated that thirty Soviet operations had been compromised in 1985–86 and detailed the efforts of the KGB to deflect from the search for a Soviet spy in the CIA. It was "virtually certain," the report said, that a KGB mole "who followed closely on the heels of CIA defector Edward Lee Howard" had penetrated the CIA and had begun to reveal operations to Moscow in July 1985 or earlier. The mole, the report added, had worked in SE division in counterintelligence. The report amounted to an accurate description of Ames, whose name was included on a list of forty people in an appendix. Yet, the report did not single out Ames, who by this time was the CIA's prime suspect.

But not necessarily the FBI's; the bureau was moving cautiously in early 1993. There was disagreement among top officials over whether there was sufficient evidence to open a full-fledged counterintelligence investigation of Ames and to obtain court approval to tap his telephones. And one key FBI analyst, who had worked with the CIA on the hunt for the mole, continued to feel there might be other suspects.

According to an intelligence source closely involved with the Ames case, the FBI faced a political dilemma. "The bureau might have gone after a great number of people at CIA," he said. "But if the bureau had opened an investigation of Gus Hathaway or Burton Gerber, or other high-level officials who had access to the 1985 cases, it would look like the bureau was attacking the agency."

R. Patrick Watson, the deputy assistant director of the FBI intelligence division at the time, said that Ames was a suspect early on, but not the only one. "Ames was one of the top two or three candidates starting in 1991," Watson said. "People sat around the table and actually voted, who was the most likely candidate. Ames got more votes than anyone else.[11] No one ever told me they had a

---

[11]The members of the joint CIA-FBI task force were polled at Jeanne Vertefeuille's insistence. The two FBI agents on the team resisted the idea of a vote. They were outnumbered. Ames got the most votes.

list and he was number one. But I was told that people at CIA felt very strongly that Ames was number one. The FBI was a little concerned that CIA was so close to the issue and did not like Ames. The FBI did not want personal animosity to put one suspect above another." Watson's meaning was clear; while both agencies later credited the CIA's Paul Redmond with reviving the mole hunt and helping to bring it to a successful conclusion, the CIA official's antagonism toward Ames was well known. "Paul Redmond," Watson said, "really disliked Ames."

Finally, in March, the FBI began to put together an investigative team. Headquarters handed the case to the Washington Metropolitan Field Office, then headed by a husky, blond lawyer from Little Rock, Arkansas, by way of Missouri, Robert M. "Bear" Bryant. Bryant turned over the day-to-day supervision of the case to John F. Lewis, Jr., a burly ex-marine and a veteran counterintelligence agent for the bureau. Lewis had a boxer's face but a soft voice, and he understood the subtleties of his craft. Under Bryant, he was the assistant special agent in charge of the field office, the ASAC (pronounced "A-sack"). It is the Washington field office, tucked away in its remote headquarters at Buzzard's Point along the Anacostia River, that handles surveillance and investigation of foreign spies in the capital. Its street agents serve on some fifteen squads that watch the SVR, the GRU, and other foreign intelligence targets. The field office in turn reports to the intelligence division at FBI headquarters in the J. Edgar Hoover Building in downtown Washington.[12]

Lewis assembled the team in great secrecy. Concerned that the mole might even be within the ranks of the FBI, he ordered that each agent selected be polygraphed. The FBI men began studying the CIA and FBI files to get up to speed on all that had gone before.

Sometime in the weeks after mid-March, the FBI had reached a decision that the target of the investigation would be Aldrich

[12]In October 1993 the new FBI director, Louis J. Freeh, changed the name of the Intelligence Division to the National Security Division and appointed Bryant its director. Lewis was named deputy assistant director of the division in November 1994 when Pat Watson retired.

Ames. FBI officials said some information from Soviet or Russian defectors had been helpful but that no defector had been able to pinpoint Ames. Pat Watson, the number two counterintelligence official at the time, declared: "There was no source that walked in and said Ames is a spy." All of the evidence pointed to Ames, in any event. By early May, the FBI was ready to move.

"We opened the case on Ames on May 12, 1993," John Lewis said. "We called it NIGHTMOVER." The code name, according to Lewis and other FBI officials, stood for both the investigation and Ames himself. At that point, TRAPDOOR, still unresolved, was supplanted by NIGHTMOVER.

It was the FBI's Jim Milburn, one of the two agents who had served on the joint mole-hunt team at the CIA, who selected the code name NIGHTMOVER.[13]

Two weeks later, John Lewis made what was to prove a key decision. He selected Special Agent Leslie G. Wiser, Jr., thirty-eight, to head the NIGHTMOVER investigation. A former navy lawyer from Level Green, Pennsylvania, a small community near Pittsburgh, Wiser had been both a military defense counsel and a prosecutor while stationed at the navy's submarine base at New London, Connecticut. Wiser had joined the FBI in 1983 when he left the navy. He had worked in foreign counterintelligence for seven of his nine years with the bureau after starting out in the FBI's Minneapolis office.

Tall and thin, with brown hair, a brown mustache, and horn-rimmed glasses, Wiser, ironically, bore a faint resemblance to his quarry, Rick Ames. He did not fit the stereotype of the laconic, grim-faced FBI agent familiar from movies and television. Wiser smiled a lot and could laugh at himself; in a serious and demanding job, he had a saving sense of humor. He also had a reputation of being quick and decisive. As his FBI colleagues knew, he was not afraid to show his emotions. When things went wrong on the Ames case, as they sometimes did, Wiser, although normally upbeat, made clear the depths of his dismay.

Wiser led a squad of seven special agents, plus a supervisor from

[13]"This is a guy who must move in the darkness," Milburn told a colleague. "Let's call it NIGHTMOVER."

the joint mole-hunt unit, an accountant, two wiremen in charge of electronic surveillance, two other team members in charge of physical surveillance, a liaison man with the CIA, and an evidence specialist.

"When we opened the case on Ames no one knew for sure that this was the man," Wiser said. "We had to find out if he was guilty of espionage. He might have been guilty of something else."

The first task was to place Ames under surveillance at both his office and home. To do so, Wiser called in "the Gs." The term is FBI parlance for the SSG, the bureau's Special Surveillance Group. The Gs are a special team of surveillance experts, selected to look like ordinary citizens. Bearded bikers, white-haired grannies with shopping bags, a young mother with a baby in a stroller, college students out jogging, street repair crews in yellow hard hats, beer-belly good ole boys in pickup trucks, young lovers kissing in the park—all may be Gs on the job. The Gs are civil servants, not FBI agents, and earn lower pay than the agents. But all are trained in surveillance, photography, and communications. They are chosen precisely because they do not resemble the public's concept of FBI agents. About fifty members of the SSG were assigned to the Ames case under Wiser.

"We were afraid the investigation might leak out," Wiser said. At "the Point," as the agents call their offices at Buzzard's Point, the NIGHTMOVER operation was tightly held. "It was very secret," Wiser said. "People in the next room over did not know what we were doing. When they asked, we said we were working on the X-files," a popular TV program. "We joked around and then they stopped asking."

John Lewis recalled some of the problems Wiser faced. "It was tough to set up surveillance in a residential neighborhood where Ames lived," Lewis said. "Strangers are noticed. We told the Gs, 'Cover him like a glove but don't get made. If there is a remote chance he will identify you, abort.' More than once our people were spotted. There was a report to the police about strangers in the neighborhood. But we didn't want to go to the local police."

The surveillance at Langley proved even more difficult. The FBI ran into a problem in trying to stake out the CIA. In January

1993, Mir Aimal Kansi, a twenty-eight-year-old Pakistani, had walked along a line of cars waiting to turn left into the CIA head-quarters and systematically gunned down the occupants with an AK-47-type assault weapon, killing two CIA employees and wounding two other CIA workers and an agency contractor. "In the wake of the Kansi case," Lewis recalled, "there was a lot of consternation on the part of CIA about allowing these unmarked bureau cars roaming around Langley." The CIA was worried that its own security force would discover the FBI cars. The FBI, to its chagrin, was forced to leave the CIA grounds. "We tried to set up outside the gate on Route 123," Lewis said.

The surveillance had a simple goal, but one that was never attained. "What we were trying to do," Lewis said, "was to see him filling a dead drop or meeting a Russian. We felt he would not meet with a Russian in this country. But if he left his office and took any documents with him we would watch him fill the drop and then try to interdict the Russian when he cleared the drop. Unfortunately, that never happened."

Ames, in fact, did visit dead drops five times between May and his arrest nine months later.[14] Ames also visited signal sites three times during this period.

But, under standing orders to avoid alerting Ames, the FBI agents and the Gs kept their distance. The SVR, as it usually does, had deliberately selected drops in remote, wooded areas. The presence of another person would almost certainly have been noticed by Ames.

Pat Watson, the FBI's number two counterintelligence official in the four years leading up to the arrest of the Ameses, understood the problem from his own years as a street agent. "Physical surveillance is one of the most delicate tasks to employ correctly in an

[14]The first of these trips took place only two days after Wiser had been named to head the investigation, and the second occurred four days later. On May 26, Ames left an "urgent" note asking for money, and on May 30 the SVR left him a large amount of cash in dead drop BRIDGE. In July, Ames retrieved money and a message promising more. On September 9, Ames left a message in a dead drop, and on October 3 he recovered a message.

espionage investigation," he said. "To attempt to take Ames to a meeting or a drop without being observed would have been extremely difficult."

The fact that Ames was a professional intelligence officer, trained in the arts of surveillance and countersurveillance, made the FBI even more wary. Ames's training was very much in the mind of both Les Wiser and John Lewis when the bureau began tailing the Ameses. "Ames was a CIA man," Lewis said. "We didn't know how good he was or wasn't."

When the FBI began its surveillance of Ames, CIA director R. James Woolsey disclosed to Anthony Lake, President Clinton's national security adviser, that a mole had penetrated the agency and had now been identified. Lake, who realized there had been a critical breach in the nation's security, immediately briefed the president. Clinton was told the bad news in the Oval Office.

The president "was interested and concerned," according to one White House official. About once a month thereafter, Lake met with the president to brief him on the progress of the FBI surveillance and investigation. Lake filled Clinton in on each new development and every detail, save one. He did not tell the president the name of the mole. The national security adviser did not know it—he had deliberately avoided learning Ames's name, lest he inadvertently let it slip out.

Ames, meanwhile, was confident that his spying had gone undetected. Only two months earlier, he had sent a message to the SVR which began: "All is well with me—I have no indication that anything is wrong or suspected." In the same letter, Ames discussed the morale of the former Soviet division, now the Central Eurasia division, personnel changes at the CIA, and information about the agency's budget. He also included a variety of classified documents, passing the whole package to the Russians through a dead drop.

On June 11, the FBI, after obtaining approval from the Foreign Intelligence Surveillance Court, began wiretapping Ames's house and monitoring his telephone conversations with Rosario. No FBI agents dressed as telephone linemen had to shinny up poles on North Randolph Street; authorized wiretaps are easily arranged through the central office of the telephone company.

On June 25, on the authority of the attorney general, FBI agents searched Ames's basement office, GVO6, in the Counternarcotics Center at CIA headquarters. They found 144 documents marked SECRET and ten marked TOP SECRET or above. Many of the documents dealt with counterintelligence or military information about the Soviet Union or the Russian Federation, and had no relationship to Ames's work in counternarcotics.

One of the top secret documents recovered from Ames's office dealt with antisubmarine warfare. The document described techniques used by Soviet and Russian nuclear submarines to try to avoid detection and tracking by American forces. This was so far afield from Ames's responsibilities that counterintelligence officials at first feared there might be another mole who had provided the document to Ames or told the SVR of its existence so that Moscow could task Ames to try to acquire it. But Ames, as it later became clear, was able to get his hands on an astonishing number of documents because of lax security at Langley.

To the FBI, the documents were further evidence that they were on target. But there was still a continuing problem of how to watch Ames without his knowing.

It was a difficulty that could be overcome if the FBI were able to place a James Bond–type transmitter in Ames's car that would give off a continuous signal, allowing the FBI to keep track of his whereabouts. But it would take time to install. Wiser developed an ingenious scheme to gain access to the Jaguar. During the week of July 18, he arranged for two agents in the bureau's Criminal Division to invite Ames and his boss, David Edger, to a meeting on narcotics traffic at FBI headquarters. Ostensibly, the meeting was to deal with the "Black Sea initiative." It was Ames's special project, a program to develop cooperation among countries in the region to curtail the opium crop. The meeting was staged for only one purpose; to get Ames to drive to the FBI.

It was vital to the plan, however, that Ames come in his Jaguar. Edger, forty-eight, was the deputy director of the Counternarcotics Center, an Oklahoman who had been a case officer in Chile, Costa Rica, and Brazil. By now, Edger knew that Ames was the subject of a counterintelligence investigation, and he was in on the plot. According to a CIA source, "David said, 'I can't use my car, it's being repaired, we'll have to use yours.' So they drove in the Jaguar to the FBI."

Ames parked in the driveway alongside the cobblestoned courtyard at headquarters and got in an elevator to go upstairs to the meeting. As soon as the doors of the elevator had closed, an FBI agent, using a duplicate set of keys he had made a few days earlier, drove the Jaguar into the underground garage. The meeting lasted half a day, ample time for FBI technicians to install the transmitter, known in the bureau as a "beacon." The work was done on Ames's Jaguar right in the FBI garage as he attended the meeting a few floors above.[15] Then the car was returned to the driveway where Ames had left it.

The same month, Ames traveled to the former Soviet republic of Georgia for the Counternarcotics Center. He showed up in Tbilisi, the capital, a few weeks after another CIA officer, Freddie Woodruff, had arrived there to run a covert operation for the agency. Woodruff, forty-five, married, and the father of three small children, was a veteran CIA officer, who had served in Leningrad, Turkey, and Africa. He had been sent to Georgia to help train its security forces to shore up the government and to protect the physical safety of its beleaguered pro-Western president, Eduard Shevardnadze.

On August 8, Woodruff and Eldar Guguladze, director of the Georgian intelligence service, took what was described as a sightseeing trip north of the capital near Mount Kazbek, the second-highest peak in the Caucasus. There were two unidentified women in the car, according to an Associated Press report. That night, someone fired a shot at Woodruff's car. The CIA man died of a single bullet in the head. Although the government never identified Woodruff as a CIA officer, CIA director R. James Woolsey, who was in Moscow for talks with Yevgeny M.

[15]For technical reasons, the FBI installers opted for the beacon alone rather than also putting in a microphone, which would have had the advantage of picking up conversations in the car. Apparently the Jaguar's electrical system is complex, and the car was difficult to bug.

Primakov, the head of the SVR, flew to Georgia to escort Woodruff's body back to the United States.

After Ames's arrest, the CIA and the FBI investigated to see if Woodruff's death might have been linked in some way to Ames's presence in Tbilisi. There was speculation that Ames might have tipped off the SVR to Woodruff's mission and that the CIA man as a result was targeted for a political assassination. Several months later, a brief account of the findings of the investigation was made public by the State Department. It said that Woodruff had passed a car that had run out of gas and that one of the occupants of the stranded car, Anzor Sharmaidze, had fired the fatal shot after he tried and failed to flag down Woodruff's car. Sharmaidze was convicted and sentenced to fifteen years' hard labor. "The results of this investigation indicate that this attack was a random act of violence and was not politically motivated," said Michael McCurry, then the State Department spokesman.

While there is no evidence to suggest otherwise, what the government did not reveal was equally interesting. Ames and Woodruff were friends who knew each other well and at one point had a financial relationship. The official account did not disclose that when Ames, with his first wife, went to New York for the CIA in 1976, he rented his house on Golf Course Island in Reston to Freddie Woodruff and his wife, Meredith. After Woolsey brought back Woodruff's body, a funeral service was held at Woodruff's house in Herndon, Virginia; Rick Ames was there.

That same month of August, Ames and his wife and son traveled to Miami Beach on vacation. The FBI went along.[16]

It was also in August that Les Wiser instituted a "trash cover" on the Ames residence—FBI-speak for going through a suspect's garbage. To do so, he did not need approval from Janet Reno or the special surveillance court, because once a citizen puts trash out on the street for pickup, it is fair game. But this was to be an especially delicate kind of trash cover.

The problem, put simply, was how to get at the trash without Ames suspecting anything. John Lewis recalled the difficulties.

[16]Ames was at the Doral. Some of the FBI agents stayed at the Fontainebleau. Ames did no spying in Miami Beach.

"We discovered he was a restless sleeper. He would get up at two or three in the morning and look out in the street."

Wiser devised a plan and turned to the Gs special Search and Response Team (SRT). Ames's trash was collected on Wednesdays. The FBI obtained a trash barrel on wheels, identical to all the others provided to homeowners in Arlington. The barrel would be placed in a van. As the van reached the Ames house in the dead of night, two men would jump out and switch barrels. Wiser had the team perform practice drills until he was satisfied that the switch could be done in seconds, noiselessly. The trash would then be taken to a nearby location—a sort of trash safe house—where it would be examined and anything of interest removed. Wiser was determined that nothing go wrong. Studying the plan, he found a potential glitch—the Arlington trash cans had individual serial numbers. Ames might notice if his trash barrel had suddenly changed numbers during the night. The trash would have to be returned to the Ames residence, well before dawn. "I wanted the same barrel back in front of his house," Wiser said.

But only a few weeks later, Bryant told Wiser to call off the trash brigade. "There was concern his antenna might be up," Wiser recalled.[17] Wiser was reluctant to give up altogether on a technique that had yielded good results for him in the past. But, for the moment, he had no choice. He brought the nocturnal trash operation to a halt.

On the morning of September 9, Ames left his house unusually early, just after 6:00 A.M. Through a mixup, the Gs arrived half an hour late and missed him. They were barely in place when Ames drove back to the house at about 6:25 A.M.

Some weeks earlier, the FBI had trained a video camera, known as "the Eye" on Ames's front door.[18] "We had remote [video] cov-

---

[17]Ames had been asking questions of Bob Wade, the FBI liaison man at the CIA, about a report that a KGB defector had told the FBI that "hundreds of Americans" had spied for the Soviets. The report had appeared in Ronald Kessler's book, *The FBI* (New York: Pocket Books, 1993), p. 433.

[18]In FBI parlance, the person or camera responsible for surveillance at a given moment is called "the Eye." Thus, an FBI agent might ask another: "Who has the Eye?"

erage," Wiser said. "We reviewed our tapes, so we knew he had gone out and come back."

It got worse before the day was over. "September 9th was Black Thursday," said John Lewis. "We missed him in the morning and then when he left Langley that afternoon we missed him leaving the agency, too. We missed him twice in one day."

At 4:00 P.M., Ames left the agency early. The FBI surveillance cars were waiting outside the gates at Langley. Ames in his red Jaguar zoomed onto the George Washington Parkway. "Ames just takes off like a bat out of hell," Bear Bryant recalled. "And we lose him."

Although the FBI had planted the beacon in Ames's Jaguar, its signals could be picked up only if the bureau's trailing car was reasonably close behind. And the beacon was not as powerful as the FBI had hoped.

Wiser was devastated. He was, he remembered, "in the depths of despair." But later that evening, the FBI caught up with the Ameses for what turned out to be a crucial surveillance. Rick and Rosario drove in the Jaguar to a parents' night at Paul's school in Alexandria. After the meeting, they drove far out of their way to a residential neighborhood of northwest Washington. With the Ameses under video surveillance, they turned into Garfield Terrace, a cul-de-sac, backed out, and returned to their home in Virginia without ever leaving the car.

They had passed a mailbox, signal site ROSE, at the intersection of Garfield Terrace and Garfield Street. To the FBI, analyzing the videotapes afterwards, it seemed clear that the Ameses were trying to check the mailbox to verify from the passenger side of the Jaguar, where Rosario sat, that a dead drop Ames had loaded that afternoon—when the FBI had lost him—had been emptied by the Russians.

Wiser was getting considerable heat from the FBI brass. His superiors let it be known to him that both Freeh, the new FBI director, and Woolsey, the CIA director, were distressed that Ames had gone operational and eluded surveillance twice in a single day.

Les Wiser decided to reinstitute the trash cover, despite Bryant's order to stop it. "I took the view that he had merely suspended the trash cover," Wiser said, "so I unsuspended it." It was a gamble, and might even endanger his career, because if he came up empty-handed again, with nothing but banana peels and coffee grounds, Bryant might not appreciate Wiser's interpretation of his orders.

Wiser decided to wait until Ames left for Ankara on a trip for the Counternarcotics Center on Monday, September 13. Two days later, in the predawn hours of September 15, a black van, its lights off, glided slowly past Ames's house. Just as they had practiced in their trash drills, two men jumped out and silently switched the barrels. The van moved on. Moments later, the FBI got its first major break in the case. They removed from Ames's trash a torn, yellow Post-it note. It said:

I AM READY TO MEET AT B ON 1 OCT. I CANNOT READ NORTH 13–19 SEPT. IF YOU *WILL MEET* AT B ON 1 OCT. PLS SIGNAL NORTH W[EEK] OF 20 SEPT TO CONFI[RM]. *NO* MESSAGE AT PIPE. IF YOU *CANNOT* MEE[T] 1 OCT, SIGNAL NORTH AFTER 27 SEPT WITH MESSAGE AT PIPE.[19]

Translated, the note, which the FBI laboratory determined was in Ames's handwriting, meant that he was ready to meet the SVR in Bogotá on October 1 but would be unable to read signal site NORTH during the middle of September. The reason was that Ames would be attending the counternarcotics meeting in Turkey that week. He asked that the Russians confirm the Bogotá date by leaving a signal at NORTH after he returned from Turkey, or by leaving a signal there, and a message in dead drop PIPE if the Bogotá meeting was canceled.

Working backwards, the FBI realized that this was the message that Ames had passed to the Russians on September 9, six days earlier. They figured it out; Ames had left the house early that morning to lay down a signal indicating that he would fill a drop

---

[19]Letters in brackets were presumably on a portion of the note that was torn away and not recovered. NORTH was a signal site on a telephone pole at Military Road and Thirty-sixth Street near Ames's house in Arlington.

later in the day. The FBI concluded that the note it had recovered from the trash was a first draft, because it also found a small piece of a second draft. Ames had put the final version in a dead drop on the afternoon of September 9 when he went racing out of Langley, eluding the FBI. Now the FBI knew exactly what the Ameses were looking for when they drove into Garfield Terrace a week earlier after the PTA meeting.

"The signal he was looking for," Wiser said, "was the erasure of the mark he had made that day. We saw nothing on the mailbox, but didn't know what it was. He was looking for 'nothing' and it was a signal."

When the Post-it note was found, Wiser was called at his home before dawn. He showered, shaved, and got in to the office a little before 6:00 A.M. He was elated when he read the note. This was it. "When we got this, we knew we had a spy," Wiser said, "and that he was active."

Wiser was waiting outside Bryant's office, smiling triumphantly, when his boss arrived.

"Wiser looked like the Halloween pumpkin," Bryant said. "I mean he was so happy it was unbelievable."

Wiser savored the moment. "I walked in and said, 'We've solved it.' I showed him the note. He asked me where we got it. So I told him, and there was a little discussion about it." Bryant, after all, had ordered Wiser to halt the trash cover.

All was quickly forgiven. "It was," said Bryant, "a marvelous piece of insubordination."

Why did Aldrich Ames, a trained CIA officer who knew the immense risks he was taking, leave incriminating notes and printer ribbons in his trash? It seemed incredibly sloppy, but Ames the CIA man was not that careless. True, he had lost his briefcase on the subway in New York and had left his safe open, but his CIA record is not replete with such violations. There was a disconnect between Ames the reckless Russian spy, driving his Jaguar into the parking lot at Langley, tossing notes to the KGB in his trash, and Ames the generally careful CIA spy. One answer to the mystery is that Ames never expected to be caught. And he also knew that if he was in turn betrayed by a defector or a CIA source, no amount of caution would really protect him.

Now, the FBI felt it had probable cause to ask the special surveillance court for permission to search the Ameses' home and to plant room bugs in his house. John Lewis was both grim and exhilarated when he saw the Post-it note. He remembered his reaction: "We're going to nail this son of a gun!

"I mean, we had the bank deposits. Sure, it looked like he had transmitted information, but was he still active? The number one question in my mind was, is he former, or still involved? We knew that we had lost lots of sources. When we found the note we had no doubts that he was 100 percent guilty and still in operation. We knew we were dealing with a live penetration."

18

ENDGAME

On September 19, two days after Ames returned from Turkey, he made airline reservations for the trip he expected to take to Bogotá at the end of the month. But ten days later the SVR signaled Ames that the trip was off.

The FBI listened in as Ames told his wife the news that day, September 29:

ALDRICH: Yeah, well, listen. There. . . there's news. No travel.

ROSARIO: Oh. . . .

ALDRICH: Yeah. . . not going.

ROSARIO: Oh.

ALDRICH: So you should ah. . . guess. . . ah. . . give CECI a call whenever you can get through to her and ah. . . tell her that. . . you know that. . . they ah. . . . My visit was canceled.

ROSARIO: Uh-huh. And does that mean you retrieve something?

ALDRICH: Yeah. Uh-huh. Yeah.

The next day, Ames canceled his airline reservations. On October 3, following the script in the Post-it note that the FBI had recovered from his trash, he picked up a message from dead drop PIPE telling him of the new arrangements for the Bogotá meet. The message was written on a piece of paper torn from the classified section of the *Washington Times*. It said:

> Are ready to meet at a city well known to you on 1 Nov. Alt dates are 2, 7, 8 Nov. If it does for you put Smile before the 17th of October. Best regards.

The message rescheduled the meeting in Bogotá for November 1 or the alternate dates and instructed Ames to put another chalk mark on SMILE, the mailbox at the corner of Thirty-seventh and R Streets, to confirm the rendezvous. On October 3, the day Ames picked up the message, he called Rosario on his cellular phone to assure her that "all is well." Later in the conversation, this exchange took place:

ROSARIO: Financially, too?
ALDRICH: Ah, yeah, ah. Wait 'til I get there.

On Saturday, October 9, Ames, Rosario, and Paul were in Pensacola, Florida, to attend the wedding of Ames's nephew Patrick, the middle son of his sister, Nancy Everly. A 1991 graduate of the U.S. Naval Academy at Annapolis, Patrick had been sent to Pensacola for his navy flight training. Paul was the ring bearer.[1]

The FBI took advantage of the Ameses' absence to make a court-authorized entry into their house, both to search and to plant bugs in it. The FBI had been wiretapping the Ameses for four months but could overhear only telephone conversations. Now, the bureau hid tiny transmitters throughout the house, in

---

[1]After the Ameses were arrested, a picture of the family, taken on the happy occasion of the wedding in Pensacola, was widely distributed. It shows a beaming, white-jacketed Ames, holding his sweet-faced son, who has a rose in the lapel of his blazer, flanked by a smiling Rosario, who is wearing designer sunglasses and discreet gold jewelry.

the Ameses' bedroom and in virtually every other room. From that day on, the FBI could listen in to room conversations as well.

The house had no burglar alarm, which made the entry a bit easier, but the FBI has declined to say how it got in. The bureau has expert lock pickers, however. The search yielded a cornucopia of espionage materials.

"The best stuff we got was from the hard drive of his computer," Les Wiser recalled. "There were some operational notes from him to the Russians and one operational note from the Russians to him. The notes made reference to signal sites and drops. He actually listed a bunch of sites and drops."

The FBI also found a key piece of evidence, a telephone number in a pocket of one of Ames's suits and the same number in his computer. "We discovered it was a number in the Russian residential compound in Vienna," Wiser said. "We believe it was the phone number of a KGB intelligence officer. That was very important because it established a clear link to Russians. The letters they sent him all said, 'Dear friend'; they never mentioned Russia."

The small team of FBI technicians and agents who went into the house downloaded the files in Ames's computer and copied data from his floppy disks as well.[2] They were careful to leave no clue that the house had been entered. They were in and gone in a matter of hours.

On Sunday, FBI computer experts began going through the file that had been electronically captured. "The floppies were write-protected," Wiser recalled. "The password on the floppies was KOLOKOL. We figured it out."

The Ameses returned from Florida after the wedding. But Ames had not yet gotten around to putting the chalk mark on the mailbox in Georgetown to indicate that he would go to Bogotá, a lapse

---

[2]The FBI explored the possibility of bugging Ames's computer so that the bureau could electronically detect and read what he might write in the future. The technology exists to pick up electronic signals from a computer screen, or even more reliably, from a keyboard, but usually the receiver must be located within 250 feet. The FBI's technical boffins concluded a computer bug was not technically feasible in this instance, and it was not done.

that appeared to irritate his wife. On October 12, Rick and Rosario had this conversation:

ALDRICH: The other thing I have to do. . . I have to take off early to put a signal down.

ROSARIO: You have to what?

ALDRICH: They would like confirmation that I am coming, that [unintelligible]

ROSARIO: Who?

ALDRICH: [unintelligible]

ROSARIO: But how do you. . . ? Do you have to lay something down in the afternoon?

ALDRICH: No. Uh-uh. Just mark the signal.

ROSARIO: Why didn't you do it today for God's sakes?

ALDRICH: I should have except it was raining like crazy.

ROSARIO: But is it agreed that. . . ?

ALDRICH: Before the fourteenth, they said.

ROSARIO: [unintelligible] Tomorrow's the thirteenth.

ALDRICH: Uh-huh.

ROSARIO: Well, honey, I hope you didn't screw up.

ALDRICH: Uh-huh.

ROSARIO: All you have to do is a mark?

ALDRICH: Yeah. Don't worry. If I didn't put it down they'd still show.

ROSARIO: Do you have time to go there and come back?

ALDRICH: It only takes fifteen minutes. There's no traffic.

ROSARIO: Should I just take [their minor son]?

ALDRICH: . . . 6:00 A.M. . . . 6:30 A.M. . . .

ROSARIO: Oh, that's early. Oh, okay.

ALDRICH: I'll just go on and do it and bang and then I'm back here.

The excerpt, released by the FBI, illustrated a recurrent motif of the wiretapped conversations, in which Rosario emerges as a sort of Colombian *kvetch* with a low opinion of her husband's trade-craft, and Ames came across, at times, like a rather henpecked spy. Rick and Rosario were discussing espionage in the same cadences that husbands and wives might use in talking about who would nip into 7-Eleven to pick up a quart of milk. It was proof that even the dramatic and dangerous can descend into the banal—at least until one realizes what they were really talking about.

Ames made his signal early the the next morning. On October 25, as Ames prepared to leave on his trip, Rosario fretted about her husband flying around with all that cash:

ROSARIO: [Losing your luggage] worries me a lot with your trip to Bogotá. It's happening more and more and you know exactly what I mean. You cannot afford to lose your suitcase and so perhaps you should use a carry-on.

ALDRICH: I am going to use a carry-on.

ROSARIO: Well, yeah, you're putting the bulk of the stuff in that suitcase, right?

ALDRICH: Sometimes, yeah, but I think I'm going to use the carry-on.

ROSARIO: You are going to have to be a little more imaginative about you always have this envelope with this big hunk, I mean really.

Three days later, Rosario was still worried about the cash. "If you get the money," she said, ". . . what I would do, would be to leave in cash, although it's a big amount of cash to leave but I guess it's better. You get the money in dollars, right?"

"Right," Ames replied.

The next day, Rosario warned, "I don't want you to bring back anything that will make them look in your luggage."

At the end of the month, Ames slipped away to Bogotá without telling the CIA. He instructed Rosario to lie and tell anyone who asked that he had gone to Annapolis.

What Ames did not know was that when he flew to Bogotá, the FBI went along. FBI agents in a parked car watched as Ames strolled through the Unicentro shopping mall, located on a street closed off to traffic. Ames headed for a bowling alley called the Bolicentro but did not go in.

A KGB officer was spotted in front of the same bowling alley.

Both Ames and the KGB man were videotaped by the FBI. Les Wiser was in Bogotá to supervise the operation.

But apparently, just as Rosario had feared, a bag went astray when Ames arrived in the Colombian capital. This conversation was recorded on October 30:

ROSARIO: [discussing the delayed bag] I am very, very nervous.
ALDRICH: I know.
ROSARIO: I know you don't give a shit about the suitcase, but I mean, okay, fine.
ALDRICH: The suitcase will turn up.
ROSARIO: Um, okay.
ALDRICH: I'm sure it will.
ROSARIO: I'm just hoping you hadn't decided to pack your. . . and you didn't have anything. . . uh.
ALDRICH: What?
ROSARIO: You didn't have anything that shouldn't have been. . . in that bag?
ALDRICH: No, honey.

On November 1, Ames telephoned Rosario in Arlington from Bogotá to report on his meeting:

ROSARIO: Why, what's up?
ALDRICH: How are you?
ROSARIO: No. Honey, it's. . . . What's up? Why are you there?
ALDRICH: No. Nothing. Nothing. I had a short meeting this evening.
ROSARIO: Oh.
ALDRICH: I came back and ELISIO [phonetic] was here and so we had a good time. [pause]
ROSARIO: Did you really meet?
ALDRICH: Uh-huh.
ROSARIO: When did you get back?
ALDRICH: [to someone in the background] When did I get back? [to Rosario] About nine.
ROSARIO: Well, honey, you don't honey, Rick. . . . Why do have to. . .

ALDRICH: Nine-thirty.

ROSARIO: . . . Why do you have to ask my mother when you got back? Don't be an asshole.

Once again, Rosario sounded much like an irritated case officer suspicious that her all-thumbs agent had somehow managed to do everything wrong, or might. On the tapes, Rosario Ames seems an eager, aggressive participant in her husband's espionage. Did he screw up? Why didn't he put the signal down, for God sakes? Use carry-on luggage, don't carry cash. Better leave the cash in Bogotá. Did he really meet the Russians on time? Ames has put a different spin on her role, ascribing it simply to wifely concern that he not be caught.

Later in the conversation, Rosario tries to soften her tone:

ROSARIO: The only reason I was upset was because I thought that it had all been for nothing and that, you know, you hadn't. . .

ALDRICH: No. No. Uh-uh. No.

ROSARIO: You're sure?

ALDRICH: Yeah. . . .

ROSARIO: . . . So what are you going to do tomorrow?

ALDRICH: I'm gonna do a little shopping in Unicentro, then I have meetings in the afternoon, and then out in the evening as well.

ROSARIO: . . . Okay, just be careful and you swear to me that nothing went wrong?

ALDRICH: Yeah. That's right.

ROSARIO: You swear?

ALDRICH: Uh-huh.

ROSARIO: Well, you don't sound too sure. You're sure? Sure, right?

ALDRICH: Sure.

ROSARIO: You wouldn't lie to me, would you?

ALDRICH: No. No. Okay?

ROSARIO: Okay.

ALDRICH: Okay. Good. . . . Just rest assured. Okay?

ROSARIO: Okay. Be careful tomorrow. Okay?
ALDRICH: Sure.

When Ames got back home in Virginia on November 3 Rosario asked him when he might have to go back to Bogotá. The FBI was listening to their bugged conversation. Ames said he would be going next time either to Caracas or Quito. And he assured Rosario that there would be "four deliveries to me over the next year to build up the financial situation. They're holding. . . one million nine hundred thousand dollars," he whispered to her.[3]

It was just a matter of time now, a question of when the right moment would come to make the arrest. But as the FBI dug deeper that month, it made an astonishing discovery about Ames's trip to Ankara in September. He had taken his laptop computer with him. He had loaded it with classified data, in violation of agency rules, and games.

Ames's boss, David Edger, the deputy director of the Counternarcotics Center, accompanied him to Turkey and asked to use the laptop to access the games. Ames could hardly refuse. Anyone else would have been nervous, because among the files was one called VLAD, which of course was the name of the KGB case officer who had met with him in Rome. But Ames had gotten away with so much for so long that, apparently unworried, he simply handed over the laptop to his superior. Edger noticed the file labeled VLAD but did not try to read it. He was startled, however, to see that Ames, against regulations, had brought files containing a huge number of classified cables and memos. When Edger returned from Turkey, he reported what he had seen to the CIA and the FBI.[4]

---

[3]The FBI calculated that by 1993 the KGB and the SVR had paid Ames a total of $2.7 million. That made Ames the highest-paid spy in the history of the world. If the $1.9 million that the SVR promised him in Bogotá in November 1993 is added to the $2.7 million, it means that Ames was paid or promised a staggering total of $4.6 million.

[4]Edger was already aware that Ames was under investigation; two months earlier, he had helped to trick Ames into driving his Jaguar to FBI headquarters, where the transmitter was installed.

In November, after his trip to Bogotá, Ames gained access in his computer to the message system of the Directorate of Operations. The floppy drives in the DO are all locked, so that it is not possible to download data and pocket it. But the floppy drives in the Directorate of Intelligence, the agency's overt side, are open. Administratively, the Counternarcotics Center where Ames worked was part of the Intelligence Directorate, so Ames had a floppy drive. He was able to use a LAN system that could tap into the DO.

Delighted with his discovery, Ames downloaded three hundred to four hundred documents, secret DO cables from all over the world, onto three floppy disks. He planned to pass the disks to the SVR in a dead drop.[5]

As 1993 came to a close, the FBI was still hoping to catch Ames in the act of filling or emptying a dead drop, but it also remained wary of getting in so close that Ames would detect the surveillance. John Lewis, Les Wiser's boss, was getting increasingly nervous. "There were several worrisome factors," Lewis said. "We felt sure they would meet him at Christmas or in January and give him a lot of money, but they didn't meet him. That raised concern that maybe he was aware of the investigation or had been tipped off by the Russians. Why aren't they coming to meet him?

"We began picking up Russian IOs [intelligence officers] in the vicinity of our surveillance. We began seeing SVR people in the area of the drops. The Russians monitor our activities. We knew the SVR had good technical coverage. They may not know what we are saying but they know where we are. We had heavy surveillance in Arlington and Langley. They must know there is a hell of a lot of activity going on around there. But fortunately they did not put it together."

As the FBI pondered when to move in for an arrest, its officials realized a deadline was fast approaching. The endgame in the

---

[5]Ames had no scheduled deliveries to make through dead drops between November 1993 and February 21, 1994, the date of his arrest. As a result, the CIA cables never got to Moscow.

Ames affair was complicated by a startling decision that had been made in Langley weeks before.

The CIA had assigned Rick Ames to go to Moscow.[6]

On February 22, Ames had been scheduled to leave for Ankara, Turkey, then Bucharest. From Bucharest. Ames was to fly to Frankfurt, where he was supposed to meet his boss, David Edger. Together, they would fly to Moscow. It would be Ames's second visit to Moscow for the CIA; he had first visited there in 1992.

In Moscow, Ames was to confer on narcotics traffic with Russian internal security officials on the home turf of the SVR, the very Russian spy service that had paid him millions of dollars for almost nine years. Later, CIA officials defended the remarkable assignment, claiming that the trip and the drug conference had been routinely scheduled weeks before. To cancel the trip, the CIA officials worried, might tip Ames to the fact that he was under suspicion. Even to send someone else might have the same result; Ames, who spoke Russian, was responsible for monitoring drug trafficking in the Black Sea region. He was the logical choice to go. The agency dithered. Over a period of a month, the date of the trip was moved forward three times, once in January and twice in February. Inside Langley, the debate went back and forth. How many more times could the trip be postponed?

It was the FBI's Les Wiser who came up with a ruse that the CIA used the third time Ames's trip was delayed. Why not tell Ames he had been selected to give an intelligence briefing to the president, or if that was not possible, to Anthony Lake? The CIA liked the idea, but scaled it back; Ames was told he would be briefing a senior member of the NSC staff.

[6]CIA director Woolsey was livid when the author reported, accurately, in *Vanity Fair* that the FBI had arrested Ames on February 21, 1994, to prevent him from getting on a plane to Moscow the next day. Kent Harrington, Woolsey's press spokesman, issued a statement to the magazine and to the *Washington Times* claiming that "at no time did anyone decide to allow Ames to actually travel to Moscow," and insisting that it was all a CIA ploy to avoid alerting him. The statement was untrue; whether or not Woolsey or his aide were aware of it, there were CIA officials who thought it would be fine if Ames got on the plane to Moscow. They were overruled by the FBI. See David Wise, "The Spy in the Jaguar," *Vanity Fair,* July 1994, pp. 88–129.

Lake approved the bogus briefing, which took place at CIA headquarters. The NSC staffer who was briefed by Ames was aware of the purpose of the meeting, but he was not told which of several CIA officers who participated in the briefing was the mole. Someone with an ironic sense of humor chose the topic of the briefing: all aspects of potential cooperation between the SVR and the CIA.

The White House sent detailed questions to the CIA in advance of the briefing, to make it seem legitimate. At the briefing, various groups of CIA specialists spoke about areas where cooperation with Moscow might be possible. When it was Ames's turn, he spoke about potential cooperation in the area of counternarcotics.[7] He suspected nothing.

The fake briefing provided a breather, but it did not solve the basic problem of whether to let Ames go to Russia. Ames was scheduled to spend a week in Moscow. Or a lifetime. Certainly, senior CIA officials from the agency's director, R. James Woolsey, down were well aware that if Rick Ames were allowed to go to Moscow again, this time he might never bother to come back.

The origins of the trip are cloaked in bureaucratic mists; nobody wanted to take responsibility for telling Ames he was going to Moscow in the first place. Ames himself is known to have suggested he go, but the CIA's dilemma was largely self-created. If it had not scheduled the trip, the agency's officials would not have had to keep postponing it. They were trapped in a box of their own making.

CIA officials insisted later that they weren't *really* thinking of letting Ames go to Moscow. The truth was very different; senior officials of the agency were divided over whether to let Ames go to Moscow.

"There were people involved in this case [in the CIA] who thought he should go," John Lewis said. "There were some people who felt there was no problem with letting him go. There were

[7]Ames and the other CIA officers who took part in the briefing were told that after the results were evaluated, there would be another meeting, this time to brief Lake. It never took place; Ames was arrested a short time later.

some people in the agency who felt he should not go. I was involved in the Howard case. I kept thinking if by any chance Ames had been alerted, they may very well not be responding to any of his signals. We would run the risk of his not returning."

In early February, about two weeks before the Ameses were arrested, Lewis said, a meeting was held to decide the issue of the Moscow trip. Officials of the FBI and the CIA met, along with Mark Hulkower, the assistant U.S. attorney who was later successfully to prosecute the Ameses. "We met with the agency, Mr. Hulkower, and others to explore the feasibility of his going to Russia. He was in the CN Center and had reasons to go there, there had been meetings in the past, there was precedent. I decided at the meeting under no circumstances would we permit him to leave."

Paul Redmond, the CIA counterintelligence official credited with giving new impetus to the mole hunt three years earlier, agreed with Lewis. The FBI official was adamant. "I said we are not going to allow him to leave under any circumstances. Paul gave a thumbs-up. He went like this"—Lewis grinned and jabbed his thumb upward to illustrate.

And that was that. The matter was settled. The FBI was not about to let Ames get on the plane to Moscow. It would arrest him first. Nine years earlier, Edward Lee Howard had slipped through the FBI's dragnet in New Mexico only to surface a year later in Moscow. There was no way that the bureau was going to allow history to repeat itself.

At the White House, Anthony Lake was briefing the president on the case once a week now, and then almost daily in the ten-day period before the arrest.

About a week before Ames was supposed to leave for Moscow, the FBI overheard him make an appointment to take his car in to Rosenthal Jaguar in Vienna, Virginia, to have the electrical system serviced. The intercepted telephone conversation created an awkward dilemma for the bureau. The Rosenthal organization, long one of Washington's major car dealerships, sold Jaguar, Nissan, Honda, Chevrolet, and many other makes. But only months earlier, eight Rosenthal employees had been convicted of conspiracy to launder drug money after they were caught in a sting operation in which the FBI had participated with local police. Detectives posing as drug dealers had purchased expensive cars for cash from the Rosenthal salesmen.

With the arrest only days away, Ames's decision to take his car in for repairs created an obvious danger. If a Rosenthal mechanic discovered the transmitter that the FBI had planted in the Jaguar, and if anything was said to Ames, the game would be over. Under normal circumstances, the FBI might have approached Rosenthal Jaguar to ask for its cooperation, although the decision to do so would have been a close call, since there was always the risk of a leak. But because the FBI had participated in MONEY MAGIC, as it code-named the sting operation, the bureau was uncertain of what kind of a reception it would get from the Rosenthal organization.

Les Wiser hesitated to make the approach. In the end he decided not to. He would hold his breath and take the risk. But, hedging his bets, Wiser had one or more of the Gs on hand in the waiting room, looking inconspicuous as usual, when Ames picked up his car. If anything was said to Ames about a strange device found in the Jaguar, the FBI would have known. Wiser's gamble paid off; the beacon was never discovered.

Now it was time for the last act. "We did not want to see him leave the country," John Lewis said. "That's why we arrested him when we did, because he was scheduled to go to Russia." The FBI even considered arresting Ames on February 22 as he was on his way to the airport, in the hope that he was taking classified documents to Moscow with him. But it was decided not to cut it that close.

Monday, February 21, was Presidents' Day, a federal holiday. Les Wiser was up very early. He had been having trouble sleeping for several weeks; he would awake at 3:30 A.M. and get up. But this morning, he felt confident.

Because it was a holiday, Wiser and Mark Hulkower, the assistant U.S. attorney, had to make special arrangements to meet with United States Magistrate Barry R. Poretz. They waited while the magistrate read Wiser's lengthy affidavit. As soon as Poretz had signed the arrest warrant, Wiser called the FBI command post in Tysons Corner. In turn, the command post called David Edger, who was standing by at the CIA. Normally, Ames, busy packing, would not have gone in to the office on a holiday. But Edger, by prearrangement, called Ames at home.

"You're leaving tomorrow," Edger said. "We have some hot information; you better get in here."

In a few moments, Ames left his house in the Jaguar. He turned right into North Randolph, then right again into Quebec Street. There, the way was blocked by two FBI cars. "Two cars with red lights came up behind him," Wiser said. "He pulled over to let them by, but they were for him."

It was all over in forty-five seconds. Under arrest for espionage and handcuffed, Ames was taken in an FBI car to the bureau's office in Tysons Corner.

There, the FBI had created an elaborate fake squad room, complete with coffee cups, to give it a lived-in look. It was all part of a psychological maneuver to try to get Ames to talk, John Lewis explained. "We had photos on the wall, big blowups, photos of his house, his drops, maps of every place he had served, to show him early on, 'We've got you.' Because we really wanted him to talk. We were trying to show he had been under investigation for a long time."

The scene was etched in Lewis's memory. "When they brought him in, he looked like the wind was knocked out of him. He was asked to sit down. When he looked around at the walls, his head sank. And he wouldn't look up."

19

THE VICTIMS

He was a big, tall man, about six foot two with an athletic build. He was from Archangel, the port city in the ice-bound far north of Russia, which might have explained his blond hair.

Sergei M. Motorin, a young major in the KGB, had arrived in Washington in 1980. He was listed as a third secretary in the Soviet embassy. Although married—his wife, Olga, had come with him—he had a wandering eye. That was of some interest to the FBI, which was always prepared to approach Soviet intelligence officers if it could find a way.

But the opportunity did not present itself for almost two years. Then the bureau got a telephone call from a friendly insurance adjuster. Major Motorin had been in a car accident. There was a hooker in the car.

The FBI's counterintelligence agents in the Washington field office began to keep closer track of the KGB officer. Not long afterward, the FBI watched Motorin walk into a store in downtown Washington and barter his operational allowance of vodka and

Cuban cigars for stereo equipment. The vodka and cigars were supposed to be used to help recruit American agents. It was clear that the major was cheating on his wife and had now committed an indiscretion that could get him into serious trouble if it became known to his superiors.

It was time for a chat. With that kind of leverage over Motorin, the FBI did not have too much difficulty in persuading him to listen, although it took several months and constant pressure. Pat Watson, who had been the FBI's deputy assistant director for counterintelligence, would not discuss the Motorin case, but he said this much: "When a Russian comes to the United States, we immediately start looking at him for recruitment. Anything that pops up on the screen that shows he has a problem, we are going to attempt to exploit that."

Another former FBI man said that the bureau tries to avoid using blackmail to recruit an agent, since someone forced into espionage is likely to be resentful and unreliable. Rather, the bureau tries to use such vulnerabilities as it can discover to open a dialogue. "We try not to be too heavy-handed," he said.

The FBI's counterintelligence agents began the recruitment of Motorin late in 1982 and held the first meeting with him in a safe house in April 1983. A year earlier, KGB Lt. Col. Valery F. Martynov had been recruited through the joint FBI-CIA COURTSHIP program. The FBI was mightily pleased; for the first time in history it now had not one but two KGB sources in the Soviet embassy in Washington.

Special Agent James O. Stassinos was assigned to handle Motorin, assisted by Mike Morton, another agent in the Washington field office. The Greek-born Stassinos, then forty-two, had grown up in Charlotte, North Carolina. He earned a law degree at Duke after graduating from the University of North Carolina and joined the FBI in 1963. Short, stocky, and dark haired, "Stass," as he was known, had handled a number of major cases and was on his way to becoming a legendary figure in the bureau.

Stassinos, drawing on his Greek background, gave Motorin the code name DIONYSUS, the god of wine, fertility, and orgies. Later, the code name was changed to MEGAS. To the CIA, Motorin was GTGAUZE.

Mike Morton's key role in the recruitment had been to act as a sort of unrelenting jack-in-the-box. Everywhere that Motorin went, Morton would pop up and buttonhole him, reminding the Russian—with the aid of FBI photographs—that the bureau knew where those cases of vodka had gone.

At the Washington field office, a special windowless, sound-proof room was set aside for the MEGAS case. There were several safes and extraordinary security measures to protect Motorin's identity.

Motorin was a Line PR officer, which meant that he was responsible for collecting political intelligence. He soon turned over to the FBI the name of every KGB officer in the embassy.

At each clandestine meeting with Motorin, the FBI gave him a modest cash payment, at first $100, later $200. But after each meeting, the bureau also put aside $500 in an escrow account, to be held for Motorin against the day that he might defect and return to America. He was told that a larger amount, perhaps $1,000 a month, would be deposited into the account after his tour was up and he went back to the Soviet Union. The escrow account is a standard device used to provide an incentive for an agent in place.

Motorin chose the name "Sam Olson" for himself; he said he liked the sound of it, and that was the name used on the bank account. It was also his code name for emergency contact. Motorin was given a telephone number that was manned twenty-four hours a day. In the event he needed to contact the FBI or indicate danger, he could call, either from Washington or Moscow, and say the name "Sam Olson."

Motorin told the FBI that he planned to divorce his wife. In addition to the hooker he had been seeing, he had a mistress at the embassy, the wife of another Soviet diplomat. The FBI, glad to keep Motorin happy, arranged for the KGB man to have assigna-tions with his mistress in a bureau safe house.

At one point, the FBI paid for a $2,000 diamond ring that Motorin wanted to give to his mistress. But the FBI worried that the gaudy ring would be noticed and raise questions. The agents talked Motorin out of it. The FBI kept the ring.

At the end of 1984, Motorin returned to Moscow on normal rotation. Six months later, Aldrich Ames handed over his identity to Sergei Chuvakhin, his Soviet contact, and Motorin was doomed.

From Moscow, Motorin had been in contact with his woman friend in the United States by telephone. The calls continued through the late winter of 1986. The conversations were recorded, and the FBI and the CIA read the transcripts. But around February, the last telephone contact took place, and soon after, Motorin was arrested in Moscow on his way to or from a meeting with a CIA officer. Much later, after Ames had been arrested, the FBI concluded that Motorin had been forced by the KGB to make the telephone calls in an effort to lull U.S. intelligence into thinking he had not been detected. A Soviet court that heard the evidence against Motorin said he had received $20,000 from the FBI, and it cited his purchase of a waterbed as proof of his Western decadence. Soon after, Sergei Motorin was shot.[1]

Valery Martynov, whose identity had been betrayed by Ames at the same time that he gave away Motorin, suffered a similar fate. Martynov, called PIMENTA by the FBI and GTGENTILE by the CIA, had been handled by Rod Carlson, Ames's boss and the man who had saved his career when Ames returned from Mexico. That fact did not give Ames pause; he betrayed Martynov in the first batch of names he handed to Chuvakhin.

The KGB had tricked Martynov into returning to Moscow by assigning him to escort Vitaly Yurchenko back home in November 1985. Martynov told his wife, Natalya, and his two young children, that he would be back in Washington shortly. The Martynovs had loved the United States, and during their tour in Washington they had traveled to New York, Annapolis, and Philadelphia.

---

[1] By coincidence, both FBI men who had handled Motorin also died prematurely, of heart attacks. James Stassinos died on May 31, 1990, at age fifty-four. Mike Morton, who was only in his forties, collapsed and died after jogging on a hot summer afternoon a little over a year later.

Ten days after Martynov flew back to Moscow, Natalya Martynova received a note from her husband saying he had reinjured a bad knee while carrying luggage and had been hospitalized. He asked her and their son and daughter to come back to Moscow. As soon as their plane had landed, Natalya realized that her husband was in trouble. Officials took the children to her mother's apartment and brought her to Moscow's grim Lefortovo prison for interrogation. At first, Natalya thought her husband might be suspected of bringing in tape recorders or other equipment and selling them. Then the KGB revealed that the charge against her husband was high treason.

Martynov's wife was questioned repeatedly by the KGB but never imprisoned. During the next two years, as KGB counterintelligence officers investigated the case, she was allowed to see her husband only four times. The last time, knowing he had been sentenced to death, she brought her son with her. Lt. Col. Valery Martynov was executed by a firing squad on May 28, 1987. He was forty-one.

Today, Natalya Martynova works as a librarian in Moscow. For Aldrich Ames, she said, she has "very sad feelings. He betrayed my husband, and my husband was executed simply because of Ames." Ames's excuse that all spies knew they were at risk is "very convenient," she said. But, she added, "You should not deal with these organizations—I mean both American and Russian—because you can be sold very quickly to the other side." Natalya Martynova had lost her husband, and her children had no father. In a quiet voice, she added, "My daughter is a grown-up girl now, but she is still crying for him."[2]

Three of the CIA agents sold by Aldrich Ames had first been betrayed by Edward Lee Howard. Two were executed and one imprisoned.

In 1985, Vitaly Yurchenko told the CIA that he had seen a cable reporting on disclosures by a KGB source, who turned out to be Howard, and who had met the Soviets in Vienna a year earlier. The cable said Howard had revealed three CIA assets: a man

---

[2]Fred Hiatt, "Russian Agent's Widow: A Shattered Life," *Washington Post*, December 17, 1994, p. A1.

Howard thought was a KGB colonel in Hungary, a sailor in the Soviet navy, and the Tass correspondent in San Francisco, who, of course, was Boris Yuzhin, the CIA's CKTWINE. Howard referred to the officer in Hungary as "the angry colonel," apparently because the man was incensed about his treatment by his superiors. Howard also fingered Adolf G. Tolkachev, GTSPHERE, the Soviet defense researcher who was reporting to the CIA on stealth aircraft technology.

As it turned out, Howard was mistaken about the colonel in Budapest, but he was not far off the mark. After investigating its own officers in Hungary, the KGB later realized that the CIA asset was a colonel in the GRU, Soviet military intelligence, who had been recruited by the agency while stationed in Budapest.

The reason that the KGB was able to identify the GRU colonel was that Rick Ames gave away his identity to Moscow. He was Vladimir Mikhailovich Vasilyev, who had been recruited by the CIA in Budapest in 1983. The CIA gave him the code name GTACCORD. The agency communicated with Vasilyev in a unique manner.

The CIA, using a laser-guided computer, embedded a concealed microscopic message in a line, a black rule, inside a copy of the *National Geographic*. The message, similar to a microdot, could be read only with the aid of a powerful magnifier; it was invisible to the naked eye.[3] A copy of the February 1983 issue of the magazine containing the secret instructions was slipped to the GRU colonel in Budapest before he returned to Moscow.

"Your package should always be in a waterproof wrapper placed inside a dirty, oily rag tied with a string. . . " the invisible CIA instructions read. It described each signal site and dead drop in Moscow that Vasilyev was to use. To mark signal site ZVONOK, for example, he was instructed to "board the number 10 trolley bus and ride in the direction of Krymsky Most. . . to the fifth stop." He was then to get off and locate a specific phone booth. "Make your mark, a 10 cm cyrillic 'R' on the building wall to the left of the phone booth and drainpipe. Make it waist high using black crayon or red lipstick so it can be seen from a passing vehicle." The

---

[3]The *National Geographic* was unaware at the time that the CIA was using a copy of its magazine for espionage purposes.

CIA said it in turn would signal Vasilyev from a car, with the license plate D-004, parked across the street from the Lenin Central Museum.

Colonel Vasilyev spied for the CIA for three years, until 1986. Although Edward Lee Howard had provided the first lead to his identity, it was Rick Ames who put the final nail in his coffin. Since the KGB now had information from two sources, it arrested Vasilyev. He was executed in 1987.

Similarly, Adolf Tolkachev was betrayed first by Howard, then by Ames. It was on June 13, 1985, the same day that Ames in Washington turned over the big list of names to the KGB, that Tolkachev was arrested and his CIA case officer, Paul M. "Skip" Stombaugh, Jr., detained. From the timing, however, it seems clear that the KGB arrested Tolkachev on the basis of its previous information from Howard. But Ames was able to verify Tolkachev's identity, and once again, his information provided additional evidence, if the KGB needed any.

In the Kremlin on September 25, 1986, according to recently declassified top-secret Soviet archives, Viktor M. Chebrikov, the chairman of the KGB, assured Soviet leader Mikhail S. Gorbachev: "Yesterday Tolkachev's sentence was implemented." The conversation continued:

GORBACHEV: American intelligence was very generous with him. They found 2 million rubles [then about $500,000] on him.

CHEBRIKOV: This agent gave very important military-technical secrets to the enemy.[4]

On October 22, 1986, the Soviet government announced that Adolf Tolkachev had been executed.

The third CIA source betrayed by both Howard and Ames was Boris Yuzhin. Howard had described him to the KGB as a Tass correspondent in San Francisco, which was as good as naming him. In 1984, when Howard fingered him, Yuzhin was already under sus-

[4]*Bulletin* (Washington, D.C.: Cold War International History Project, Woodrow Wilson International Center for Scholars, Fall 1994) Issue 4, p. 84.

picion because of the CIA camera disguised as a cigarette lighter that he had dropped in the Soviet consulate in San Francisco.

Yuzhin had gone back to Moscow in 1982 and was placed under surveillance as soon as Howard pointed to him. But, once again, when Ames confirmed Yuzhin as a CIA source, CKTWINE, the KGB had the evidence it needed to arrest him.

Boris Yuzhin, whom the FBI called RAMPAIGE, was one of the lucky ones, if serving time in the Soviet gulag can be called that. Arrested in 1986, he escaped execution but was sentenced to fifteen years for high treason, thanks to Ames. On February 7, 1992, after six years under harsh conditions in the gulag, Yuzhin was one of ten political prisoners released from the notorious Perm-35 prison camp in the Urals under an amnesty granted by Boris Yeltsin, the new president of Russia. Gray haired at fifty-three, he now lives in northern California with his wife, Nadya, and daughter, Olga. He is trying to build a new life.

Vladimir V. Potashov, code-named SUNDAY PUNCH by the FBI, was the young disarmament specialist who fed information to the CIA while working in Moscow for the prestigious Institute of the USA and Canada Studies. Arrested on July 1, 1986, he too was sent to Perm-35, sentenced to thirteen years.

To know what it was like to be betrayed by Ames one has only to listen to Potashov recount his ghastly experiences. After being interrogated about a hundred times at Lefortovo prison, always under bright lights, Potashov was shipped east. "After Lefortovo," he said, "there was a seven-day trip to Perm in a cage with fifteen murderers all with TB. In Perm, I was doing hard labor. I was a transporter worker hauling five hundred pounds of metal parts in a handcart. I had to push the cart, and my right shoulder joint broke." Potashov and the other prisoners worked ten hours a day six days a week.

Although only thirty-seven, Potashov aged rapidly in the gulag. "I was in Perm five years and seven months. The doctor told me I had bones like a sixty-five-year-old man. I lost all my teeth from bad or radioactive water in the camp. I has beaten with iron rods by KGB agents, my bones were broken. In September 1991 I did a twenty-four-day hunger strike. I lost forty pounds."

A few months later, Potashov was released in Yeltsin's amnesty. His young wife was frightened by his arrest, and prison cost him his marriage; they were divorced while he was in Perm. With the help of the CIA, Potashov came to the United States, remarried, and now lives along the seacoast in the southern part of the United States. In the fall of 1994, his wife had a son, Potashov's first child.

Potashov was debriefed by the FBI in March 1994, shortly after Ames's arrest. Although Potashov assumed that Ames had betrayed him, neither the CIA nor the FBI would say so. Potashov, determined to find out the truth, filed a request with the FBI under the Freedom of Information Act and wrote to Helen F. Fahey, the U.S. attorney in Alexandria, who had jurisdiction over the Ames prosecution. On September 20, Fahey wrote to Potashov's attorney, confirming the betrayal: "I have been advised by a Special Agent of the FBI with supervisory responsibility for the Ames case that Vladimir Potashov was, in fact, betrayed by Ames's espionage."

Not all of the CIA agents whose identities were given to the KGB by Ames were executed or imprisoned; a few managed to escape. Of those who did, the strangest story of all is that of Sergei Fedorenko, the UN official whom Ames had handled as a CIA agent in New York in the mid-1970s.

During those years, according to Fedorenko, he turned over unclassified government publications and think-tank reports to the KGB at Ames's direction. Fedorenko gave the materials to Vladik Enger, the KGB man later convicted of espionage and returned to Moscow in a trade for a group of Russian dissidents. "Ames made Xerox copies and handed them to me," Fedorenko said. "And I passed them to Enger, to keep them happy and off my back—and to find out what they were interested in. There were Rand Corporation and other think-tank reports, unclassified assessments from the CIA, on CIA letterhead. They loved those. And congressional materials. They wanted anything on aerospace technology."

But Fedorenko also passed other data to the KGB on his own. "To play it on the safe side, if I was going somewhere on a trip, I would invent a report, 70 percent untrue. The KGB approached me many times. I said okay, I am traveling, I am meeting with some people in Boston or Washington. I will share whatever publications I get, speeches, research papers. And I gave those to the KGB. It was called protecting your ass."

At the same time, of course, Fedorenko was providing information about the Soviets to the CIA and the FBI. Fedorenko's CIA crypt was GTPYRRHIC. His FBI code name was MYRRH. And the young FBI agent who handled Fedorenko jointly with Rick Ames in New York was Pat Watson. Sixteen years later, Watson was the number two FBI official at headquarters supervising the investigation of Rick Ames.

After Fedorenko returned to Moscow in 1977, he was out of touch with the CIA for twelve years. Ames did not immediately give Fedorenko's name to the KGB in 1985. Perhaps because Fedorenko was an agent he had personally handled, perhaps because of the friendship he had formed with his agent, Ames did not include Fedorenko in the initial batch of names he handed over. But after a while, Ames was running out of names. During the three years he spent in Italy, he was out of the loop of the Soviet division. And so in Rome in 1987, it was so long, Sergei. Business is business, and Ames wrote a message to the KGB fingering Fedorenko.

The FBI recovered the computer that Ames had used and sold while in Rome, but it was empty. When the FBI searched Ames's home, however, it found diskettes with files dating back to the time that Ames was in Rome. One of the files was the note to the KGB that identified Fedorenko.

Instead of arresting Fedorenko, the KGB allowed him to continue his work at the Institute of the USA and Canada Studies in Moscow. He even assisted in some speech writing and consulting work for Mikhail Gorbachev's national security council. Then, in the fall of 1989, Fedorenko was permitted to travel on the first of several trips to the United States.

Fedorenko came to Washington. He was having dinner with an American friend at the Hotel Madison when his old case officers, Rick Ames and Pat Watson, along with another FBI agent, walked into the dining room. They could not approach Fedorenko, since he was not alone. They waited until he went to the men's room and there slipped him a note asking him to meet them later in one of the hotel's rooms.

After dinner, Fedorenko went up to the room. According to Fedorenko, Rick Ames looked like he had seen a ghost. He must have wondered why Fedorenko hadn't been shot or thrown in prison. "He was frightened, with a shaky voice, and totally obsessed with asking irrelevant questions," Fedorenko recalled. In retrospect, Fedorenko said, he is convinced that Ames was "trying to find out if I knew" that Ames was working for the KGB.

"Ames was asking a lot of detailed questions. Pat was there and sort of surprised, and shut Ames up a couple of times. I made some teasing remarks, I let him know I could see he was nervous. I did not know why. He was sweating like hell."

Fedorenko went back to Moscow but returned to the United States half a dozen times in 1990, and in November, he stayed. It was soon after that Paul Redmond and Milton Bearden arranged for the hostile polygraph, and the CIA dropped Fedorenko. But Fedorenko claimed that the polygraph was rigged and unfair; he said later that the CIA had asked him very personal questions, including several about his sex life. Fedorenko said that upset him and skewed the results.[5]

Redmond was suspicious that Fedorenko alone among the CIA's agents had not been arrested, and he believed that GTPYRRHIC had not given truthful answers. The CIA suspected that Fedorenko was a double agent under Moscow's control, which would have explained why nothing happened to him.

"I had a big fight with the CIA," Fedorenko said. "They didn't like the fact that I didn't tell them I was staying here for good. They were suspicious that I was still walking around. But the KGB never had any tangible evidence on me. They had to catch some-

---

[5]Fedorenko also said the customary preinterview was skipped and he was put right on the machine. "The polygraph operator's first comment was, 'If you were not a provocation, we could be friends.'" Then, he said, the operator asked: "How did you survive?" The obviously hostile tone of the questions angered him, Fedorenko said, and contributed to the unfavorable outcome.

one red-handed. By the time Ames gave my name I was on the team that was writing position papers for Gorbachev. My father-in-law is still alive, but that did not protect me. Although he did tell me I was under KGB surveillance."

Ames much later offered, in effect, another explanation of why Fedorenko was untouched. He said that he had personally known only "two or three" of the agents he betrayed—and Fedorenko would have to be one of these. He claimed he disclosed their identities only after he was convinced that they would not be harmed. He said he told the KGB, "There's no need to do anything. I don't think you need to do anything. I had confidence that nothing would happen to them, and nothing did."[6]

It was a novel claim, that one could turn over the name of a Russian CIA agent to the KGB on condition that they be left alone. Fedorenko's account of his meeting with Ames at the Hotel Madison—he said Ames was frightened and "sweating like hell"—suggests that Ames was surprised and scared that his old friend was still alive and well.

Even before Ames was arrested, it had also occurred to U.S. counterintelligence officers, Paul Redmond among them, that one reason the KGB decided not to arrest Fedorenko was the very fact that he *was* Ames's agent. The American officials reasoned that the KGB would worry that taking action against Fedorenko might turn a spotlight on Ames—the last thing Moscow wanted. In the world of black mirrors, reflections are often the opposite of the image that is projected.

Once the CIA had dropped GTPYRRHIC, he was in danger of being forced to return to Moscow. But the FBI came to his rescue. Pat Watson remembered the information that Fedorenko had provided to the American government in the 1970s. The FBI, Watson argued, had to look at the entire record and at Fedorenko's contribution to the United States, not just at one polygraph exam. In Moscow, Fedorenko had been under investigation by the KGB for years; he had been living in a fishbowl. The information he had

---

[6]Ames made this claim in an interview with reporter Martha Raddatz on National Public Radio. Transcript, *Morning Edition,* NPR, February 16, 1995, p. 2.

given to the CIA and the FBI had proved accurate. In Watson's view, Fedorenko was not under KGB control. Now after many years, he had returned; should he be thrown back to Russia, is that the way we treat people who enter into a relationship with the U.S. government? Watson's arguments prevailed.

The FBI declined to comment at all about the Fedorenko case. But one official confirmed that the bureau had intervened to help its former agent. "The position the FBI took is we aren't going to throw him back to the wolves," he said. With the assistance of the FBI, Fedorenko applied and was granted immigration status and permission to remain in the United States.

On the day of Ames's arrest, the FBI, armed with a court warrant, conducted an exhaustive searched of Ames's house, office, and cars. A total of fourteen statements from the Dominion Bank of Virginia in the name of Sergei Fedorenko were found in the Jaguar and in the house. According to Fedorenko, Ames, at the suggestion of the FBI, had agreed to let him use his address for the bank statements during the period in 1989 and 1990 when Fedorenko was traveling back and forth to Moscow. In the 1970s, the CIA had put money aside in an escrow account for Fedorenko. "Now I have it," Fedorenko said, "but that was not the money in the bank account" found in Ames's house. He said the account in Virginia, which held more than $10,000, was money from a pension and lecture fees.

With his wife, Helen, whose picture in *Vogue* had so upset Andrei Gromyko, Fedorenko now lives in this country and teaches at a small college in New England.

When Ames pleaded guilty to espionage on April 28, 1995, federal prosecutors released a document listing the CIA cryptonyms—but not the true names—of eleven agents betrayed by Ames. Of these, six had been executed. Some of the crypts were accompanied by brief descriptions of the person. One that carried no description was GTBLIZZARD.

GTBLIZZARD was Sergei Ivanovich Bokhan, a powerfully built, dark-haired officer of the GRU, Soviet military intelligence, who in 1985 was serving his second tour in Athens under cover as the embassy's first secretary. In fact, he was deputy resident of the

GRU. Bokhan, then forty-four, had had arrived in Greece three years earlier.

Bokhan had been providing the CIA with the names of Greek agents working for Soviet intelligence and information on how the Soviets were acquiring Western military technology in Greece. In May, Bokhan was summoned by Georgi Borisovich Maslovsky, the GRU resident.

Bokhan had been recalled to Moscow, Maslovsky explained. His son, who was in the military college in Kiev, was having trouble with his grades; it would be best if he spoke to the young man in person. Officially, Moscow could not bring Bokhan back for family reasons, Maslovsky explained; so as far as the record would show, headquarters was ordering him back to discuss official business. But as both men knew, this was done all the time, a device to bring back officers from the field for family reasons.

Maslovsky's explanation sounded humane. But GTBLIZZARD smelled a rat. As far as he knew his son was doing fine in school. He suspected the worst. He resisted the order from Moscow. But Maslovsky insisted, and finally Bokhan agreed to go. On a Friday in May he was driven to the airport, but, by a small miracle, or perhaps by design, Bokhan arrived late for the plane.

He contacted the CIA. David Forden, the former chief of the Soviet division, where he was Ames's boss, had become chief of the Athens station the previous year. He, too, decided the situation did not look right. GTBLIZZARD would have to be exfiltrated.

Forden set the plan in motion; Bokhan could not just be taken to the airport and put on a plane for Washington; the KGB would be watching. He would have to slip out of Greece by a clandestine route. Meanwhile, Bokhan was told his trip to Moscow had been postponed but he would have to leave during the week.

On Saturday he told his wife Alla he had to meet someone. He left the house, taking a sports bag with him. On Monday, his wife went to see Maslovsky with the key to her husband's office safe. Sergei left the house on Saturday, she said, and didn't come back. Since it was Monday by now, the KGB, which was immediately alerted, suspected that Bokhan's wife was involved in his disappearance.

The KGB quickly searched Bokhan's house and found several tape recorders but no evidence of his spying and no clue to his whereabouts. But BLIZZARD was already en route to safety. At Moscow's insistence, however, the Greek government turned over his wife and seven-year-old daughter to the Russians. Soon after Bokhan disappeared, the Greek government arrested a Greek naval officer and two businessmen; all three were reported to have been part of a Soviet spy ring in Greece. The timing indicated clearly that Bokhan had provided the information about the spy ring to the CIA, which in turn had decided to share it with the Greek government.

There was an ironic postscript to Bokhan's narrow escape from Rick Ames's betrayal. About a month after BLIZZARD vanished from Athens, his boss, Georgi Maslovsky, was ordered home. The reason: Nikolai Tikhonovich Krestnikov, the KGB resident in Athens, was suspicious that Maslovsky, the GRU chief, might somehow be implicated and defect as well.[7] Maslovsky was ordered to leave Athens for home on a passenger ship. The ship stopped in Istanbul en route to its Soviet port, but Maslovsky, who was accompanied by KGB agents, was not allowed to leave the ship.

Sergei Bokhan lived for a time in a town house near CIA headquarters in Virginia. He later moved to New York, where he planned to marry a Russian emigrée. Like most defectors, he has a new identity, acquired with the assistance of the CIA.

Like Bokhan, Oleg Gordievsky, as already recounted, managed to escape from under the noses of the KGB in Moscow. He had worked for British intelligence for eleven years, rising to the position of resident in London before he was suddenly called home in May 1985. Ames has said he believes he turned over Gordievsky's identity to the KGB in June. "Ames gave up Gordievsky," said Pat Watson, "but we believe there are other reasons he was recalled in May. In a world of shadows there are a lot of unanswered questions, pieces of information that many times are not consistent. It is very difficult to sort them out and not go off in the wrong direc-

---

[7]It was not a good tour for Krestnikov; in February 1986, one of his own KGB officers, Colonel Victor Gundarev, also defected to the CIA. He now lives in the United States.

tion. The fact that Gordievsky was recalled on May 16 would indicate the Russians were suspicious of him before that for some other reasons."

Those who escaped death or imprisonment were the exceptions, however. The story of most of those betrayed by Ames did not have happy endings. Consider the fate of these other agents given away by Ames:

GTMILLION, Lt. Col. Gennady Smetanin of the GRU, was stationed in Lisbon in the early 1980s when he dropped a letter in the mailbox at the home of a U.S. military attaché. In the note, the colonel volunteered to provide information. If the Americans were interested in his offer, he wrote, respond with an ad in a local paper worded a certain way.

Some of the CIA officers in the Lisbon station were suspicious of the walk-in and thought he might be a double agent under Soviet control. David Forden, then the chief of the Soviet division, remembered the lesson of the Cherepanov papers, a well-known episode in the history of Soviet operations. Aleksandr Nikolaevich Cherepanov was an officer of the KGB's Second Chief Directorate. In the fall of 1963 he handed a package of documents to an American couple in Moscow, pleading that the papers be taken to the American embassy. When the documents arrived, two senior embassy diplomats considered the papers a provocation and returned them to the Soviet government over the vehement protests of Paul Garbler, the CIA station chief, who argued that a man's life was at stake. Garbler managed to photograph the papers before they were returned. Later, the Soviet defector Yuri I. Nosenko reported that Cherepanov had been caught and shot.

Forden overruled the Lisbon station. The ad was placed. And Smetanin, now GTMILLION, began providing a lot of solid intelligence. In 1985, he was recalled from Lisbon. Unlike Sergei Bokhan in Athens, he went back. He was executed.

GTFITNESS, Gennady Grigorievich Varenik, was a KGB officer in Germany. He was stationed in Bonn and his cover was that of a correspondent for Tass, the Soviet news agency. Varenik, who was a CIA source, disappeared in 1985. According to Oleg Kalugin, the former chief of counterintelligence for the KGB, "Varenik was abducted from Germany, brought back to Moscow, and executed." Kalugin, who broke with the KGB after resigning from the intelligence agency in 1990, said that Varenik "may have been lured from Bonn to Berlin," and spirited over the border into East Germany. "A recall to Moscow would always be suspicious," Kalugin said. "It would have been easier to get him to Berlin."

To avoid arrest for his highly public criticism of the KGB, Kalugin ran for office as a member of the Supreme Soviet and won, giving him immunity from prosecution. "When I was a deputy, a member of parliament, Mrs. Varenik came to me to find out if her husband was alive. I said unfortunately no, he has been shot as a spy."

GTWEIGH, Leonid Polyshuk, was a KGB officer serving in Africa when he was suddenly recalled to Moscow, arrested, and shot.

GTCOWL was Sergei Vorontsov, a KGB officer stationed in Moscow. Among the information he provided to the CIA was a description of the "spy dust" chemicals that the KGB used to track the movements of American diplomats in the Soviet capital.[8] COWL provided information to the CIA about other KGB counterintelligence measures directed at the CIA in Moscow. He was arrested and executed.

GTJOGGER, as previously noted, was Lt. Col. Vladimir M. Piguzov, a senior KGB officer in Indonesia. When Piguzov had returned to Moscow from Djakarta, he was assigned to the Andropov Institute, the KGB training academy in a forest northwest of Moscow. Piguzov rose to the position of Communist party secretary at the institute, which made him the number two official at the school. He had access to the names of students there and to

---

[8]The disclosure by Washington in August 1985 that the Soviets were using spy dust caused a furor. The chemical, nitrophenylpentadienal (NPPD), was an invisible powder that the Soviets sprinkled on the steering wheels or doorknobs of CIA officers in the Moscow station so that traces would be left on the hands or clothing of Soviet citizens with whom they came in contact. U.S. government scientists analyzed and tested the substance for six months and concluded early in 1986 that in the levels used by the Soviets, the spy dust "does not pose a health hazard." The tests also found that luminol, a second tracking chemical used by the KGB, was not dangerous to humans.

where they would be assigned after graduation. Piguzov, who revealed to Langley that David Barnett, the former CIA officer in Indonesia, had spied for Moscow, was then, in turn, betrayed by Ames and executed.[9]

And finally, most tragic of all from the CIA's point of view, it was TOPHAT's turn. In 1980, Gen. Dimitri Fedorovich Polyakov, the CIA's GTBEEP, had returned to Moscow for the last time. He had spied for the United States for eighteen years and was living out his years peacefully in Moscow with his family. Other than Oleg Penkovsky, whose CIA code name was HERO, Polyakov was considered the most valuable spy in the agency's history.

Until Aldrich Ames turned him in.

In 1990, the Soviets announced that General Polyakov had been caught and, they later said, executed on March 15, 1988.

The CIA did not know what had gone wrong. Then Ames was arrested, and it knew. Jeanne Vertefeuille does not like to talk about it, even now. Polyakov had been one of a kind. "He didn't do this for money," she told a colleague. "He insisted on staying in place to help us." Tears came in her eyes when she spoke of the general.

"It was," she said, "a bad day for us when we lost him."

[9]In his book *The First Directorate* (New York: St. Martin's Press, 1994), Oleg Kalugin, the former KGB counterintelligence chief, tells how he met Barnett in Vienna and paid him $80,000 on the spot to spy for Moscow. Kalugin implies that it was Edward Lee Howard who identified the CIA source inside the KGB residency in Indonesia. But Kalugin explained to the author in 1995 that he wrote his manuscript, and the reference to Howard, in 1991—before he knew of the existence of Aldrich Ames. In his book, Kalugin also reported that the KGB man in Indonesia, whom he did not name, was executed. It is clear that he is describing JOGGER.

20

AFTERMATH

Before dawn on the morning of Ames's arrest, the FBI was in place, watching his house in Virginia. At precisely 7:50 A.M., the surveillance team knew he did not plan to leave to signal the SVR that morning; he had run out of time.

From observing the pattern of his movements, the FBI agents had learned that Ames was always required to mark a signal site before 8:00 A.M.—and there was no site close enough for him to reach in ten minutes.[1]

The timing was of particular interest to the FBI. Ames was in custody by midmorning, but there was an operational reason why his arrest on February 21 was not announced publicly for twenty-four hours. The FBI had decided to pretend it was Aldrich Ames.

About five minutes before 8:00 A.M., more than two hours in advance of the arrest, an FBI agent drew a chalk mark at a signal

[1]Signal site NORTH was located close by, on a telephone pole at Military Road and Thirty-sixth Street in Arlington. It was about three minutes away. But it was only used by the KGB to signal Ames, not the other way around.

site across the Potomac in Georgetown. The FBI hoped to see a Russian intelligence officer respond to the signal and go to a dead drop. Had that happened, the presence of an SVR officer at the signal site and the drop would have been additional evidence that could have been used against Ames.

"We made his mark for him on the mailbox at Thirty-seventh and R," John Lewis said. "It was our hope to draw them out. But we didn't make the right mark. They have vertical and horizontal lines and sometimes the KGB changed them. We drew the line the wrong way."

Counterintelligence is in the details. It was only much later, after debriefing Ames, that the FBI discovered what had happened. Les Wiser explained it. "The chalk mark was made at SMILE, the mailbox at Thirty-seventh and R. We drew the line horizontally. Vertical means danger, we know now. Horizontal was nothing. Because they had changed the signal site from SMILE. They had switched it to JOY, an electric utility box at Reservoir Road and Thirty-fifth street.

"The vertical line was specifically the danger signal. On February 21, we did draw a Russian out. They checked every day for the 'danger from me' signal, a vertical line at SMILE, JOY, or TAD.[2] They checked all three every day. When they saw the horizontal line, it probably confused them. They may have thought he was in danger and nervous and drew it the wrong way. Or that he forgot it was no longer a signal site."[3]

At the White House, Anthony Lake had been intensely curious about the identity of the mole, but had carefully avoided that

[2]TAD was also on Reservoir Road. All three sites were near each other in Georgetown. Had SMILE still been in use as a regular signal site, which it no longer was, the chalk mark drawn by the FBI would have activated dead drop BRIDGE on Massachusetts Avenue.

[3]Ames was indeed in danger, but he didn't know it. The attempt to draw the Russians out raised the interesting possibility that if the SVR had checked the mailbox just after 8:00 A.M., it would have had about a two-hour advance warning that Ames might be in trouble. At that point, it would have made little difference. But in the event, the SVR did not check for the chalk mark until after lunch, in the early afternoon. The FBI watched them do so.

knowledge. After the arrest, he finally learned the name for the first time. He revealed it to the president and showed him several FBI photographs of Ames as he was caught and handcuffed.

On the morning of Tuesday, February 22, the FBI announced the arrest of Aldrich and Rosario Ames.

Irwin Rubenstein nearly went off the road. The retired foreign service officer, one of Ames's regular luncheon group in Mexico, was driving back with his wife, Estelle, to their home near Fort Lauderdale, Florida, after an overnight stay in Melbourne. "I was zooming down one of the big interstates in Florida and I heard the tail end of a news story," Rubenstein recalled. "I just caught the words 'Aldrich Ames and espionage.' I said, 'What the hell is that?' I had to wait forty-five minutes to hear the news come up again. I said, 'Oh, my God.' He never gave any hint that he was disloyal."

Rich Thurman was working in his office at the State Department. "Someone said, 'Look what's on CNN, they've arrested a big CIA spy.' I looked at the television and my jaw dropped. I was torn up by it for weeks. I still am. I can't believe what he did. I still have some affection for Rick. I considered him a good friend. I'm still amazed that someone could be out of control for so long and never show it."

David Samson got the news in a telephone call from Washington. "I found out from Judy Thurman. She said, 'Isn't it awful about Rick and Rosario?' She was terribly distraught. She kept saying, 'Isn't it awful?' I thought they had been in a car wreck. She said it was awful. I thought it must be a bad wreck. Then she said, 'They're spies.' I was stunned."

Joseph F. Lynch, who had been Ames's boss in Turkey more than two decades earlier, had retired to Cape Cod. At first, when he saw the story in the local paper, he did not connect the name to his former subordinate of so many years before. Then he saw Ames's picture. "Oh, my God," Lynch said.

Roman Popadiuk, who had hosted Ames at two lunches at the White House and shown him around the West Wing and the Situation Room, had a different reaction. *If I had the guy in front of me, I probably would have wrung his neck.*

On the same day that the FBI arrested the Ameses, the bureau's agents went back to his office at CIA, this time armed with a warrant, to search it more thoroughly than they had been able to do the previous June.

In the Counternarcotics Center in the basement of the new headquarters building, the agents entered Room GV06, a large open area with a lot of desks and dividers. At the far end of the room were two private offices. The one on the right had a sign on the door: RICK AMES.

Inside the office, which had beige walls and gray trim, the FBI found several documents stamped TOP SECRET. One of the documents, discovered in a file cabinet under a bookcase, was entitled, "What Angleton Thought." It suggested that Ames had a more than casual interest in the mole hunt that had taken place at the CIA thirty years earlier. The document was written by Cleveland C. Cram, a Ph.D. Harvard historian who was a longtime CIA officer and twice a station chief. In 1975, Cram began a six-year study of the Angleton era, in the course of which he became the preeminent CIA expert on the controversial counterintelligence chief.[4]

The document found in Ames's office consisted mainly of what agency insiders called Angleton's "secret speech" of April 1966, which had been taped and transcribed when he delivered it to his senior staffers. Angleton, euphoric, had just returned from a trip to Norway, The Hague, France, and England with his favorite defector, Anatoly Golitsin, in tow. He had not told his superiors at CIA about the trip. He was mightily pleased with the results. In his speech, he related how he had warned the other friendly intelligence services in each country of a monstrous KGB plot to send out false defectors, after Golitsin, to confuse the West.

As it turned out, however, an official of Dutch intelligence, skeptical of Angleton's secret presence in his country, had tipped off the CIA station that the counterintelligence chief was in town. The station cabled headquarters, causing a huge flap when Angleton returned to Langley.

---

[4]Cram produced an approximately four-thousand-page study of the Angleton epoch that remains locked in the CIA's vaults. Cleveland C. Cram, *History of the Counterintelligence Staff 1954–1974* (Langley, Virginia: Central Intelligence Agency, 1981), classified, unpublished study.

Cram had personal knowledge of these events because he was the station chief in The Hague who had alerted headquarters to the trip. And since the world of intelligence is fairly small, it is of passing interest that one of the officers serving under Cram at the time was Jeanne Vertefeuille. She did not care for Angleton and was amused that the Dutch service had blown the whistle on the secretive counterintelligence chief.

A second top-secret document, found inside a green folder in the same file cabinet drawer, was entitled "SHAMROCK Analysis." Ames had probably acquired the document when he worked in the Analysis Group of the Counterintelligence Center beginning in the fall of 1990. SHAMROCK was the joint CIA-FBI code name for a KGB walk-in who had been run by the bureau in New York during the 1960s. When he went back to Moscow, the FBI turned the case over to the CIA. Angleton immediately labeled SHAMROCK as a false volunteer.

About 1965, the CIA's Soviet division prepared a two-volume study of the case. SHAMROCK had provided what seemed to be good information. He never reappeared in the West and never made contact again, so his fate was unknown. In the CI Center, Ames could sift through old files. He was in a position to tell the KGB about CIA sources who might still be in the Soviet service or retired but still living. That was TOPHAT's fate, and it may have been SHAMROCK's.

After Ames was given time to take in the details of the fake squad room at Tysons Corner, he was moved to an interview room. He declined to say anything, other than to observe, gloomily, that if the FBI had arrested him, it probably had a pretty good case. Rosario Ames was taken to a separate interview room and questioned by Yolanda M. Larson and John Hosinksi, the two agents who had arrested her at her home. Rosario Ames at first denied, and then admitted, that her husband had received money from the Russians and was a spy for Moscow.

As Rosario began to open up to the two FBI agents, a short, compact young man with dark brown hair slipped into the room and listened to part of the interview. At thirty-six, Mark Hulkower, a young assistant United States attorney, was embarking on the biggest case of his career. Helen Fahey, the U.S. attorney, had turned the prosecution over to Hulkower, not only because he was smart and energetic but because he had successfully prosecuted three past espionage cases.[5]

For four years, Hulkower had worked for Williams & Connolly, the prestigious Washington law firm founded by the late Edward Bennett Williams. But he left in 1989 after deciding he wanted experience as a prosecutor. "My grandfather was a baker," he said in describing his modest roots. His grandfather had emigrated to America and found work in a bakery in the Bronx, where many East European Jews had settled in New York. Hulkower remembered a time when his parents had so little money that the family moved in with friends on a chicken farm in New Jersey. After a while, his father prospered, becoming a successful businessman and president of several shoe companies. When Hulkower was eight, they moved to Hartsdale, in Westchester. He grew up in the New York suburb.

After graduating from Cornell, he did not go to law school right away. Instead, he took off for England for three years, where he managed the first Hard Rock Café, on London's Hyde Park corner. Abandoning the restaurant business in 1981, he enrolled in law school at Georgetown University. After earning his law degree, he clerked at the U.S. Court of Appeals in Washington, joined the Williams firm, and then Fahey's staff. A friendly man, devoted to his young family, Hulkower was also a tough-minded prosecutor. Working with Les Wiser and the other FBI agents who had inves-

---

'Hulkower won convictions of Frank A. Nesbitt, a former marine sentenced to ten years in 1991 after he passed signals intelligence secrets to the KGB, which had flown him to Moscow from Bolivia; Frederick C. Hamilton, a researcher for the Defense Intelligence Agency, who received a three-year sentence in 1993 for passing classified documents to Ecuador while he was stationed in Peru; and Steven J. Lalas, a State Department employee who received fifteen years in 1993 for selling secrets to the Greek government.

tigated Ames, as well with CIA officials, Hulkower immersed himself in the case until he knew every detail. Rick and Rosario Ames, he was certain, were going to prison.

The telephone call to Plato Cacheris from Magistrate Barry Poretz came on the morning of February 22. Donna Coffman, Cacheris's tall blond secretary, put it through on the speakerphone. Poretz's voice boomed out. A CIA officer, Aldrich Ames, had been arrested for espionage. His considerable assets had been frozen by the government. Would Cacheris serve as his court-appointed lawyer?

Cacheris was sitting at his Early American polished mahogany desk in his seventh-floor office on Connecticut Avenue in downtown Washington. One of the capital's most respected criminal lawyers, Cacheris was clever and fast on his feet in the courtroom, but he had a rock-solid reputation for integrity. He also earned $400 an hour keeping very rich clients out of jail; the job that Poretz was offering paid $60 an hour.

But it was also the sort of high-profile case that lawyers, especially Washington lawyers, find it hard to resist. During Watergate, Cacheris had represented former attorney general John N. Mitchell. In the Iran-contra scandal, he had represented Oliver North's secretary, Fawn Hall, invariably described in the press as statuesque, who operated her boss's shredder and took documents out of the Executive Office Building concealed in her boots and dress.

Lawyers do not like to offend judges. Poretz made it clear he hoped that Cacheris would represent Ames. "I said I would," Cacheris recalled.

The son of Greek immigrants, Cacheris grew up in Washington and went to law school at Georgetown. He dressed like a fashion plate, in tailored Savile Row suits and expensive British shoes. He drove a white Porsche Carrera 2. He had built a private all-weather tennis court—friends called it "the John Mitchell Memorial Court"—on the grounds of his imposing home in Alexandria, not far from the city jail where Ames and his wife were being held. At sixty-four, Cacheris was sleek and a trifle portly, but he kept active with frequent workouts on his tennis court and a regular weekly doubles match.

That afternoon, Cacheris stopped by the U.S. attorney's office in Alexandria to pick up the complaint and sign in as Ames's lawyer. In the evening, he called on his client. They took the handcuffs off Ames so he could shake hands. Ames was impressed, and pleased, to have Plato Cacheris as his lawyer.

Poretz had appointed William B. Cummings, the former U.S. attorney in Alexandria, to represent Rosario Ames. Both Rick and Rosario were being held without bail.

When the arrests were announced, President Clinton called it "a very serious case" and lodged a protest with Moscow. But Clinton said the case should not undermine overall relations between the United States and Russia, and he made it clear he would resist any congressional efforts to cut off the administration's $2.5 billion aid package to Russia.

Still, the White House had to do something to react to the embarrassment of the Ames affair. Four days after the arrests were announced, Washington expelled Aleksandr I. Lysenko, the SVR resident, who had only recently replaced Ivan Gromakov. The Yeltsin government, in turn, expelled James L. Morris, the CIA station chief in Moscow.

Almost from the start, there was speculation that Ames would enter into a plea bargain with the prosecutors. The CIA, in particular, was anxious to question Ames to find out, if possible, exactly what agents and operations he had betrayed, information it badly needed in order to assess the full extent of the horrendous damage he had wreaked.

But there was no assurance that this would happen, and in the meantime, Mark Hulkower had to prepare to prosecute Ames. Hulkower started lining up witnesses. With John L. Martin, chief of the internal security section at the Department of Justice, he flew to England to meet with Oleg Gordievsky, GTTICKLE, the MI6 source whose name Ames had provided to Moscow.

Fifteen years earlier, when Hulkower had managed the Hard Rock Café, he would walk past London's posh Grosvenor House hotel. It was far beyond his means. This time, he and Martin stayed there, albeit at a government rate.

"Gordievsky would have been the expert witness in the case,"

Hulkower revealed. "He would have reviewed all the documents and testified that they reflected classic KGB methods. One document referred to a meeting at an 'iron site.' Gordievsky explained that the phrase 'iron site' was classic KGB—if anything goes wrong, go back to this one place which will always remain, like iron."

Ames and his wife were denied bail by Judge Poretz at a hearing on March 1. According to Cacheris, both the Ameses had "great expectations that she would get out on bond and she did not. He was very disappointed." But Cacheris was able to establish at the hearing that the FBI had never seen or photographed Ames actually meeting with any KGB agents.

Despite that, the government had a mass of documentary evidence. "We received the inventory of items," Cacheris recounted, and he showed the list to Ames. "His reaction was, 'Gee, did I leave all that there?' Which fits the sloppiness of the whole operation."

Cacheris stalled for time. "We discussed with the prosecutors a continuation of everything so we could view the evidence they had seized, so we could assess the case, and if we thought we should engage in plea-bargain discussions, it would give us more time. We made arrangements through the FBI to bring the materials that were considered secret to the jail, so that we could present them to Ames to show him the quality and quantity." Looking over the documents, Ames now realized with dismay just how much evidence the FBI had been able to gather after it went inside his home, installed bugs, and downloaded his computer.

"We felt these intrusions were illegal," Cacheris said. "I wrote him [Ames] a letter in which I counseled him there were significant legal issues which in my judgment should be tested, and I suggested he plead not guilty. But the letter also said that because I recognize he wanted to aid his wife and son I would not impede his desire to plead guilty."

Even with a celebrated lawyer, Ames had virtually no hope of avoiding a life sentence for espionage. All he could do was to try to bargain to reduce the time Rosario would serve, so that she would eventually get out and be able to take care of their son. He had scant room to maneuver.

According to Cacheris, Ames during their meetings was "placid, calm, resigned, thoroughly in control of himself. He was never distraught, upset, out of control." That was not always the case, however, during three joint meetings that were held with Rosario and her lawyer, William Cummings. "His wife is much more emotional than he is, and he exhibited emotion because of that, and during discussions about his son. His eyes would water when we discussed arrangements for his son."

After reading over the government's evidence against him, Ames told Cacheris to throw in the towel. "We began to discuss plea negotiations at his insistence. I said, 'I can't do a thing for you under these circumstances.' He said, 'I understand that, but I want to take care of Rosario.' The plea arguments with Hulkower and later at the Department of Justice were over how much time she would have to serve. We wanted three years; they wanted seven."

Finally, the deal was cut; if Ames cooperated fully with the CIA and the FBI, Rosario would be sentenced to just over five years, but would serve about four and a half years with good behavior. Aldrich Ames would be sentenced to life with no possibility of parole. Ames and his wife would have to agree to forfeit all of their assets, including the house, the Jaguar, and the money in their bank accounts, and to forgo any profits from book, movie, or television deals.[6]

April 28, 1994, was a cool, clear sunny day in Alexandria. Before dawn, the press had started to gather outside the federal courthouse, and by 8:45 A.M. when the sentencing of Aldrich Ames was to begin, the building was surrounded by a mob of reporters and television cameras, boom microphones, and cables.

Only twenty-seven people were allowed to squeeze into Judge Claude M. Hilton's tiny courtroom. Rick and Rosario, in prison garb, sipped water and chatted quietly with each other in the moments before the court convened. Rosario, looking exhausted, clutched at a crucifix around her neck. She was the first to stand before the bar. She pleaded guilty to conspiracy to commit espi-

---

[6]Later, the government permitted the Ameses to hold on to their properties in Colombia. Everything else was forfeited.

onage and to defraud the United States of tax revenue. Her sentencing was put off until after Ames's debriefings.

Aldrich Ames stood. Mark Hulkower informed the judge that Ames had been indicted by a federal grand jury on two counts of conspiracy to commit espionage and conspiracy to commit tax fraud. He had promised to "cooperate fully" with the government.

"How do you plead to count one?" Judge Hilton intoned.

"Guilty."

"And to count two?"

"Guilty."

Hulkower said that before the sentencing, he believed the record should show that Ames's crimes "caused people to die as surely as if the defendant had pulled the trigger. And [with] all the talk about assets, penetrations, compromise and intelligence information, all of the spy lingo which has been bandied about in this case, it is easy to forget that what we are talking about, Your Honor, are people."

And then Hulkower, without mentioning Dimitri Polyakov's name, or the code names GTBEEP or TOPHAT, began talking about him. "In the 1970s a Russian general who was disturbed by the course his country was taking volunteered to help this country by giving information to the CIA. He didn't want money. He did it, he said, because it was right." Because of Ames, the general "was arrested and executed by the KGB." He and others died "because Rick Ames wasn't making enough money with the CIA and wanted to live in a half-million-dollar house and drive a Jaguar." He asked the court to sentence Ames to life in prison without parole.[7]

Then Ames spoke at length. With Rosario weeping behind him, he said "I bitterly regret" the catastrophe he had brought upon "my wife and son." He said he felt "profound guilt and shame" and the "deepest sympathy" for the Soviets he had betrayed. "We made similar choices and suffer similar consequences."

It was a disingenuous comment. Ames was suggesting that

---

[7]There is no longer any parole in the federal system. Since 1987, when parole was abolished, prisoners sentenced for federal crimes must serve their full sentences.

those Soviets who worked for the CIA had also betrayed their country and took the same risks as he did. But ten of Ames's victims were shot; in the United States there was no death penalty for espionage in peacetime.

Ames then launched into a bitter denunciation of the government's treatment of Rosario. She had not known he was a Russian spy for seven and a half years, he insisted, and he said she had pleaded with him thereafter to break off his relationship with Moscow. He had been able to "manipulate her, even to blackmail her" into silence. Fearing "my sloppiness, verging on recklessness," she had cautioned him to be careful in his contacts with the Russians.

On the day of her arrest, she had made incriminating statements, he said, but the government then dropped her because it found so much evidence in their house "that she was no longer important to the prosecution's case against me." The government had tried "to depict Rosario as an active and scheming participant in my espionage." It had even made public her secret contract with the CIA in Mexico "to blacken her reputation in Colombia."

Finally, Ames said he felt "regret and shame" for his "betrayal of trust, done for the basest of motives." But, he said, he did not believe "that our nation's interests have been noticeably damaged by my acts. . . ."

He recounted his spying for the KGB and said two reasons had shaped his decision. He had come to dissent "from the decades-long shift to the extreme right" in American foreign policy. And second, "I had come to believe that the espionage business, as carried out by the CIA. . . was and is a self-serving sham, carried out by careerist bureaucrats who have managed to deceive several generations of American policymakers and the public about both the necessity and the value of their work." Shades of Acapulco. Rick Ames, the spy *manqué*, was finally speaking out.

"Frankly," he added, "these spy wars are a sideshow which have had no real impact on our significant security interests over the years." He had a few more comments, and then he was through.

Judge Hilton leaned forward. "It will be the sentence of the Court, Mr. Ames, that. . . you be committed to the custody of the Attorney General to serve a term of life."

Amid much anticipation, the first debriefing of Aldrich Ames took place at the Tysons Corner office of the FBI on April 29, the day after he was sentenced to life in prison. Ames was brought there under guard from the Alexandria jail. Now American counterintelligence officials would begin to learn the truth.

The debriefers were in place around a polished conference table. From the FBI there was Les Wiser, James Milburn, and Special Agents Mike Donner and Rudy Guerin. Mark Hulkower represented the U.S. attorney's office. There was only one person from the CIA, a small, gray-haired woman who might have been mistaken for a librarian, or a schoolteacher, or somebody's grandmother.

When all of the officials were assembled, Ames was brought in in handcuffs. As he entered the room, the officials stood up. The handcuffs were removed.

Ames spotted her right away. He had seen her around the Soviet division.

Mole hunter and quarry were finally face-to-face.

Ames nodded to her.

"Hi, Jeanne," he said.

"Hi, Rick," said Jeanne Vertefeuille. And for the first time in a long while, she allowed herself a smile.

Ames leaned across the table and shook hands with each of the debriefers, including Vertefeuille, although he hesitated for a moment before shaking hands with Hulkower, the man who had put him and Rosario in prison. But then he did.

Everyone sat down, and Ames made an opening statement. He had participated in a number of debriefings on the other side of the table, meaning when he was a CIA officer doing the debriefing, and he would handle it in a professional manner, like he would have done in his former role.

The debriefers went along with that. They were treating Ames with respect, even though many, including Vertefeuille, felt nothing but personal animosity toward Ames and intense loathing for what he had done. But the name of the game was to extract as much information as possible from Ames; if that meant treating him like a fellow professional—which is what he badly seemed to want—then they would.

Rudy Guerin, young and bespectacled, looking more like an English professor than an FBI agent, led the debriefing. Did Ames know of any other moles in the CIA? No. In other agencies of the United States government? No. The questioning went on.

It was near lunchtime, and sandwiches were brought in. Ames chain-smoked through the session, which lasted a few hours, and ate two sandwiches.

Guerin led Ames through the history of his espionage for the KGB and the SVR. When Ames came to the part about his fear after Moscow had rolled up the CIA's agents all at once in 1985, the debriefing took a dramatic and unexpected turn.

He had talked to the KGB in Rome about the swift arrests of the agents he had betrayed. He had told them how frightened he was that the loss of the agents might lead the CIA to look for a mole and jeopardize his safety. And the Soviets had asked, what can we do to help you, is there anyone you can blame? The KGB, in other words, was suggesting that Ames provide the name of another CIA officer, someone who could be framed.

Ames looked at Jeanne Vertefeuille, who sat across the table from him.

"You're not going to like this," he said, "but I gave them your name."

It was an electric moment. The debriefers could hardly believe their ears.

Aldrich Ames had given Jeanne Vertefeuille's name to the KGB. So that Moscow, perhaps with help from Ames, could plant clues that *she* was the mole!

There was something else. He knew, Ames added, that Vertefeuille was on the special task force that was trying to find the penetration at Langley. He could not be sure, he said, but he thought he had also passed that secret to the KGB.

*　　　*　　　*

The Alexandria city detention center is a modern, red-brick building that sits in an isolated area, close by the beltway that rings the capital. Accompanied by Plato Cacheris, I took the elevator to the third floor and entered a tiny room, number 303. The heavy door slammed behind me and locked. There were bare white cinder-block walls, a small table and chairs. No windows. Opposite the door I had entered was another door, with a small glass panel at chest height, leading to the cell blocks.

I waited, and in a few moments I saw him through the glass. A uniformed guard unlocked the door, and Rick Ames entered. The guard left. We were alone.

Ames was wearing a khaki shirt with the word PRISONER emblazoned on the back in large letters, and dark pants. A tall man, broad shoulders, mustache, thick glasses, and jug ears. Very self-possessed. We shook hands and sat down at the little table. Cacheris handed Ames some interview requests and other correspondence that he had brought and some yellow pads Ames had asked for. Ames took a moment to shuffle through the papers. He looked for all the world like a business executive opening a meeting. The president and CEO of Rick Ames, Inc.

He was friendly, upbeat, almost jovial. It was June 2, 1994, only a little more than a month after his sentencing, and it was apparent that he had not yet felt the full impact of prison and of the bleak future that awaited him. The debriefings had begun, he said, and as he talked it was clear that he was enjoying the interaction with his old colleagues from CIA and the FBI. They were treating him like a professional, as long as he kept talking. And surely he derived some pleasure not only from the human contact with his former peers but from telling them in detail how he had successfully deceived them and carried on his espionage for almost nine years.

The FBI debriefers, he said, were people from both headquarters and the Washington field office. The sessions were "friendly" and "professional." The government's representatives, he said, had dropped any hostility toward him. The questioning was taking place on Mondays, Wednesdays, and Fridays, sometimes all day, in three locations—the FBI's northern Virginia field office at Tysons Corner, the Washington field office at Buzzard's Point, or in a room in the Alexandria jail. Les Wiser was usually present for the FBI.

"Hulkower was there for four hours yesterday," Ames said. "The other day they brought in a couple of actual members of the surveillance team. They were very excited to finally get a chance to meet their actual target." Ames smiled, as though he savored all this.

I expressed some amazement at the fact that the CIA had placed him in charge of the Soviet counterintelligence branch—in the bear's mouth, as it were—at the very time when he was most vulnerable. He was getting divorced, he needed money, he was drinking.

Ames nodded. Had I talked to his friends, he asked? I mentioned two former CIA officers he had known well at Langley.

He had to be careful, Ames said, not to reveal any classified information to me. Rosario's sentence depended upon his compliance with the plea agreement, which barred him from disclosing classified information about either the CIA or his spying for the KGB.

He expected she would get five years, he said. He was very bitter about his wife's sentence, "because she did nothing." The media had ignored the part of his statement in court in which he said the government had used her as a way to punish him. The government has been unfair to her.

I said I understood his view and his contention that Rosario was only trying to protect him. But the wiretaps were part of the public record, and the excerpts that had been released appeared to show that his wife had participated in his activities.

His eyes turned to ice.

I thought he might break off the interview, but he did not.

Shifting to other subjects, I asked him how he had acquired the KGB code name of KOLOKOL, which means "bell" in Russian. What was its significance?

"I chose the name KOLOKOL," he said, "because of Herzen. And his newspaper." Aleksandr Herzen, the nineteenth-century Russian revolutionary writer, exiled in Paris, then in England, published an influential weekly journal, *Kolokol,* which was banned in Russia but widely read.[8]

Ames became quite animated in talking about Herzen and the roots of his KGB code name. "KOLOKOL means bell," he said, "and the bell is important in Russian history." Ames mentioned the Ivan the Great bell tower in the Kremlin.[9] It was also his own idea, Ames said, to sign his letters to the KGB with the letter K, short for KOLOKOL.

Since he had spent his career as a CIA case officer and a counterintelligence official, what was his view of why the FBI had not seen him filling or emptying a dead drop?

"There are some good explanations for that," Ames replied.

"They did not want to get in too close?"

He smiled and said, "That's right."

The interview was winding down, and Cacheris pushed a buzzer to summon a guard. Early in our conversation, I mentioned that I had met his former boss, Yevgeny Primakov, the head of the SVR, and other officials of the KGB and the SVR.

During the few minutes while we waited for the guard to come, Ames asked me what I thought of Primakov. He seemed very interested in my views. I told him an anecdote about my first meeting with Primakov, which had taken place in Moscow a few years earlier when I was researching an article for the *New York Times Magazine.* Ames listened intently; he seemed hungry for news of the SVR.

Then the guard arrived. We shook hands again and Ames was taken away. The heavy door slammed behind him with a loud metallic clang.

---

[8]Herzen founded *Kolokol* in London in 1857. He was a socialist and to an extent a forerunner of the Russian Revolution in the twentieth century. Herzen did not believe in Hegel's view of history as inevitable; he thought that the fate of nations was decided by chance—and human will.

[9]The enormous Czar Bell, at the foot of the tower, is described as the largest bell in the world.

21

ROSARIO V. RICK

As Rosario Ames was questioned by FBI agents in the hours after her arrest, she insisted at first that the source of all the money was their wonderfully charitable friend, "Robert," from Chicago.

Then she admitted the truth. As Les Wiser testified at a hearing on March 10, 1994, she "amended her statement to say that the money, and she was referring to their unexplained wealth, came from the Russians in return for Mr. Ames spying."

Once that hurdle had been crossed, Yolanda Larson, the pregnant FBI agent, gently asked Rosario when and how she had learned that her husband was a spy. It was then that Rosario related the story of the wallet.

In 1991, Rosario said, she had needed a small wallet to fit in her purse and remembered that Rick had the little red one he never used. She looked in a drawer and found it. And inside she discovered a mysterious note, the contents of which had alarmed her. Later, in debriefings by the FBI after her guilty plea, she elaborated. The note had referred to a meeting in an embassy in "the city where your mother-in-law lives."

She had asked Rick for an explanation, but he had been evasive. She continued to press him: Why was her mother mentioned in the note? What is this? And about two weeks later, Rick took her to Germaine's, the Vietnamese restaurant on upper Wisconsin Avenue above Georgetown. Over dinner, Rosario maintained, Rick confessed that he was spying for the Russians. It was the Russians who had paid the money, not "Robert." He had been a spy since 1985.

Later, during the plea-bargain negotiations over Rosario's sentence, she changed her story again. She now believed she had found the note in 1992 rather than in 1991.[1] In his own debriefings, Aldrich Ames told essentially the same story about the wallet and the dinner at Germaine's.

While the account of how and when Rosario discovered her husband was a spy may be true, there are some problems with it. At a press conference after the Ameses had pleaded guilty, Helen Fahey, the U.S. attorney, was asked if she believed that Rosario had thought all along that the money had come from investments. "We cannot prove otherwise," Fahey replied.

It would have been very difficult to verify or disprove what the Ameses were saying. But it was also true that at this point the government had no great interest in challenging Rosario's story. Her participation in her husband's crimes had been demonstrated by the wiretaps in 1993, so it was not necessary for the prosecution's case to establish whether she might have known the truth earlier than she admitted. In fact, in the months after Rosario's guilty plea, the government's diminished interest in the question of Rosario's knowledge actually coincided with her own interests.

---

[1]Rosario Ames may have moved up the date by a year because Rick Ames said he told his wife the truth in August 1992, the same month that he wrote to the SVR: "My wife has accomodated [sic] herself to understanding what I am doing in a very supportive way." Of course, the change in the date also meant that Rosario claimed she had known of his espionage for perhaps a year and a half instead of two or three years.

Having worked out a plea bargain that would give Rosario a relatively light sentence in exchange for her husband's cooperation, it was not to the advantage of the government to pursue the issue of whether she had known of, or participated in, Rick's spying all along. Because if she had, the prosecutors might then have had to justify the lighter sentence for Rosario.

The truth about the extent of Rosario's prior knowledge may always remain elusive. But it can be examined. To paraphrase the familiar incantation of Senator Howard Baker of Tennessee during the Watergate hearings, what did Rosario know and when did she know it?

Rosario, to begin with, was a paid CIA asset in Mexico. Once she went on the payroll, she was not an innocent, an espionage naïf. She was well aware that her husband worked for the CIA in a sensitive job and that he had access to valuable secrets.

Rosario Ames was also a Ph.D. candidate universally described by her teachers and friends as an intellectual and a brilliant scholar. Yet she apparently accepted without question that a vague friend in Chicago, whose last name was never offered and whom she had never met in all the years of their marriage, was somehow the source of an endless river of money, of tens, and hundreds of thousands, eventually millions, of dollars that Rick was stashing away in Swiss bank accounts.

Could she have known *nothing*? In 1985, in the summer before the Ameses were married, Rosario went out to Chicago and enrolled in a philosophy course at the University of Chicago. That summer, in the second week of July, there was a lecture by a famous author, and Rick and Rosario's mother, Cecilia, joined her in Chicago and together they attended the lecture. Where was Robert?

Ames had begun his spying that spring and had received his first $50,000 on May 17. He has said he explained away the money as a loan from "Robert." Perhaps he had not yet told Rosario about "Robert," but if he had, since they were all in Chicago, would it not seem likely that Rosario might have inquired about the possibility of meeting Rick's old and good friend, the presumed source of the $50,000 he had already received from the KGB? But, apparently, there was no talk of "Robert" on the Chicago trip.[2]

According to Ames, "After, after I started getting the money. . . what I finally did was, I had told Rosario that the first $50,000, I prepared a cover story. . . . There was an old friend of mine who, that I had asked for a loan, that I had known back in college days in Chicago. And I had done a big favor for him once. I never described what it was, but I would ask him for a loan to get us sort of out of the financial hole. Then later, however, I had to account for more money. . . . And what I told her was that this friend of mine, I only identified him to her as Robert, and his associates were interested in investing money in Europe. And that while I was in Rome, I would look after some of their investments and manage them. . . . And I would get a commission."[3]

In the six or seven years that Rosario says she knew nothing, "Robert" was never further identified by Rick, and Rosario apparently managed to suppress any curiosity she may have had about the anonymous and incredibly generous investment wizard in the Windy City.

At the very least, Rosario should have known there might be something illicit about the money that was pouring in, because she and Rick were not reporting it on their income taxes. Not any of it. For eight years, Rick and Rosario Ames signed false federal tax returns, reporting only that they were living on Rick's modest government salary. It was one of the counts to which each pleaded guilty.

And why were there not one but *two* stories that were told to explain the Ameses' extraordinary wealth to their friends and family? Most friends were led to believe that the money came from an inheritance Rosario had received after the death of her father. Rosario knew that was false. She could hardly tell that story to her

---

[2]Ames had attended the University of Chicago briefly and undoubtedly had made some friends in that city. However, the FBI was unable to establish that Ames had a specific person in mind when he invented the story of "Robert." Government investigators do not believe that "Robert" existed.

[3]Senate Interview, pp. 46–47.

mother, of course, since Cecilia knew better.[4] But others were told that the Ameses had been fortunate in their investments. If Rosario really believed the story about "Robert from Chicago," then why was it necessary to mislead most of their friends into thinking that the money had come from her family? Why the lie?

Rosario says she was terribly upset about the reference to her mother in the famous note in the wallet. But she did not voice any objections when Rick and Cecilia went to the American embassy in Bogotá in 1989 to execute a fraudulent gift letter, a letter claiming that the half a million dollars that came from Rick's Zurich account, and which he used to buy the house in Arlington, was a gift from her mother. Rosario has said she didn't know that her mother had signed the letter.

Since both Rosario and later her husband told essentially the same story about the note in the wallet and dinner at Germaine's, it may have happened. On the other hand, if the Ameses had wanted to coordinate their story, there was ample opportunity to do so. There were at least three meetings between Rick and Rosario and their lawyers during the plea-bargain phase, and the couple was able to exchange notes through their attorneys in the Alexandria jail. They also rode in the same police car on the way to one or more court hearings. Rick Ames did not recount the wallet story until after April 28, more than two months after Rosario had first told it to the FBI.

It is also conceivable that they had agreed upon their story in advance; perhaps, if caught, Rosario was to say she found out the truth about Rick a year before, or two years before. Plato Cacheris discounted any thought that the story was contrived. "I don't think they concocted it," he said in an interview. "If it was an advance agreement, why not say she knew nothing? Because they didn't know about the electronic surveillance."

[4]Rosario may not herself have talked about her supposed inherited wealth to friends, but she heard Rick do so and said nothing to dispute the story. As Rick Ames has said, "I allowed a presumption to grow up that her family had money, so this was the source of our relative affluence." Senate Interview, p. 47.

But Rick Ames, a CIA counterintelligence specialist, would have known that if the FBI ever caught up with him, it would tap his phones for some substantial period of time before the agents moved in. If their story had been worked out in advance, he would know enough to suggest that Rosario not try to claim total ignorance. Ames, however, might have hesitated to broach to his volatile wife such an explosive subject as the possibility that they might one day be caught. Rosario Ames has described herself as "very high-strung, very emotional."[5] Raising the delicate question of what to say if they were ever arrested might not have been popular topic with Rosario.

It may well be that Rosario Ames did find a note in 1991 or perhaps in 1992 that led her husband to confide the truth. But that does not answer the larger question of what Rosario thought was really going on in the six or seven years before that, when the Ameses went from being virtually broke to the lifestyles of the rich and famous. These were the years when the Ameses were concealing their income from the government and telling two different stories about the source of their sudden wealth.

It seems reasonable to suppose, given all the facts, that during these years Rosario Ames did not *want* to know the truth. Far better to look the other way. She may, in short, have adopted a "don't ask, don't tell" policy.

In fairness to Rosario Ames, it should be noted that she did not have access to any CIA secrets (other than the ones that Rick brought home and put in his computer), she was not accused of passing any documents or information to the Russians or of meeting with any Russians for purposes of spying, and she was not herself paid any money by the KGB or the SVR. But she did actively advise and encourage her husband in his espionage activities for the Russians.

Whenever she learned the truth, she was under no legal obligation to disclose it to the authorities. Contrary to popular opinion, it is not a crime to fail to report a crime. Rosario was not convicted for failing to turn Rick in, or even for spending tens of thousands of dollars knowing that the money had come from the Russians.

[5]ABC News, *Primetime Live*, October 20, 1994, Transcript, p. 2.

There is no federal law against spending money gained from espionage. Even after she knew that Rick was a criminal, it was legal for her to spend the money—which she did, in large amounts—because spending the money in itself was not a crime. If it were, the wives of Mafia dons and bank robbers would be prosecuted, and they are not.

On April 28, Judge Hilton postponed Rosario's sentencing until August 26 so that both she and her husband could be questioned by the government, and to allow ample time for the FBI and the CIA to determine if Rick Ames was living up to his agreement to cooperate. On August 11, Rick was transferred from the Alexandria detention center to a new federal maximum security wing of the federal penitentiary at Allenwood, Pennsylvania.[6]

As the date for sentencing Rosario approached, Judge Hilton granted a month's delay, until September 23, to allow more time for the government to question her husband. Then, the day before Mrs. Ames was to be sentenced, she suddenly dumped William Cummings and hired a new lawyer. He was John P. Hume, who also represented the government of her native Colombia in Washington. Sentencing was again put off, as is usual when a new lawyer enters a case, until October 21.

Hume proved an adroit public relations man. Just before the sentencing, he invited Sally Quinn of the *Washington Post* and Diane Sawyer, the coanchor of ABC television's *Primetime Live,* to interview Rosario Ames. The hope was to portray Rosario as a victim and to build public support for a lighter sentence.

Quinn is a talented writer who built her reputation in Washington by deftly skewering the celebrated and the pompous,

---

[6]Allenwood, where some of the Watergate defendants served their time, had gained a reputation as a sort of country club prison for white-collar criminals, with tennis courts and minimum security. That was not the case in the wing in which Ames was housed, however. While the debriefings continued, he was held in what amounted to solitary confinement, allowed out of his cell for only an hour a day, his mail censored by the CIA and his phone calls restricted. The treatment was extremely harsh, but the government was not about to let Ames mix in the general prison population, at least until the debriefings were over.

an art at which she has no peer. But this was to be a different sort of story. Quinn wrote a lengthy, generally sympathetic article that led the newspaper's "Style" section and occupied a full page inside. Rosario's tale was "compelling and heartbreaking." Her husband had manipulated, and threatened, and controlled her. She felt "totally trapped." Rosario talked about the wallet and "Robert from Chicago." As for the money, "She thought nothing of it, she says, because lots of people have investments."

Their sex life had deteriorated, Rosario complained. By the time Paul was born, "she says, Rick had become almost totally impotent. . . ." Rosario also made public a letter from Rick in which, among his faults, he listed "impotence: drinking: my side business. . . ." But Rick was apparently not always impotent, because he demanded sex, and "I remember telling him several times that I didn't like to be raped because that's the way I felt." Rosario Ames, in short, was a victim of spousal abuse by an impotent husband who was also a rapist. She never wanted to see Rick again, she said, "not after knowing that he's caused people to die."[7]

It was much the same on *Primetime Live*. Rosario told Diane Sawyer that after learning that Rick was a Russian spy, she had repeatedly told him "you have to stop." Sawyer also mentioned Rick's letter listing his "drinking, impotence." Then the program cut to Bogotá, and Paul jumped into the room wearing a Batman costume. Sawyer explained that the boy was being cared for by his grandmother.

At the outset of the interview, Sawyer asked Rosario Ames how she felt about her husband now.

"I despise him," she said.[8]

Facing four or five years in prison and separation from her young son, one can hardly fault Rosario or her attorney for trying to build public sympathy for her. The PR campaign did not, however, impress the judge. But it did irritate the prosecution.

On October 21, back in Judge Hilton's courtroom again, Rosario

[7]Sally Quinn, "The Terrible Secret of Rosario Ames," *Washington Post*, October 19, 1994, pp. C1, C4.

[8]ABC News, *Primetime Live*, October 20, 1994.

Ames rose to denounce her husband as "a master liar and manipulator." She knew nothing. "For the first seven years of our marriage I remained ignorant of his sinister spying." Rick, she said, had even insinuated that if he were caught, she and Paul might be killed by the KGB. She had seen a report in the press about the millions the SVR might be holding for her and her son, but "I certainly will not accept their blood money."[9] She grieved for her husband's victims, and "I weep for their wives and children."

"I beg you, Your Honor, Paul needs me, Paul is innocent, he did nothing wrong," she said in a trembling voice. "I beg you to be merciful. . . . Please understand that you are not only sentencing me, but Paul, too."

Her attorney, John Hume, described Rosario as "a victim of the worst form of spousal abuse."

Mark Hulkower rose to respond.

What he found most troubling, he said, was Mrs. Ames's "complete abdication of any responsibility for her own conduct. As each day goes by, Mrs. Ames takes less and less responsibility for her conduct and goes further in her attempts to convince this court and the world at large that she never did anything wrong. . . ." She had granted "selective interviews" toward this end. In 1992, after learning of her husband's spying and the source of the money, he said, "Mrs. Ames happily spent $6,000 of the KGB's money on a weekend shopping spree in New York including more than a thousand dollars on fancy restaurants and more than $2,000 on clothing and shoes. In one weekend."[10]

[9]The story Mrs. Ames cited had been published in the *Washington Post* the day before. It reported that Rosario Ames herself had informed the FBI on the day of her arrest that Rick had told her the Russians were holding between $1 million and $2 million for him. The story said that unidentified U.S. officials believed the SVR might regard that money as a "debt of honor" and attempt to deliver it to Ames's wife and son. See Walter Pincus and Bill Miller, "U.S. Feels Russia May Settle 'Debt of Honor' With Ames," *Washington Post*, October 20, 1994, p. A4.

[10]The $6,000 was spent by both the Ameses on their New York weekend. Most of the credit card slips were signed by Rosario. The couple dropped $320 at La Côte Basque, a pricey restaurant on Manhattan's East Side, $1,500 at an electronics store, and a modest $200 at a Cole-Haan shoe store.

Although Rosario had claimed she pleaded repeatedly with her husband to stop spying for the Russians, in the "thousands of hours" of recorded conversations and wiretaps "not once do you hear Mrs. Ames criticize her husband for working for the KGB. Not once do you hear Mrs. Ames tell her husband to get out of this dirty business. If she was constantly begging him to quit, wouldn't it appear on tape at least once?"

In a memorandum Hulkower submitted to the court, he reviewed the plea agreement that made Rosario's sentence dependent on her husband's cooperation. Ames's cooperation, he said, had been "substantial." There were some topics on which the debriefers believed that "Ames has not been completely forthcoming." But he had provided "significant new information about espionage activities not available from other sources."

Judge Hilton then sentenced Rosario Ames to sixty-three months for conspiracy to commit espionage and twenty-four months for conspiracy to evade taxes, the sentences to run concurrently. Soon afterward, she was sent to the federal prison in Danbury, Connecticut. With time off for good behavior and for the months already served after her arrest, she could be released in about four and a half years, around August 1998.

Rosario Ames was certainly far less culpable than Rick, as her sentence reflects. If not for her husband, she would probably be back in her native land, explaining Hegelian philosophy, if that is possible, to graduate students in Bogotá. Instead she is behind bars and separated from her son.

On the other hand, Rosario Ames clearly enjoyed spending the SVR's money even after she knew the truth about its origin. In one conversation recorded by the FBI late in 1993, Rick tells Rosario there is a bill of over $10,000 at Neiman Marcus. But not to worry, he said, he had paid $9,600 of the total in cash.[11]

The debriefings of Aldrich Ames went on all summer and continued for months after Ames had been moved to Allenwood.

---

[11]Had he paid more, of course, the department store would have had to file a Currency Transaction Report with the Treasury.

In many areas, Ames provided details about his spying to the CIA and the FBI that only he could have known.

Ames helped the FBI, for example, to identify his KGB and SVR handlers. In Bogotá, as Ames and "Andre," his contact, strolled past the same bowling alley, the FBI took videos of the Russian. "We had Rick do a composite sketch of Andre," an FBI man said. "The video matched the sketch. He viewed the video and confirmed it for us that it was Andre." Armed with the video and Ames's description, the FBI was able to identify the man as Yuri Karetkin of the SVR.

But there were lingering doubts that Ames was telling all he knew. It would stand to reason, especially once Rosario had been sentenced, that Ames might try to hold back some information. His loyalty, as he had made abundantly clear, was to the SVR, not to the CIA. In the unlikely event that Ames would ever end up in Moscow, he would undoubtedly like to be able to tell his superiors in Yasnevo that he had withheld certain data, that he had not told all.

In his memorandum to the court, Mark Hulkower placed the government's doubts on the record. "The debriefers suspect, but cannot prove, that he is still withholding information, and a polygraph given Ames on September 20, 1994, supports this concern."

Hulkower did not elaborate, and neither the FBI nor the CIA have said what information Ames is suspected of holding back. But according to one official with access to the debriefings, Ames failed a polygraph test in which he was asked when he began spying for the KGB. Despite this, the FBI was confident that Ames did in fact begin his spying in the spring of 1985.

Both Rick and Rosario had failed at least one other question on their polygraph tests.

"He failed on whether he was withholding information about how his wife learned he was spying for the KGB," the official said.

"She failed on when and how she learned he was a spy."

22

WOOLSEY ON
THE BURNING DECK

He knew it was coming, of course, the earthquake that hit Langley on February 22, 1994, with the disclosure in large black headlines and all over television, that a "CIA spy couple" had been arrested by the FBI. The nightmare of a KGB mole inside the Central Intelligence Agency had finally come true.

Jim Woolsey, the quintessential Washington insider, had been around the capital for twenty-five years, long enough to know that the arrests of Aldrich and Rosario Ames would not be a one-day story. This one wasn't going to go away easily. It would register in the upper levels of the Richter scale.

Before it was over, the CIA had been shaken to its foundations, its uncertain future was in the hands of a presidential commission, Congress was furious at the director, and Woolsey had abruptly resigned. Public confidence in the CIA was at its lowest ebb since the disclosure by a Senate committee in the mid-1970s of the agency's assassination plots, drugs tests, mail opening, and other high crimes and misdemeanors.

There had been no hint of disaster in the beginning. Woolsey had impressive credentials and an enviable record of experience in Washington. A lawyer with close ties to the defense and national security establishments, he had moved easily in and out of government in a variety of backstage jobs under both Republicans and Democrats. He was a hybrid, a combination of private citizen and public servant indigenous to the habitat inside the beltway.

The son of a lawyer, he was born and raised in Tulsa, Oklahoma, graduated from Stanford University, and, like President Clinton, went on to Oxford as a Rhodes scholar. Like Bill and Hillary Clinton, he earned his law degree at Yale.

He spent two years in the army after law school, starting in 1968, first as program analyst in the Pentagon during the last months of the Johnson administration. Then he worked for Paul Nitze on the SALT I arms-control delegation. He moved to Henry Kissinger's National Security Council staff briefly in 1970 during the Nixon administration. For three years after that he served as general counsel of the Senate Armed Services Committee under the powerful John C. Stennis of Mississippi, the committee's veteran Democratic chairman. During those years it began to be whispered that the man to see, the behind-the-scenes power in the committee, was R. James Woolsey. No longer a lowly Defense Department analyst, Woolsey now was in a position to influence the Pentagon's multibillion-dollar budget.

In 1973, Woolsey left the Hill and joined the Washington law firm of Shea & Gardner, where he remained for four years until he was named undersecretary of the navy in the Carter administration. After two years in that job he returned to his law firm as a partner. He served on various government commissions during the Nixon and Reagan administrations and as a delegate to the strategic-arms talks in Geneva during the 1980s, earning him the sobriquet of the Republicans' favorite Democrat. Woolsey during those years became a confidant of Brent Scowcroft, President Bush's national security adviser, serving with Scowcroft on two commissions that studied the MX missile and strategic forces. In 1991, Bush named Woolsey as ambassador to the talks on conventional forces in Europe.

Woolsey, in short, was a conservative Democrat who had worked closely with the Republicans. He was a director of Martin Marietta, a major military contractor, and other defense companies.

Despite the Rhodes scholar and Yale law school ties, Woolsey was not close to the Clintons. He first met Bill Clinton in 1991 at a dinner organized by Pamela Harriman, the doyenne of the Democratic party. Three months before the 1992 presidential election, Woolsey joined a group of conservative foreign-policy specialists who endorsed Clinton. When Clinton, following his election as president in 1992, was searching for a CIA director, Woolsey had the support of Senator David Boren, from Woolsey's native Oklahoma, then the chairman of the Senate Intelligence Committee. In Little Rock on December 22, the president-elect named Woolsey director of Central Intelligence on the same day he announced Warren M. Christopher as his choice for secretary of state.

There were problems almost from the start. Woolsey took over the CIA on February 5, 1993, ten days after Mir Amal Kansi had murdered two CIA employees and wounded three other men in the shootings outside Langley headquarters. The agency was shaken by the tragedy. The CIA, already a target of critics, was now a target of a terrorist.

But Woolsey hit the ground running, determined to be an aggressive battler for the CIA. At a time when the agency was having to justify its very existence in the aftermath of the cold war, Woolsey and the administration asked Congress for more money, not less.[1]

During the presidential campaign, Clinton promised to trim $7 billion from the intelligence budget over five years. At first, as the Clinton administration looked for ways to trim the deficit, the intelligence budget seemed a fat target. Woolsey fended off the budget cutters.

"Yes, we have slain a large dragon," Woolsey told members of the Senate Intelligence Committee at his confirmation hearing in

[1]Woolsey asked for about $29 billion for all the intelligence agencies, a figure that was slightly higher than the existing budget but lower than Clinton had asked for during the presidential campaign. Congress cut about $1 billion from the total.

February. "But we live now in a jungle filled with a bewildering variety of poisonous snakes. And in many ways, the dragon was easier to keep track of."

Woolsey had a good point; the danger of nuclear Armageddon might be greatly reduced, but regional conflicts by third-world countries that might acquire nuclear weapons posed an increasing threat. Whether the new jungle required the same huge budgets for intelligence was much less clear, however.

And some powerful members of Congress found Woolsey's aggressive personal style off-putting. Dennis DeConcini of Arizona, the new chairman of the intelligence panel, clashed with Woolsey in what soon developed into a raging personal feud. It began during the fight over the intelligence budget, which DeConcini wanted to cut and Woolsey defended.

"Woolsey," said one veteran Capitol Hill hand, "is very smart, and a prodigiously hard worker. But he had to win every battle. He had an attitude of, 'I don't care if I lose the war, but I'm going to win this battle.' He alienated everybody. The least bit of criticism, he would pounce on it like a tiger."

For bureaucrats, the first rule of dealing with Congress is to be deferential. Members of the House and Senate like to be stroked. Woolsey wouldn't do it, and he paid a large price for his pugnaciousness. To some, it also seemed as though Woolsey, in his first big, high-profile job in Washington, had succumbed to the seduction of power, the government car with its scrambler telephone, the security men in dark suits always at his side, the mystique of heading not only a powerful agency but a secret one.

The CIA director's combative personal style continued to draw attention. "Woolsey is bald and wears glasses," said one critic. "A James Bond he's not. He looks like a classic nerd, the kid with the violin case walking through the bad neighborhood. So he has to prove himself the toughest kid on the block."

Since Woolsey knew the Ames case was about to surface, he was ready to react. When the arrests came, Woolsey moved swiftly to try to contain the political and intelligence damage. He tried to stay ahead of the curve. He wanted to know, he announced, why "it took from 1985 to early 1994 for arrests to be made."

Woolsey ordered three separate investigations. The first and most sweeping was by the CIA's inspector general, Frederick P. Hitz. Next, Woolsey ordered a "damage assessment" of the Ames case, a traditional exercise in which an intelligence agency that has been penetrated tries to figure out which of its secrets have been compromised, and indeed whether it has *any* secrets left. The Damage Assessment Panel was headed by Rich Haver, the director of the Intelligence Community Management Staff.[2] The panel, among other things, had the task of trying to determine which of its compromised assets may have become double agents under KGB control, feeding Langley and Presidents Reagan, Bush, and Clinton false information. And Woolsey also named a special panel to make long-range recommendations to try to fix the agency's problems.[3]

Frederick Hitz, the inspector general, was a former DO officer and Washington lawyer who had been the agency's legislative counsel and then deputy chief of the European division under William Casey. Congress, annoyed that it could not get access to the reports of the CIA inspector general, enacted a law in 1989 creating an independent inspector general for the agency. President Bush named Hitz to the job. He worked for the CIA and for Woolsey, but he could be removed only by the president.

With a staff of twelve investigators, Hitz dug deep into the Ames case. His detailed, 486-page classified report—373 pages long with 113 pages of appendices—issued in September, was a devastating indictment of the agency's handling of the Ames case and the management of the Directorate of Operations. Hitz's central con-

[2]The Intelligence Community Management Staff was the successor to the Intelligence Community Staff, the unit that Aldrich Ames, as "Rick Wells," had used as cover when he first began his authorized meetings with the Soviets in 1984.

[3]The CIA panel was made part of a the Joint Security Commission that had been created by the CIA and the Pentagon in 1993. The panel set up after the Ames case was headed by Jeffrey H. Smith, a Washington lawyer who was also commission chairman, and it was advised by Brent Scowcroft, Harold Brown, the former secretary of defense, and Douglas Gow, the former chief of FBI counterintelligence.

clusion was that Ames could have been caught a lot sooner. The agency and the DO simply had not responded adequately to the agent losses.

Hitz singled out twenty-three individuals, including three past CIA directors—Casey, Webster, and Gates—for criticism. The Hitz report was the beginning of the end for Woolsey. It created an enormous problem for the CIA chief: how to react.

Woolsey had been in charge of the CIA for only one of the nine years that Ames had spied for Moscow. By the time he arrived at Langley, the search for the mole was all but over. The FBI had opened its formal case on Ames only four months after Woolsey became CIA director. But how the CIA handled the public and congressional outrage after the case broke was Woolsey's responsibility.

And Woolsey had presided over the agency during the final stages when key decisions had to be made. He was director, for example, during the months when Ames was told he was going to Moscow for a narcotics conference, and he was director during the ensuing waffling within the DO over whether or not to send him, and the repeated postponements of the trip. And it was Woolsey who had permitted his chief CIA public relations man to deny that there was any thought of sending a mole to Moscow, when, in fact, the matter was not settled until the date of the trip approached and the FBI put its foot down; Rick Ames, the FBI ruled, would not be allowed to get on that plane.

Woolsey also blundered after the arrests by going on NBC's *Today* show on April 19 and announcing that he expected there would be other moles uncovered. There would be "quite a few" spy scandals, Woolsey said, and the agency had leads to moles "in several parts of the American government." Correspondent Jamie Gangel, who does not mince words, said that it sounded like "you're out here trumpeting now, 'We ain't the only ones.'"

Woolsey replied: "People should not have the impression that the Ames case is the only major counterintelligence case that they're going to see. They're going to see a number of these over the years to come." The FBI was furious that Woolsey seemed to be saying the government was honeycombed with moles, which reflected adversely on the bureau, since the FBI had the responsibility for finding spies. The next day, Woolsey was forced to back-track. "I should have limited myself to saying 'leads,' not 'cases,'" he said.

Woolsey was enraged at what he perceived as Ames's gift for manipulating the news media through interviews from his prison cell. He compared Ames, unfavorably, to Benedict Arnold. Woolsey thought that Arnold, at least, had some redeeming features. Ames, Woolsey said, was trying to "reinvent himself" as someone who had acted for political motives. To consider Ames's views on the CIA seriously, he said, would be "a little bit like taking John Gotti as an authority on the FBI."[4]

The agency, from Woolsey on down, sought to counter Ames's public relations efforts by discounting him as a "mediocre" officer who had performed poorly in his CIA career. There was a problem with this, however, since Ames had been given a number of important jobs, including handling Shevchenko and Yurchenko, two high-level defectors. Ames, in truth, was an intelligent man with a sharp, analytical mind. If he was incompetent, why was he given important jobs? Woolsey finessed the contradiction by saying that in some areas, Ames had performed well.

"We couldn't say he was a complete buffoon," one CIA official confided. "So Woolsey hit on the 'partial buffoon' theory."

But the more Woolsey spoke about Ames, the more he became identified with the case. It was true that others had directed the agency for most of the nine years that Ames had betrayed every secret he could get his hands on. But this was of little comfort to Woolsey. The Ames case had hit him in the face with the full force of a lemon pie thrown by some spiteful vaudevillian in the sky. Woolsey's dilemma was what to do about it.

He decided he wouldn't censure his predecessors as CIA director—that simply wasn't done, and besides, Casey was dead and both Webster and Gates strongly maintained that they had never been fully briefed on the problem.

Woolsey faced an additional difficulty: There was no smoking gun in the Ames case. There was no single individual whom

---

[4]*Larry King Live,* CNN, May 9, 1994, Transcript, p. 8.

Woolsey could point to and say: He was the one who let Aldrich Ames get away with it. Perhaps Gus Hathaway, by virtue of his title of chief of counterintelligence, came closest to filling the bill, but he was retired and long gone from the agency. Hathaway was indeed on Hitz's list, but there many others who could and should have done more.

The political theorist Hannah Arendt has characterized bureaucracy as "rule by Nobody."[5] It is a classic rule of a large organization that nobody claims responsibility for anything. Who should be punished and how?

Woolsey finally selected eleven current and former CIA employees on the Hitz list to discipline, all but one from the Directorate of Operations. The problem that Woolsey faced was that most of those he chose to reprimand were beyond his reach. Of the eleven persons selected, seven had already retired or, in one case, was just about to retire. Four were still on the payroll.

Woolsey's excruciating dilemma, boiled down, was this: Would it be fair to crack down hard on the four employees still working for the CIA by firing them, when the other seven could not be touched? Woolsey's choice was even more complex: Of the four persons he believed most at fault, three had already retired, and one was about to retire.

It was even worse than that. One of the four current employees was none other than Ted Price, the chief of the Directorate of Operations—the nation's top spook. Could Woolsey afford to fire him?

Congress, as Woolsey knew, wanted heads to roll; the Hill wanted to see blood on the floor. So, in fact, did many of the younger DO officers, who suspected from the start that Woolsey and the agency establishment would protect the old boys.

Woolsey was trapped. For all of his feisty, often arrogant manner, he had a deep sense of fairness and a perhaps misplaced loyalty to the DO that would not permit him to fire only those who

[5] Hannah Arendt, *Crises of the Republic* (New York: Harcourt Brace Jovanovich, 1972), p. 137. Bureaucracy, Arendt adds, is "an intricate system of bureaus in which no men, neither one nor the best, neither the few nor the many, can be held responsible."

happened still to be within his grasp. He decided simply to issue eleven letters of reprimand.

The decision doomed him, as he must have known it would.

Woolsey announced the reprimands to the press and to the congressional intelligence committees on September 28. The only one of the eleven persons reprimanded whom Woolsey named was Ted Price.[6] Price had been Hathaway's deputy in the Counterintelligence Center. After Hathaway retired, Price moved up in March 1990 to head the center for ten months. During three months of that period, Ames worked for him in the center's Analysis Group. Price knew that Ames was considered a security risk.

"I have decided that those who were responsible for allocating resources to the mole hunt before it entered a new and more vigorous phase in early 1991 deserve reprimands," Woolsey told the House Intelligence Committee. His statement covered Price; it also applied to Hathaway and others whom he did not name. "Accordingly, I have issued a reprimand to Mr. Price for his failure to devote additional resources during the ten-month period that he served as director of the Counterintelligence Center in 1990." In effect, Woolsey was saying that Price should have given Jeanne Vertefeuille more help.

It was an extraordinary public reprimand for the nation's top spy. But Woolsey immediately followed it up by saying he was not about to fire Price. "I have confidence in Ted Price's ability and professionalism, and I have asked him to stay on as Director of Operations."

The second-highest-ranking CIA official reprimanded was Burton Gerber, who, ironically, was deputy inspector general under Hitz at the time of the IG's investigation of the Ames case. Since Gerber was a potential target of the investigation, he was prohibited from participating in the probe. Gerber was reprimanded because he had been head of the Soviet division in 1984

---

[6]Normally, the CIA does not identify anyone who works in the Directorate of Operations. Price could be named because he was a semipublic figure whose name had often appeared in print. Woolsey, following tradition, did not name the others.

when Ames began his authorized meetings with Sergei Divilkovsky and also because he headed the division in 1985 when Ames walked into Chadwick's and handed Sergei Chuvakhin some seven pounds of CIA documents, including the names of virtually all of the CIA's Soviet agents.

The third official reprimanded, Jack Gower, also illustrated Woolsey's dilemma. Gower had been the deputy chief of station in Rome during Ames's tour there. After Ames's arrest, a cable went out from headquarters to all stations, asking agency personnel to tell what they knew about Ames. When Ames was in Rome, it will be recalled, drinking his lunch, three women in the station complained about his long absences in the afternoons and his neglect of his work. Their complaints were brushed off.

"After the arrest," a CIA source said, "one of the women who had served in the Rome station under Gower wanted to come forward and tell what she knew about Ames.

"The woman was overseas, in the CIA station in Tegucigalpa, Honduras. She got the cable and tried to tell about the situation in Rome. Guess who her station chief is? Jack Gower. And he refused to let her send it. She came back to headquarters and made an official report.

"There's more to the story. One of the women, an ops officer, had developed a relationship with senior Czech civilian, an intelligence guy in Rome. She asked for some guidance from Ames. What to do next? She got no satisfaction from him, because he was drunk all the time, and she went to Jack Devine, who had replaced Gower as the deputy COS, and complained that Ames would not help her and Ames was drunk all the time. She complained to Devine, who brushes her off and does nothing."

Clearly, the Rome station was not interested in disciplining Aldrich Ames. So Woolsey reprimanded Gower, since he had been the number two man in the station. But the chief of station, Alan Wolfe, had retired. Woolsey could have fired Gower for failing to crack down on Ames, but Wolfe, Gower's boss, was beyond reach. Woolsey contented himself with sending both Gower and Wolfe letters of reprimand.

The fourth person still employed at CIA whom Woolsey reprimanded was the official responsible for coordinating Ames's polygraphs. Hitz had recommended that three former directors of security at CIA be disciplined because Ames, on his polygraphs, had never been asked questions about his finances. Woolsey decided that there was not a close enough connection between the mismanaged polygraphs and the failure to catch Ames sooner to justify action against the former OS chiefs.

Besides Wolfe and Hathaway, the other retired CIA officials who received reprimands ranging from harsh to light were Clair George and Richard Stolz, two of Price's predecessors as deputy director for operations, and two former chiefs of the Soviet division, Milton Bearden—who actually kept trying to kick Ames out of the Soviet division—and David Forden, who had the misfortune to have headed the division when Ames was made Soviet branch chief for counterintelligence after his return from Mexico. Finally, Woolsey reprimanded James Anderson, who had been chief of the Washington station when Ames failed to file all of the reports of his meetings with Chuvakhin.

He also announced, without mentioning his name, that he was promoting Paul Redmond to the new position of special assistant for counterintelligence in recognition of his role in catching Ames. And he praised the officer, "dogged and determined for seven hard years," who had pursued the mole.

Again, because she was an officer of the DO, he did not identify her as Jeanne Vertefeuille.

Woolsey, of course, could have fired Ted Price, Burton Gerber, and Jack Gower. Perhaps it would have been unfair, but as President Kennedy once suggested, life is not always fair. It would have sent a clear message to the agency and to the public at large that the CIA would no longer tolerate the relaxed, old-boy atmosphere of the DO, the culture that had permitted a mole to operate with impunity for nearly nine years after it was apparent, almost from the start, that the agency had been penetrated.

But Woolsey, who had no experience in espionage, had allied himself early on with the DO, which knows very well how to co-opt directors who come in from the outside, how to wow them with spy tradecraft, and gadgetry, and the glamour of the dark world of espionage. Welcome to Langley's version of Skull and Bones, and here is your invisible ring. You are one of us now.

There was no way that Jim Woolsey was going to fire the head of the DO. The reaction was predictable. Congress, and many editorial writers, howled that Woolsey had let the old boys off with a slap on the wrist. The Senate Intelligence Committee noted that no one had been "fired, suspended, demoted or even reassigned" in response to "the greatest managerial breakdown in the CIA's history." Woolsey's disciplinary actions, it said, were "seriously inadequate."[7]

Then, if it were possible, matters got worse. Milton Bearden, the tall Texan who ran the CIA's covert war against the Soviet-backed regime in Afghanistan, was ending his long career as station chief in Bonn. There was to be a good-bye ceremony for Bearden at the CIA station in the American embassy in Germany. Two of his senior colleagues in the agency decided it would be a nice gesture to honor Bearden with a plaque. (Bearden, of course, was the official whom Woolsey had not named but had said was about to retire.)

Frank Anderson, the chief of the CIA's Near East division, telephoned N. John MacGaffin, Price's deputy, in October. Anderson told MacGaffin he was flying to Bonn to say farewell to Bearden and present him with a memento of his years of service. MacGaffin wished him well and thought no more about it.

The following week, Woolsey was in Detroit to meet with executives of the auto industry. One of his assistants called MacGaffin and Anderson and summoned them to Detroit. The two officials flew out, having no inkling that they were in trouble.

When they met with Woolsey, they soon found out they were. The CIA director made it clear that he regarded their approval of an award to Bearden as a direct affront, since Woolsey had reprimanded the station chief. MacGaffin and Anderson, surprised by the onslaught, argued that they had not given Bearden an agency "medal," it was a plaque with no official status. Anderson, in his comments in Bonn, they pointed out, had made no reference to

[7]Senate Report, p. 87.

Ames or to the period when Bearden supervised Ames. They had meant no offense to the director.

Woolsey, already sensitive to widespread criticism that he had been wimpish in his reaction to the Ames case, would not buy it. He told the two high-ranking officials they would have to "step aside" from their current positions. Woolsey offered them lesser jobs. Both refused and chose to retire instead. The story leaked out, and Woolsey, who had been assailed for not firing anybody, was criticized for overreacting to the Bearden affair. To his critics, there were echoes of Captain Queeg in all this, and who stole my strawberries? But MacGaffin and Anderson were through.

As Woolsey struggled to cope with the fallout of the Ames case, he made a number of internal changes at CIA to try to tighten the net against future counterintelligence disasters. He overhauled personnel and computer security and ordered a fresh evaluation of the DO. In May, President Clinton signed a directive reshuffling counterintelligence and, in an unprecedented step, requiring that the chief of the CIA's Counterintelligence Center be an FBI agent.

But Congress was determined to do something on its own about the CIA. Senator John Warner, the Virginia Republican, sponsored legislation to establish a seventeen-person commission on the future of American intelligence. President Clinton appointed former defense secretary Les Aspin, the chairman of the President's Foreign Intelligence Advisory Board (PFIAB), as chairman of the group. The commission was required to report by March 1996.

The commission was created over the active opposition of Woolsey and greeted with something less than enthusiasm by the White House. For Woolsey, it meant that as director, he would have seventeen people looking over his shoulder. He did not attempt to conceal his distaste for the commission:

"I don't think it really is necessary. . . frankly. But I think it could do some useful work, if it has. . . the right attitude. And if it comes into being, we'll work with it."[8]

Both the Senate and House intelligence committees were hard

---

[8]Woolsey interview, *MacNeil/Lehrer Newshour*, September 28, 1994.

at work investigating the Ames case. On November 1, the Senate panel produced a detailed, more than two-hundred-page report that was highly critical of the "gross negligence" by the agency and its officials in the Ames case. Then on November 30, the House committee weighed in with its own report criticizing both the CIA and, to a lesser degree, the FBI.

While there had been speculation for months that Woolsey would have to go, the White House did not, apparently, force him to walk the plank. Following the shock of the November 1994 election that gave the Republicans control of both houses of Congress for the first time in forty years, Bill Clinton had enough problems without creating a new one by firing his director of the CIA.

So it seemed as though Woolsey had weathered the storm and would stay. He said repeatedly that he had no plans to leave. As late as December 22, he was in his office at Langley headquarters, interviewing candidates to replace his executive assistant, the powerful Janet Andres, a foreign service officer on loan to the CIA who was leaving to become consul general in Frankfurt.

Over Christmas, Woolsey huddled with his wife, Suzanne, and their three sons at their home in suburban Maryland. He reached his decision.

It came as a complete surprise to most of his colleagues at the CIA and elsewhere in Washington. On December 28, the CIA, in a terse statement, announced that Woolsey was resigning. In a letter to President Clinton, Woolsey said the job's demands were such that he had not been able to spend enough time with his family. Clinton accepted his resignation "with regret," but the White House was caught off guard.[9]

In his last appearance before the Senate Intelligence Committee, Woolsey faced Senator Arlen Specter, the Republican chairman who had replaced his nemesis, Dennis DeConcini. Specter

---

[9]On February 9, 1995, Clinton named a retired air force general, Michael P. C. Carns, fifty-seven, as the new director of the CIA. Carns abruptly withdrew on March 10 after conceding he may have violated immigration laws when he brought a young Filipino man, the nephew of the family's cook, to the United States. Clinton the same day offered the CIA job to John M. Deutch, the deputy defense secretary.

asked if Woolsey could assure the committee there would never be another Ames case.

No CIA director "should ever give a guarantee" that there would not be another mole, Woolsey replied. He had put in place reforms, he said, "to reduce the likelihood of another Aldrich Ames." But "absolute assurances" should not be given.

On January 9, CIA employees gathered in the cavernous lobby of the old headquarters building to say good-bye. Woolsey made an unpublicized speech. It was very difficult to operate an intelligence agency in an open society, Woolsey told the spies. "You are in the job of stealing secrets. . . . We do our very best to hide these acts from all and sundry. That is what we are about."

He had made some wrong calls, he confessed, and some right ones, and he had tried to work for "changes in the culture of the agency." The CIA had to work in ways that were consistent with American values.

The wagons were still drawn in a circle at Langley. It is "vital that none of us let the outside world, whether wearing the guise of an editorial writer, a United States senator, or anything else," divert the CIA from its mission of upholding the Constitution and those values.

The applause echoed through the cold marble lobby, and then R. James Woolsey was gone, the eleventh victim of Aldrich Ames.

"THEY DIDN'T WANT
TO KNOW"

The Aldrich Ames case reveals that the CIA, often portrayed as a wily covert manipulator of global events, is in fact a tired bureaucracy, living in the past, wearing blinders, and deeply flawed.

In the wake of the fiasco, the agency was portrayed in caricature as a bunch of bumblers and clowns, Keystone Cops unable to spot a mole who drove a Jaguar into headquarters every day and carried out classified documents by the pound. Its mistakes in the case are too many to list, its old-boy blindness to the idea that one of their own, a member of the club, could be a traitor, indefensible.

It need not have happened that way.

In the fall of 1985, the Central Intelligence Agency lost almost all of its agents in the Soviet Union. Over time, it learned that ten had been executed and many others sent to prison. Vital technical operations, including electronic eavesdropping on Soviet communications, were also destroyed. In all, three dozen agents were lost, and perhaps hundreds of secret operations—the precise number may never be known—were compromised.

It was clear, or should have been, that something had gone terribly wrong. The possibility that all these agents had been arrested because they or the CIA all made operational mistakes defied the law of averages and common sense. Some other explanation—a compromised code, for example—was possible, but remote. Everything pointed toward a human penetration. A mole.

To the senior officials of the Directorate of Operations, it was a hideous, unthinkable possibility—that a Soviet agent inside the CIA was betraying the agency's operations to the KGB. Faced with a disaster of such apocalyptic proportions, the agency might have been expected to turn Langley upside down until the mole was found and rooted out. To put everything else aside until the overwhelming problem was solved. To pull out all the stops. To launch a major investigation.

It did not.

A full year after the agents began vanishing, Gus Hathaway, the new chief of counterintelligence, finally appointed a small Special Task Force to study the problem. But the task force consisted of only four persons, two of them retirees.

Jeanne Vertefeuille and her tiny staff were not trained in criminal work. She was assigned one young investigator to explore every lead—including the many false trails obligingly provided by the KGB. She worked with great dedication over almost eight years and never gave up. She stayed with it to the end, and beyond—as Ames's debriefer in prison. But it was clear from the resources allocated to her that finding the mole was not a high priority among the CIA's leaders.

Why?

"They didn't want to know," said one intelligence official whose job it was to analyze the Ames case thoroughly. "If you find a mole, you have to deal with him. It becomes embarrassingly public, like the Howard case."

The evidence suggests that neither William Webster nor Robert Gates, the two CIA directors who presided over the agency during most of the mole hunt, was told very much about what was going on. Their contention that they were advised that only a handful of agents had vanished is supported by the report of the House Intelligence Committee. "They were not given a full appreciation of the magnitude of the losses or the fate of the assets," the report concluded. Webster and Gates were told that the mole-hunt unit was studying a troubling problem "rather than the most serious operational disaster that had befallen the Agency."[1]

"No one ever told us we had a mole or any evidence of a mole," Webster said. "Ames wasn't on the screen; no name was given to us. They [the task force] tried hard with very little to work with. . . . I never knew the numbers were higher. Not until Ames was arrested."

Robert Gates, Webster's successor, insisted that he was not kept informed. "Until Ames's arrest," Gates said, "I was still under the impression there were a half dozen or so compromises. No one ever told me they had identified the mole or told me Ames's name. Their failure to come to me and tell me they had the mole—my God, I would have told the President. Maybe not the name, but I would have said we have a mole and we know who it is."

Why did the Directorate of Operations keep successive CIA directors in the dark? The intelligence official who studied the Ames case suggested one answer. "The DO will never tell the director about a problem because they're afraid the director might tell them how to fix it. That's always the problem. The guys in charge aren't told and don't want to know."

The culture of the DO was clearly a major factor in why it took almost nine years to catch Aldrich Ames. Woolsey himself warned that the Directorate of Operations could no longer be run as "a fraternity—much less a white male one" in which "once you are initiated you're considered a trusted member for life."[2] The DO's officers, although many are bright and well educated, are convinced that they know best. The DO is a self-protective secret society that is its own worst enemy. Lapses by its members are cov-

---

[1]House Report, p. 61.

[2]Address to Center for Strategic and International Studies, Washington, D.C., July 18, 1994, prepared text, p. 25.

ered up. Outsiders, even within the CIA, are not to be trusted. The press and Congress least of all. This "us against them" mind-set is the reason that the House and Senate intelligence committees, which are responsible for congressional monitoring of the agency, were told almost nothing about the agent losses for nine years, although the law requires the CIA to keep the people's elected representatives fully informed of its activities.

The universal cry of the bureaucrat, "It didn't happen on my watch," was another important cause of the Ames debacle. The agency lost all of its Soviet assets in a short period beginning late in 1985, but then the damage tapered off. There were continuing losses, but not as many. The reason, in retrospect, is clear: Ames was in Rome from 1986 to 1989, and out of the loop. He had access to all sorts of cables and CIA documents but to many fewer identities of agents. One proof of the fact that Ames was running low on names is that he finally gave away his own agent and friend, Sergei Fedorenko, in 1987, during his posting in Rome. So, during that period the new officials in charge at the CIA swept the problem under the rug, which is to say they virtually ignored it. It hadn't happened on their watch. Besides, Jeanne Vertefeuille and her little group were working on it; not to worry.

Ames, of course, should never have been assigned as the chief of the Soviet counterintelligence branch in the first place. He had been reported to headquarters for alcohol abuse in Mexico and had openly complained to colleagues about his financial problems, including the cost of the divorce he was going through. With all of these vulnerabilities he was put in one of the most sensitive jobs in the entire CIA, a post that gave him access to the innermost secrets of the agency's operations against the Soviet Union.

The Angleton legacy was yet another factor that allowed Aldrich Ames to spy undetected for nearly nine years. Angleton gave counterintelligence a bad name. In his quest for a mole, he destroyed the careers of so many loyal officers that afterwards, counterintelligence was downgraded. The better CIA officers, if they could, avoided assignment to CI work. Angleton was so sure that the Soviet division's sources were under KGB control that he succeeded in bringing operations against the Soviets to a halt at the height of the cold war. In the wake of the Angleton era, "the pendulum swung to the other extreme."[3] The agency's ability to find traitors was curtailed, its officials wary of repeating the mistakes of the past.

After Ames went off to Rome in 1986, he made no effort to conceal his wealth. He began living high and bought his first Jaguar. People in the Rome station knew that, but somehow the news never reached the mole hunters in Langley.

Even after the CIA was finally alerted in 1989 to Ames's lavish lifestyle, it took more than four *years* to catch him. The FBI was not called in until two years after the CIA received its first, belated tip. By then, in 1991, the CIA knew:

- Ames had spent his career in the Soviet division, and when he was counterintelligence chief of the Soviet branch, he had access to all the cases that were blown in 1985.
- Ames and his wife were living like millionaires and spending lavishly in Rome and Washington.
- Ames had not reported all of his meetings with Russian officials.
- Ames was an alcoholic who literally ended up in the gutter in Rome, often could not work after lunch, and got drunk about three times a week.
- Ames asked questions of colleagues about Soviet cases he had no need or reason to know about.
- Ames drove a Jaguar into the CIA parking lot each day, and had owned one in Rome as well.
- Ames had paid more than half a million dollars in cash for his house.

While it is true that Ames did not wear a Russian fur hat into his office at CIA, as the cartoons later depicted him, the list was at least an indication that he might bear looking at. Nevertheless, it took another three years before he was arrested.

The 1988 CIA-FBI Memorandum of Understanding, which William Webster and William Sessions had signed to prevent

[3]House Report, p. 59.

another Edward Lee Howard debacle, proved meaningless. The Ames case was not formally referred to the bureau until 1993, four years after Ames fell under suspicion, although the two agencies were cooperating at the working level as far back as 1986.

Within the CIA, the Office of Security did not talk to the mole hunters, and the polygraph operators did not talk to the Office of Security. At times, in fact, it appeared that nobody was talking to anybody, which was fine for Rick Ames and the SVR.

The FBI, too, dragged its feet, although at the most, it did so for a few months, not for almost nine years, as the CIA did. The CIA formally turned the mole hunt over to the FBI in January 1993, yet the bureau hesitated and did not open a case on Ames until May 1993. During those months, the bureau moved with an excess of caution. Partly it did so, however, out of fear that there might be another mole in addition to Ames. In part, it was slow off the mark because bureaucracies move ponderously. Traditional rivalry with the CIA was also to blame; the FBI was reluctant to take the CIA's word that Ames was the culprit, and the only one; it waited until it arrived at that hypothesis on its own.

The FBI knew back in 1985 that Ames had failed to report all of his meetings with Chuvakhin, yet it did not aggressively pursue its efforts to get the CIA to require Ames to file the missing reports. The bureau also knew in 1992 that Ames had made bank deposits after his meetings with Chuvakhin. It did not act on that information. Once Ames was the target, however, the FBI performed well. Bear Bryant, John Lewis, and Les Wiser and his team of men and women were professional and efficient. At any moment, a mistake could have blown the investigation sky high and alerted the target. Yet not once did the field agents and the Gs put a foot wrong. Ames never suspected he was under surveillance. And he was caught.

But he might have been caught five or even eight years earlier had the CIA been looking harder. Had that happened, lives could have been saved, and the damage contained.

Who is Rick Ames? Why did he betray his country? The answers, if there are any answers at all, must be sought on several levels. One can start with the obvious, with the outer surface of the man, and then seek to go deeper and inward.

The story can begin with Ames's father. Carleton Ames was a drunk who worked for the CIA, married a woman thirteen years his junior, and had an undistinguished career in the agency.

Rick Ames was a drunk who worked for the CIA, married Rosario, a woman eleven years his junior, and had a career that, while a good deal more satisfying than his father's, had essentially stalled.

Carleton Ames worked for James Jesus Angleton, hunter of moles.

Rick became a mole.

A psychologist might have a field day with this set of facts, but even if it is argued that their significance is marginal, the parallels are not without interest and relevance to the case. Ames in all probability would not have ended up in the CIA if his father had not worked there. The CIA, like alcoholism, tends to run in families.

Again, continuing to explore the surface, the outer level of the man, Ames in 1985, "the year of the spy" and the year he began spying for the KGB, was a forty-four-year-old GS-14 earning about $50,000 a year. His first marriage had failed, which did not enhance his self-esteem. Although he had a good job in counter-intelligence as Soviet branch chief, his career was not on the agency's fast track. He knew he had little or no chance of ever becoming a station chief or a division chief; his poor fitness reports would come back to haunt him.

He was about to marry Rosario, a woman whom he regarded as coming from an "upper-class" family.[4] Debts were mounting, including the cost of the divorce from his first wife, and Ames in his own words, felt "embarrassed. . . humiliated" to have "lost control" of his finances.[5] Describing the money pressures he felt that spring, he spoke of "my own sense of failure, inadequacy, and fear. . . ."[6]

---

[4]Ames corrected Senator DeConcini on this point. The chairman of the Senate Intelligence Committee had characterized Rosario as "middle class." She came from a family that was "upper class. . . actually," Ames said. Senate Interview, p. 49.

[5]House Interview, p. 2.

[6]Senate Interview, p. 26.

Love is wonderful the second time around. It is not unreasonable to suppose that Ames was determined that this time would be different. His marriage would succeed. He would provide for his new, "upper-class" wife in appropriate style. He would somehow break free of his status as a midlevel government drone, forever trapped by a modest salary and a limited future.

The answer to all these problems was literally in his hands. He knew the value of the secrets that came across his desk each day. Secrets that to the KGB were, to use Ames's own words, "beyond price."

And it was all too easy to rationalize that those first few names he turned over in April were worthless, a scam. "What I did in April. . . instead of robbing a bank, I decided to rob the KGB," Ames said.[7]

Once he had the first $50,000, however, Ames couldn't stop. He professes to be puzzled as to his motive, to have been "sleepwalking" through the next stage, when on June 13, 1985, he walked into Chadwick's and handed over the identities of every agent he could think of to the KGB.

It is not really all that puzzling. Ames had found an endless pot of gold at the end of the rainbow. So, yes, he did it for the money. But that was not all.

He did it as well, by his own admission, to eliminate any CIA sources who might learn of his identity and betray him in turn. There was a certain murderous logic in destroying the potential witnesses against him. Each time he gave the name of a CIA agent to the KGB, there was one less person around who might somehow discover that Ames was a mole for Moscow. It was an insurance policy for which, in ten cases, death was the premium.

But descend for a moment to a second, deeper, level in the mind of Aldrich Ames. There are other CIA or government employees frustrated in their careers who have both access to sensitive secrets and financial problems. They do not betray their country.

Aside from pure greed, Ames was also a man who had lost faith

---

[7]House Interview, p. 63.

in himself and his institution. When Ames, on the day he was sentenced to life in prison, spoke in court of his disillusion with the CIA and with U.S. policy, the agency's officials, led by Woolsey, were quick to say that he was a traitor and a money-grubber who was trying to reinvent himself, to mitigate the heinous nature of his crimes by cloaking himself, retrospectively, with bogus political motives. While there may be an element of truth in this argument, it also seems clear that Ames, by the early 1980s, was unhappy both with the direction of U.S. foreign policy and with his profession as a CIA spy.

On the beaches of Acapulco and in other conversations with his friend David Samson, for example, Ames made clear his strong disagreement with Ronald Reagan's attacks on the Soviet Union as the "evil empire." He expressed his fear that the Soviets, if they felt cornered, might react violently and dangerously. Moreover, he had become disillusioned with his own career prospects.

Although Ames says "I was never a seriously disgruntled employee," he was never a DO insider, either. "I was not a fast-tracker. I was not an old boy."[8] And, he says, "I became convinced that the practice of espionage in this century has grown into almost a positive evil."[9]

In interviews after his arrest Ames also talked of a desire to shorten the cold war by "leveling the playing field" between the two superpowers.[10] Here his arguments become both convoluted and unconvincing. Ames said the KGB and the Politburo believed the CIA had "penetrated all the levels of Soviet society." By revealing that the CIA had only infiltrated the KGB, Ames said, he felt "this gave the Soviet leadership and. . . Gorbachev, some assurance that the United States. . . was not pulling the strings secretly in Soviet society and that he didn't have to listen to conservatives in the KGB or elsewhere who would argue that we were. As well as dispel a lot of the thinking about aggressive American intentions." Ames added: "The 'leveling the playing field' was some-

[8]House Interview, p. 59.
[9]House Interview, p. 76.
[10]Tim Weiner, "Jailed, Turncoat at C.I.A. Tells of a Long Betrayal," *New York Times*, July 27, 1994, p. B10.

thing I did feel strongly about, still do to some extent. But, again, it's more in describing the effect of what I did rather than the reasons for doing it."[11]

One should not make too much of all this, and cold cash and personal greed remain Ames's obvious, principal motives. But his betrayals for money took place against a backdrop of political disaffection and disillusion with his own profession. His frame of mind made it that much easier for Ames to become a spy for Moscow.

Descend to a third, even murkier level. There is in many, perhaps all, of us an impulse to visit the dark side of the moon, to eat of the forbidden fruit.

In Acapulco, Rick and his friend David Samson talked, entirely in a joking vein, about how to approach the KGB without being caught. It was the sort of idle fantasy in which more than one CIA officer has indulged. Only Ames turned it into reality.

To understand this darkest level of Rick Ames, we have to look no further than his own words. True, his comments about himself are necessarily suspect, perhaps self-serving. But his interviews, in particular those with the House and Senate intelligence committee chairmen, are remarkably self-revelatory, just as his comments about the CIA and its flaws are thoughtful and often accurate, in spite of their notorious source.

It is clear from his comments that Ames did more than deliver secrets. He switched sides. "I. . . threw myself at the KGB. Lock, stock and barrel."[12] "I simply delivered myself to them with the information that I had. . . . It was. . . a switching of loyalties."[13] "I formed a new identification. . . with the KGB or with my handlers in the KGB."[14] Rick Ames had stepped through the looking glass. He *wanted* to belong, to be accepted by the very enemy he had fought all his life. In the end, he identified more with the KGB's First Chief Directorate than with the CIA.

It seems clear that working for the Russians, quite aside from

[11]House Interview, p. 47.
[12]Senate Interview, p. 20.
[13]House Interview, p. 7.
[14]House Interview, p. 76.

the money, was fulfilling some deep psychological need in Ames. They treated him like a hero. The KGB respected him, or said it did. The KGB gave Ames the recognition that he had not achieved in the CIA. It paid him $2.7 million dollars and promised $1.9 million more. That is a lot of reassurance.

It set aside land for a dacha, land that "belongs to You forever." It praised him for his talents.

Its officers undoubtedly assured him, accurately, that he was the most valuable spy of the cold war. He had not intended to keep working for Moscow, Ames claims, but *"I was dependent on that relationship, in a strange sort of way"* [italics added].[15] It was not a completely unusual transference of loyalties. Oleg Penkovsky, the most valuable GRU spy for the CIA and MI6, insisted on donning and being photographed in U.S. Army and British army colonels' uniforms. He wanted some tangible reassurance that he really belonged to the American and British side.[16]

There are varying theories about Ames's recklessness, why he made no effort to conceal his wealth or his spying, driving a Jaguar to the CIA and leaving documents in the trash.

Kati Spillmann, a Zurich psychoanalyst who has studied the case, said, "The striking fact is that Ames was spending money in a way that could only attract attention. One possible reason may be that Ames subconsciously wanted to be caught because of guilt." Dr. Arthur Ourieff, a Los Angeles psychiatrist, suggested that Ames's actions might be attributed to "a grandiose vision of himself. He thought he knew more about the CIA than anyone else. He, Rick Ames, could never be caught."[17]

Did Ames make a difference in the broad course of history? Probably not. In the late 1980s, communism disintegrated in

[15]Senate Interview, p. 101.

[16]The photographs, of course, were retained in the files of the CIA and the British intelligence service. It would have been impossibly risky for Penkovsky to have taken the pictures with him back to the Soviet Union.

[17]Ames, interestingly, said as much in a 1995 interview on National Public Radio with reporter Martha Raddatz. "I was too confident of—you know, basically, incompetence on the part of the agency. You know, I counted on that." Transcript, *Morning Edition*, NPR, February 16, 1995.

Eastern Europe and then in the Soviet Union. The CIA itself did not make much difference in the ultimate outcome of the cold war. From the Bay of Pigs to Iran-contra, its covert warriors hatched one disaster after another. Its analysts misjudged almost every major development in the post–World War II world, including the most spectacular misjudgment of all—the flat-out failure to predict the collapse of the Soviet Union.

But Ames did succeed in depriving America of valuable intelligence, of military and political information, by destroying the sources who were providing it and causing ten of them to be executed. He did more than betray agents; he also transmitted important intelligence, political, and military information to Moscow.

Although the point has not been much publicized, Ames also compromised significant technical operations. The damage assessment team that studied the case in great secrecy after Ames's arrest confirmed that he also gave away to the KGB a number of NSA and CIA technical operations, including those aimed at intercepting Soviet and Russian communications. As early as November 1986, the chief of the Soviet division's Counterintelligence Group noted in a memo that two CIA technical operations had been blown. There were, as it turned out, many more.

Is there another mole? "There's always another mole," said Skip Brandon, who was acting director of the FBI's intelligence division as the bureau closed in on Ames. But the idea of a confederate working in tandem with Ames, he added, "is beyond the pale of tradecraft. The documents Ames got were probably just due to lax security. I can't imagine their risking one high-level mole for the other."

As damaging as the betrayals were, in the end the greatest damage Ames did was to the agency itself. He made it look foolish, the butt of cartoonists, at the very time when the agency was at its most vulnerable, cast adrift by the end of the cold war, desperately seeking new roles and missions. Now its future is uncertain, its structure and prospects under scrutiny by a presidential commission.

There were, to be sure, a handful of people at CIA, including the woman who was the chief mole hunter, who did try to find the culprit, even when the agency's top management appeared not to care.

And when the old bulls of the Directorate of Operations, many scattered now and retired in the Sun Belt, gather at their golf outings and meetings, they can remind each other that in order for Aldrich Ames to have betrayed all those spies, the CIA had to have recruited them in the first place.

For all of its mistakes and defects, the CIA, or an intelligence service, is still a necessity in a dangerous and unstable world. The perils of a nuclear war between the superpowers have given way to the menace of nuclear proliferation in the third world and global terrorism. A president needs an intelligence service to provide the information on which to base foreign policy and national security decisions.

Ames has contended, with some accuracy, that many of the agents he betrayed were simply providing information about the opposition service, KGB—although this was certainly not true of all of them. General Polyakov, Oleg Gordievsky, and others were providing intelligence of a much broader nature. But during the cold war even intelligence about the KGB was significant because the Soviet system rested on three pillars of power—the party, the army, and the KGB. As one high-level former CIA official argued, "Ames did more than destroy sources on the KGB. But even if you are only penetrating the KGB you are penetrating one-third of the country. These aren't just gumshoes, they are part of the power structure in every ministry, and in the military."[18]

Ames has argued that the Russians, too, were betraying their country. In his self-justifying rationalizations to the court that sen-

[18]The Russians had no doubts that Ames had provided enormously valuable service to the KGB in destroying the CIA's sources of information. Quite aside from the $4.6 million they paid or promised to him, the officials in Yasnevo received extraordinary commendations. In 1986 the prestigious and rarely given Order of Lenin, the second highest award in the Soviet Union, was bestowed upon Viktor I. Cherkashin, the KGB counterintelligence chief in Washington who the FBI believes was the officer who met with Ames in the Soviet embassy; Anatoly Kireev, chief of Directorate K, the KGB's counterintelligence arm in Moscow; Valentin Novikov, the deputy director of Directorate K; and four other officials. The seven KGB officials were almost certainly recognized because of the Ames coup.

tenced him to life in prison, he implied that he faced the same risks as did those he betrayed. But there was a moral difference. The Soviet Union, to which Ames sold his loyalty, was a dictatorship that maintained a vast prison system to repress all dissent. Many of its citizens wanted only to leave the country if they could. The United States is a democracy to which people all over the world fight to come.

There was a practical difference as well. Ames risked prison if caught; the Russians he betrayed were risking their lives. Ames knew that. He knew that when he sold secrets to Moscow, the United States had no death penalty for espionage in peacetime. He knew that the Soviet Union did. He was, it might be argued, a kind of serial killer.

Ames betrayed his country. He betrayed his colleagues. He betrayed his friends. He destroyed his marriage. He put his wife in prison. In perhaps the most unforgivable sin of all, he deprived his son of a father. And he deprived himself of his freedom.

From his prison cell in Allenwood, he has granted interviews to CNN, the BBC, National Public Radio, and others. But in time, the media interest will taper off. The television, radio, and newspaper interviews will stop.

Then Ames will be left alone in his cell to ponder what he has done. If his imagination roams, he may even think of what it must be like to stand in thin prison clothes in the snow or cold at dawn in Moscow and face a firing squad, to feel the bullets slam into your body in that terrible instant as your life ends.

In prison, Ames still wears his wedding band. He hopes to remain married. He has exchanged some letters with Rosario. He hopes to see his son one day, although it will be painful to explain to Paul why his father is in prison. Above all, he clings to the hope of a trade, an exchange of spies that would suddenly, miraculously set him free. He could live in Moscow, like Philby, or perhaps in that dacha the KGB had promised him, on the land by the river.

It is a forlorn hope, and the ultimate irony of the Ames case. A trade could happen, of course; they have in the past. But the cold war is over. American intelligence officials say there is no one they know of imprisoned in Russia whom they want back in exchange for Aldrich Ames. At one time there were agents of great value to America who might have been traded.

But Ames killed them.

In his maximum security prison cell Aldrich Ames will, of course, have time to reflect on all this. On the journey from River Falls to Burma, to Ankara, to Mexico, and Rome, to Allenwood, to reflect on the trail of broken dreams and broken lives that he left behind on his voyage of betrayal through the secret world.

APPENDIX

THE VICTIMS

Following are the ten Soviet agents working for the CIA who were executed after their identities were disclosed to the KGB by Aldrich Ames. Their CIA code names, all beginning with the letters GT, and in some cases their FBI code names, are listed, along with a brief description of each victim. The government has not made this list public; it was compiled by the author from intelligence sources.

GTBEEP: Dimitri Fedorovich Polyakov, FBI code name TOPHAT. General of the GRU, Soviet military intelligence.

GTGENTILE: Valery F. Martynov, FBI code name PIMENTA. KGB lieutenant colonel stationed in Washington.

GTGAUZE: Sergei M. Motorin, FBI code name MEGAS. KGB major stationed in Washington.

GTJOGGER: Vladimir M. Piguzov, KGB lieutenant colonel stationed in Indonesia.

GTACCORD: Vladimir Mikhailovich Vasilyev, GRU colonel stationed in Budapest.

GTCOWL: Sergei Vorontsov, KGB officer in Moscow who revealed spy dust to the CIA.

GTMILLION: Gennady Smetanin, lieutenant colonel of the GRU stationed in Lisbon.

GTFITNESS: Gennady Grigorievich Varenik, KGB officer stationed in Germany.

GTWEIGH: Leonid Polyshuk, KGB officer stationed in Africa.

GTSPHERE: Adolf G. Tolkachev, Soviet defense researcher in Moscow.[1]

---

[1]Tolkachev was arrested after CIA defector Edward Lee Howard gave his identity to the KGB; on the same day he was arrested, Aldrich Ames also revealed his name to the KGB, providing confirmation that he was a CIA agent. Tolkachev was executed September 24, 1986.

AUTHOR'S NOTE

I began work on the Aldrich Ames case on the day his arrest was announced, a little more than a year ago. At midmorning on February 22, 1994, the phone rang in my office in Washington. It was the Canadian Broadcasting Company calling. Did I know that a CIA "spy couple" had been arrested?

The CBC interviewed me, the *Times* of London wanted an article within three hours, NBC sent a crew to film me that afternoon for the nightly news, and I appeared on CNN's *Crossfire* that evening. *Newsweek* asked for an article, the television magazine shows were calling and it went on like that for days, with the telephone ringing off the hook, and calls coming in from as far away as Scotland and Austria.

The reason for the worldwide interest was plain. As the dimensions of the case gradually emerged, it became clear that Aldrich Ames—aside from being the highest paid spy in the history of the world—was also the most damaging mole inside the Central Intelligence Agency since the CIA was created in 1947.

In the entire history of the cold war, there had never been anyone like Aldrich Ames. He betrayed three dozen CIA and allied agents, caused at least ten of them to be executed, and sold perhaps hundreds of CIA operations to the KGB. The damage he did to the nation and to the CIA itself was incalculable. And all the while, he was driving his Jaguar into Langley headquarters, his colleagues apparently oblivious to the carefree displays of wealth by Ames and his wife, Rosario.

I began work almost immediately on a lengthy article on the case for *Vanity Fair*, and within weeks I was deep into the research for *Nightmover*. My previous book, *Molehunt*, had chronicled the destructive hunt for a mole in the CIA by James J. Angleton, and before that I had written *The Spy Who Got Away*, the story of Edward Lee Howard, another CIA officer who betrayed secrets to Moscow. The Ames case combined elements of both of those stories, and as I was soon to discover, involved some of the same players inside the CIA.

To research this book, I conducted more than 450 interviews with almost 200 persons. Although much of the text is based on these interviews, there are additional references to court documents, congressional reports on the Ames case, and other sources, and these are cited in the footnotes.

One of the first questions I wanted to answer was, who is Aldrich Ames? Almost nothing was known about his family background. I contacted his sister, Nancy Everly, who agreed to meet with me. She proved to be an exceptional woman whose strength in coping with the tragedy that struck her family won my admiration. Mrs. Everly, while devastated and completely apalled by her brother's actions, has remained loyal to him as a sister. In a series of extraordinarily frank interviews, she helped me to understand the Ames family background in great detail and provided some of the exclusive family photographs included in the book. I am enormously grateful to her. More family history, and additional photographs, were also generously contributed by Donald B. McIntyre and his wife, Susan, Ames's aunt and uncle.

David T. Samson, who became Rick Ames's closest friend when Ames worked for the CIA in Mexico City more than a decade ago, provided valuable insights into Ames's frame of mind at that time and later. It was Samson who first dated and then introduced Ames to his future wife, Rosario Casas. Ames, in turn, was later best man at Samson's wedding. I am especially grateful to David Samson for the many hours he spent in recalling his close friendship with Ames and Rosario, and for the photographs he provided. Rich and Judy Thurman and Irwin Rubenstein were other good friends of Ames who provided additional background about his life, and I am grateful to them, as well.

I interviewed Aldrich Ames in the Alexandria City Detention Center not long after he was sentenced to life in prison, and have also corresponded with him. In our meeting, he provided certain information that proved very important to the book. Ames subsequently granted a great many television and print interviews, and where I have drawn upon these sources, they are cited as well.

I am indebted to both the prosecutor and the defense counsels for the considerable time they took to share their views with me. Mark J. Hulkower, the assistant U.S. attorney, who was the governments's lead counsel in the case, helped me to thread my way through the maze of Swiss bank accounts and clarified other aspects of the case; I am deeply grateful for his patience and assistance. Plato Cacheris, the celebrated and gracious criminal lawyer who represented Ames, was always open to my questions and in several interviews and conversations provided valuable background to the plea bargaining and the formal proceedings in the case. His insights are greatly appreciated. My thanks go as well to his then associate, Preston Burton.

Writing a book about a man who worked for two secret agencies, on both sides of the cold war, presents special problems of attribution. Some of my most valuable CIA and other sources made it clear that the best way I could thank them would be by omitting their names from the author's acknowledgments and by not quoting them in the text. Given the secret nature of their work, and having been anonymous all of their lives, these men and women preferred to remain that way. They have placed their trust in me, and I have respected their wishes. They know who they are.

Wherever possible, however, CIA, FBI, and other sources are identified by name and quoted directly. Many of the interviews I conducted were with present or former CIA officers and FBI agents who had direct knowledge of Ames and of the efforts, ultimately successful, to identify and to arrest him.

From the start, researching the life and espionage career of Aldrich Ames presented a considerable challenge. His work for the CIA was carried on in great secrecy, and his spying for the KGB and its successor, the SVR, was concealed for almost nine years. As his FBI code name suggests, he moved by night in a clandestine world.

By finding many of those who had worked alongside Ames in the CIA, however, I was able to reconstruct the details of his career, as he moved from Langley, to Turkey, to New York, to Mexico City, and back to headquarters. At the same time, I traced his double life as a spy for Moscow in Washington, Rome, and finally at CIA headquarters.

I also wanted to know a great deal more about the victims of Aldrich Ames, the ten who were executed and the many others who were imprisoned. I was able to learn the identities and CIA code names of all ten of those executed because of Ames, as well as the names of several who were imprisoned, and some who escaped.

I was fascinated to discover the identity of the CIA's chief mole hunter, Jeanne R. Vertefeuille, the woman who refused to give up and worked the case for more than seven years. I learned of her background and details about the other members of her highly secret team. I thank all of those who helped me in this endeavor.

The CIA is a secret intelligence agency, and the Directorate of Operations, in which Ames spent his career, is its most secret part. The CIA, not surprisingly, did not throw open its files to me. However, the agency's director, R. James Woolsey, was helpful in making available a limited amount of background information early in my research, which I greatly appreciate. And the agency's public affairs staff was diligent in answering specific questions where it felt it could do so. My thanks in particular go to Carolyn M. Ekedahl, the CIA's chief of media relations, and to Mark

Mansfield, the agency's spokesperson. Both were admirably patient with my seemingly endless list of questions and answered them when they could.

A number of former CIA officers were generous with their time. While most cannot be named, a few can. I owe particular thanks to William H. Webster, the former director of both the CIA and the FBI who helped me to understand the beginnings of what became the search for the mole. I am grateful as well to Robert M. Gates, who succeeded Webster as CIA director, to William E. Colby, whose tenure as CIA chief preceded Ames's spying, to Richard J. Kerr, former CIA acting director, as well as to Dean Almy, Milton A. Bearden, Robert H. Campbell, Paul Garbler, Donald F. B. Jameson, S. Peter Karlow, George Kisevalter, Newton S. Miler, Hugh J. McMillan, Colin R. Thompson, and Lawrence M. Wright. The list of those who prefer to remain anonymous is much longer.

The FBI made available a number of its counterintelligence officials and special agents. My thanks in particular go to Robert M. "Bear" Bryant, assistant director in charge of the National Security Division, John F. Lewis, Jr., the deputy assistant director, and Special Agent Leslie G. Wiser, Jr., as well as to Tim Caruso, the assistant special agent in charge in New York City, James Holt, Michael P. Kortan, unit chief in the FBI's national press office, and Jennifer Spencer, public affairs specialist.

A number of former FBI officials also provided invaluable assistance. The list must begin with John F. Mabey, who for the first time told the story of how General Dimitri Fedorovich Polyakov, TOPHAT, was recruited by him to work for the United States. I will always be grateful for the trust he placed in me.

I am indebted as well to William S. Sessions, former director of the FBI, former Ambassador James E. Nolan, Jr., who was the deputy assistant director of the FBI's intelligence (now national security) division; to Phillip A. Parker, his successor; R. Patrick Watson, who held that post when Ames was arrested; Harry B. "Skip" Brandon, former acting chief of the division; Edward J. O'Malley, former chief of the division; and former Special Agent Bill Smits.

Many others deserve my thanks, including Dr. Edward Adelson, Daniel Brandt, president of Public Information Research, Sergei Fedorenko, Giles FitzHerbert, Victor Gundarev, John W. Holmes, Oleg Kalugin, the former chief of counterintelligence of the KGB, Ruth Kiker, James H. Lesar, Dr. Arthur Ourieff, former Ambassador Roman Popadiuk, Vladimir Potashov, Christine S. Ritchie, Professor Philip Robbins, of The George Washington University, Thomas B. Ross, Special Assistant to the President, Arkady N. Shevchenko, Kati Spillmann, Professor Irene Thompson, of The George Washington University, and Susan J. Williams. Margaret L. Anderson, Kathryn Strok Hartzler, John Hoofnagle, and Wes Sanders, four of Ames's high school friends, were kind enough to share their recollections of him with me, and they have my gratitude.

Several writers and colleagues in the press were generous as well, including Seymour M. Hersh; Andrew J. Glass, chief of the Washington bureau of the Cox newspapers; Mike Edwards, assistant editor of the *National Geographic*; Daniel Schorr, senior news analyst of National Public Radio; Elizabeth Bancroft, editor of the *Surveillant*; Anthony Summers; Gene Randall, of CNN; Jeffrey T. Richelson; Victor Simpson, of the Rome bureau of the Associated Press; Katherine A. Foley, deputy director of information services, the *Washington Post*; Barclay Walsh, of the *New York Times* Washington bureau; Maria Cristina Caballero, in Bogotá; and Hugo Martínez McNaught, in Mexico City.

A special word of thanks must go to the superbly professional editors and staff of *Vanity Fair*, with whom it was a pleasure to work on "The Spy in the Jaguar" (July 1994), the article that began my research on the Aldrich Ames case. They include Graydon Carter, editor in chief; Wayne Lawson, the executive literary editor; Maria Recapito, his then assistant; Anne Phalon; and Paula Gillen.

I am especially indebted to Adrian Zackheim, the executive editor of HarperCollins, whose enthusiam and support from the outset made this project possible, and to Sterling Lord, my friend and literary agent of many years, to whom this book is affectionately dedicated.

No words of appreciation would be adequate to thank Angela E.

Lauria, who provided the principal research assistance for the book. She hit the ground running and never stopped. I am grateful as well to my brother, William A. Wise, who provided valuable additional research assistance, and to Eve Sawyer, who helped to keep my newspaper files current.

Most of all, I thank my family, my wife Joan, and my sons, Christopher and Jonathan, whose love and understanding were always there, even when I was not, as I worked to produce *Nightmover*.

DAVID WISE

Washington, D.C.
March 20, 1995

INDEX

ABOUT THE AUTHOR

David Wise is America's leading writer on intelligence and espionage. He is coauthor of *The Invisible Government*, the number-one
bestseller widely credited with bringing about a reappraisal of the
role of the CIA in a democratic society. His most recent book is
Molehunt. He is also the author of *The Spy Who Got Away*, *The
American Police State*, *The Politics of Lying*, and coauthor with
Thomas B. Ross of *The Espionage Establishment*, *The Invisible
Government*, and *The U-2 Affair*. Mr. Wise is the author of three
espionage novels, *The Samarkand Dimension*, *The Children's Game*,
and *Spectrum*. A native New Yorker and graduate of Columbia
College, he is the former chief of the Washington bureau of the
New York Herald Tribune and has contributed articles on govern-
ment and politics to many national magazines. He is married and
has two sons.